When You Lie Down & When You Rise Up

Daily Readings in Shemot - Exodus

Rabbi Jonathan Allen

Preface by Eitan Shishkoff

When You Lie Down & When You Rise Up
Daily Readings in Shemot - Exodus
ISBN 1-901917-10-X
Copyright © 2011 Jonathan Peter Allen

Cover Design by Naomi Allen

Typeset in Times New Roman, Viner Hand, Aquaduct, Briner Pro

Where Scripture quotations are unattributed, they are the author's own translation.
Otherwise they are attributed and taken from:

CJB   Complete Jewish Bible, Copyright © 1998 by David H. Stern. Published by Jewish New Testament Publications, Inc., Clarksville, Maryland, U.S.A. www.messianicjewish.net/jntp Used and adapted with permission.

ESV   The Holy Bible, English Standard Version, Copyright © 2001 by Crossway Books, a division of Good News Publishers. www.gnpcb.org Used by permission. All rights reserved.

GWT   GOD'S WORD Translation. Copyright © 1995 God's Word to the Nations. Used by permission. www.godsword.org All rights reserved.

JPS   Tanakh - The Holy Scriptures, Copyright © 1985 by The Jewish Publication Society www.jewishpub.org All rights reserved.

Living   The Living Torah, by Rabbi Aryeh Kaplan, Copyright © 1981, Maznaim Publishing
Torah   Corporation, New York

Message   The Message by Eugene H. Peterson, Copyright © 1993-96, 2001-02. Used by permission of Navpress Publishing Group. www.navpress.com All rights reserved.

NASB   New American Standard Bible, Copyright ©1960, 1962, 1963, 1968, 1971, 1972, 1973, 1975, 1977 by The Lockman Foundation. www.Lockman.org Used by permission.

NIV   Holy Bible, New International Version, Copyright © 1973,1978,1984 by International Bible Society. Used by permission of Zondervan. www.zondervanbibles.com All rights reserved.

NKJV   New King James Version, Copyright © 1982 by Thomas Nelson, Inc. www.thomasnelson.com/consumer Used by permission. All rights reserved.

NLT   Holy Bible, New Living Translation, Copyright © 1996. Used by permission of Tyndale House Publishers, Inc., Wheaton, Illinois. All rights reserved.

NRSV   Holy Bible,New Revised Standard Version, Copyright © 1989, 1995. Division of Christian Education of the National Council of the Churches in Christ in the United States of America

RSV   Holy Bible, Revised Standard Version, Copyright © 1952, 1971. Division of Christian Education of the National Council of the Churches in Christ in the United States of America

Published by Elisheva Publishing Ltd.
www.elishevapublishing.co.uk

Contents

Preface

Does the world really need this book, yet one more *Torah* commentary? After reading Jonathan Allen's stimulating analyses of the Book of Exodus-Shemot, my answer is --- yes. Allen's work is intellectually, academically and spiritually substantive without being stilted, overly technical or simply boring. While there is a growing body of *Torah* commentary by Messianic Jewish authors (Resnik and Feinberg for example), it is still a fresh field. For those desiring a perspective on the Books of Moses that integrates reflections from the New Covenant authors, this volume and its companions provide a valuable addition, showing respect and relevance for both Jewish and Gentile readers.

"*The Scriptures are a source of life, because they point us to the source of all life*" (p.195) is a statement the author makes, which guides him throughout. I found in "When you Lie Down and When you Rise Up" engaging insights into the biblical text. Allen takes us on concise, rich explorations of the *Torah*'s verses, giving color and texture with well-chosen references to rabbinic and biblical writings. You may not agree with all of his interpretations, but the process of interacting with his conclusions will sharpen your own understanding and increase your appetite for the manna of God's word.

Speaking of Moshe's communication with Israel, Allen writes: "*In order for people to be able to accept a foundational truth, it has to be explained and presented to them in a clear and understandable way; if this is not done, then their understanding of and therefore their commitment to it will be weak. It is necessary ... to communicate the message in clear and unambiguous language ... (in order to) bring the hearers to a decision by asking them to respond*" (p.98). Here is a key to Allen's own heart and his motivation for writing. Here he lays out both his goal and his method.

His aim is to follow the example of Moshe, who repeatedly challenged Israel to respond to the words of the Most High. By shedding renewed light on this ancient document from God, my colleague ushers us into the time-honored, continuing conversation of sages, prophets, apostles, teachers and Messiah Yeshua concerning the meaning of *Torah*. Jonathan Allen's aim is to bring us repeatedly to the point of evaluation and decision in the real conduct of our lives. May this book do that for you as you enjoy the Exodus journey with Jonathan --- as I have.

Eitan Shishkoff
Tents of Mercy, Kiryat Yam, Israel

Introduction

Exodus - the Book of Names - is the book that formally records not only the entry of the Jacob family to Egypt, but also narrates their exit from Egypt as a people some four hundred years later. Including the theophany and *Matan Torah*, the Giving of the *Torah* at Mt. Sinai, the book lists also the instructions for and fulfillment of the construction of the tabernacle, the place where God was to dwell in the midst of our people as we travelled through the desert towards the Promised Land.

Covering ritual and relationship, slavery and freedom, free-will and compulsion, the *Torah* does not shrink from cataloguing both big and small in the process of creating *Am Yisrael* - the People of Israel. Join in the conversations that have been going on about and within the text for almost as long as the text has existed.

These commentaries on the weekly *Torah* portion have been written over the course of seven years: one per portion, per year. They have grown as we have grown; they have developed as our knowledge and understanding of the Hebrew texts, the classic and modern commentators has also developed. Like us, they are themselves a work-in-progress. They step in turn through the seven readings or *aliyot* into which the weekly portion is divided, to offer seven commentaries in each portion. You can read one at a time for each day of the week, or dip into them on an *ad hoc* basis.

These commentaries on the weekly *Torah* portion have been written over the course of seven years: one per portion, per year. They have grown as we have grown; they have developed as our knowledge and understanding of the Hebrew texts, the classic and modern commentators has also developed. Like us, they are themselves a work-in-progress. They step in turn through the seven readings or *aliyot* into which the weekly portion is divided, to offer seven commentaries in each portion. You can read one at a time for each day of the week, or dip into them on an *ad hoc* basis.

This work is, in a sense, "old hat" in that they have been published week by week on our website: *http://www.messianictrust.org.uk* and, indeed, new commentaries continue to be published each week. Please do visit the website or sign up for the weekly e-mail to join in the ongoing conversation and have your say on the thoughts presented.

We have resisted the temptation to rewrite or enlarge the earlier commentaries, believing that their value lies in what - we trust - God has been saying, rather than in the cleverness (or otherwise) of the words or the number of citations. We have nevertheless taken the opportunity to remove some spelling mistakes and typographical issues, hopefully without inserting a fresh collection during the collation and editing phase.

It is true to say that the body of Messiah outside the Messianic Jewish world has largely ignored and rejected the work of the Jewish rabbis in discussing and processing - often at great length - the words of *Torah*, God's foundational revelation to the patriarchs and the people of Israel. This has been a significant loss to the body, as many early insights into the multiple layers of meaning and nuance within the text have essentially been denied to the believing community. One of the aims of these commentaries has been to share some of the insights, commonly held among Jewish people from Second Temple times - the times of Yeshua's (Jesus') own earthly ministry - and successive generations, with the wider body of Messiah. In particular, it is our desire and - we believe - calling, to encourage our own people to re-discover the riches of the rabbinic writings and hear the ancient voices and conversations afresh in the light of our faith in Yeshua, the Jewish Messiah.

Technicalities

We usually follow the Ashkenazic division of the *parasha* into the seven readings in which the text is read during the *Torah* service on *Shabbat*.

As this is a work based upon the Hebrew Bible, we have followed a number of conventions of the Jewish world that may need some explanation:

a. names: we use Hebrew names for Yeshua (Jesus), Rav Sha'ul (the Apostle Paul), the patriarchs, Moshe and Aharon, the books of the *Torah* and the individual *parasha* names; this is of no doctrinal significance, but is part of our culture as Messianic Jews

Avraham	Abraham	B'resheet	Genesis
Yitz'khak	Isaac	Shemot	Exodus
Ya'akov	Jacob	Vayikra	Leviticus
Moshe	Moses	B'Midbar	Numbers
Aharon	Aaron	D'varim	Deuteronomy

b. the chapter and verse numbering of the traditional Hebrew text: this is occasionally different from the conventional English numbering and most often only varies by one or two verses; we usually follow the numbering of the Bible version from which we are quoting

There is one commentary for each of the seven *aliyot*; seven commentaries in each portion. These can be read one at a time for each day of the week, or dipped into on an *ad hoc* basis. Each commentary contains a short Hebrew text, its transliteration into an English character set and an English translation, followed by a commentary based upon the text, some verses or passages for further study and some application suggestions.

Leap years - the Jewish calendar has seven leap years in each nineteen year cycle, when we add an extra month to the year - often a challenge to the *parasha* sequence. In non-leap years, some of the portions are traditionally read together; in leap years, they are read separately. The reader will find that while the double portions have full coverage, the single portions do not have a full complement of seven commentaries each.

Citations from the ancient Jewish writings - the Mishnah, the Talmuds and the Midrash Rabbah are accompanied by their appropriate references.

The prefix *"m."* means Mishnah, *"y."* the Jerusalem Talmud, *"b."* the Babylonian Talmud. Each part of Midrash Rabbah is given its Hebrew name, for example Shemot Rabbah. Talmud references give the page (or folio) number in normal type, while the side *a* or *b* in italic.

References to the classic commentators show their names in the Aquaduct font; there are brief biographical details listed for each named source in the Biography section at the end of the book. These are intended to provide a frame or context from which the commentator speaks. Author and book names also share the Aquaduct font and can be found in the Bibliography section, at the end of the book.

Terms and expressions in an italic typeface are explained in the Glossary section at the end of the book. This provides definitions of some of the other documents, languages and factual information that are referenced in the commentaries, or explain some of the terms that may be unfamiliar to modern readers or those from a less Jewish-friendly background.

Quotations from the Scriptures themselves are shown in Brinar Pro font so that they are distinct from the commentary text.

One particular Jewish convention is used with such frequency that although it has glossary entries, we felt that we should explain it here as well. It is Jewish custom not to use or pronounce the tetragrammaton covenant name of God in an inappropriate or irreverent way in order to fulfill the commandment not to take God's name in vain. Jewish custom is therefore to use one of two allusions to allow the name of God to be used and referred to in a "safe" way. Obviously, the tetragrammaton appears many times in the Hebrew biblical text. When formally read or used in a worship context, the word is pronounced *Adonai*; on other occasions it is pronounced *HaShem*, which literally means "The Name". You will find these words used in many places in the commentaries.

Every book that includes transliteration of Hebrew words into an English alphabet has its own particular style. The purpose of the transliteration is to provide a pronunciation that also reflects the different letters where possible. We denote the Hebrew letter *chaf* by 'ch', *khet* by 'kh' and *kof* by 'k'. A *chaf* with a *dagesh* (a dot in the middle of the letter) is also shown as 'k'. We represent both *sin* and *samech* by 's' and *tzadi* by 'tz'. Dipthongs are usually shown by adding an 'i' or 'y' to the ordinary vowel letter. We generally follow modern Israeli pronunciation, so *vav* has a 'v' sound and *tav* and *tet* are both always 't'. In particular we do not follow the Ashkenazic custom of pronouncing a *tav* without a dagesh as 's'.

We do not take account in this book of *Rosh Chodesh* or the "special" *shabbaton* during the year, such as *Shabbat Shekalim* or *Shabbat Shuva*, when some of the ordinary readings may be replaced by an otherwise out-of-sequence reading. Readings for the festivals will be found at the end of the normal weekly readings, before the reference sections.

שְׁמוֹת

Shemot - Names

Shemot / Exodus 1:1 - 6:8

רִאשׁוֹן	Aliyah One	Shemot/Exodus 1:1 - 17
שֵׁנִי	Aliyah Two	Shemot/Exodus 1:18 - 2:10
שְׁלִישִׁי	Aliyah Three	Shemot/Exodus 2:11 - 25
רְבִיעִי	Aliyah Four	Shemot/Exodus 3:1 - 15
חֲמִשִׁי	Aliyah Five	Shemot/Exodus 3:16 - 4:17
שִׁשִּׁי	Aliyah Six	Shemot/Exodus 4:18 -31
שְׁבִיעִי	Aliyah Seven	Shemot/Exodus 5:1 - 6:1

שְׁמוֹת א׳

Shemot - Names - 1

Shemot/ Exodus 1:1 - 17

Shemot/Exodus 1:1 And these are the names of the Sons of Israel, the ones coming to Egypt

וְאֵלֶּה שְׁמוֹת בְּנֵי יִשְׂרָאֵל הַבָּאִים מִצְרָיְמָה

Mitzray'mah   ha'ba'iym   Yisra'el   b'ney   sh'mot   v'eyleh

Rashi connects this verse with the promise that God gave Avraham: "Look up at the sky, and count the stars - if you can count them! Your descendants will be that many" (B'resheet 15:5, CJB), and a verse from the prophet Isaiah: "Turn your eyes to the heavens! See who created these? He brings out the army of them in sequence, summoning each by name" (Isaiah 40:26a, CJB). At this point, the start of the story of our departure from Egypt, it is as if Rashi is reminding us that as children of Avraham not only are we numbered as the stars of the sky, but like the stars, each of us is sufficiently important and precious to God to be known individually by name. *HaShem* is about to call our people out of Egypt, "with an outstretched arm and with great judgements" (Shemot 6:6, NASB), but each one of us is to be counted and called by our names.

Now the verse from the prophet continues, "Through His great might and His massive strength, not one of them is missing" (Isaiah 40:26b, CJB). At the same time, *Chazal* tell us that not all of the descendants of Israel left Egypt; whether they didn't think it would work, were too young, too old or too sick to travel, or had slightly higher ranking jobs that they didn't want to leave, we don't know. Similarly, when the exiles returned to Jerusalem from Babylon (under Ezra, Nehemiah and Zerubabel) we know that only a relatively small number chose to return to *Eretz Yisrael* - many chose to remain behind in Babylon. Even today, when the State of Israel and a number of religious charities are doing all that they can to encourage Jews from around the world to make *aliyah* and return to Israel, there remain significant numbers of Jewish people, particularly in the USA and Europe, who simply don't want to live in the Land at this time and are voting with their feet to stay put. Can all those people have frustrated God and made His word null and void? It's a question of understanding the call and how it works.

Writing to the believers in Rome, Rav Sha'ul said, "we know that God causes everything to work together for the good of those who love God and are called according to His purpose" (Romans 8:28, CJB). So we know that God calls people to enter into relationship with Him and, as Yeshua said, "For God so loved the world that He gave His only and unique Son, so that everyone who trusts in Him may have eternal life" (John 3:16, CJB), that relationship is available to everyone. What matters is whether people respond to that call and accept God's invitation. Yes, God does know each of us individually and knew our names before we or our parents did, but He does not force Himself upon us; He calls and cajoles, "for it is not His purpose that anyone should be destroyed" (2 Peter 3:9, CJB), but the choice is ours.

Further Study: Matthew 22:1-14; Psalm 139

Application: Ask God to show you how you have responded to His call on your life up until today. Have you preferred the leeks and onions of Egypt, or have you followed the example of our father Avraham and left everything to go with Him to a land that He will show you?

שְׁמוֹת ב׳

Shemot - Names - 2

Shemot / Exodus 1:18 - 2:10

Shemot/Exodus 1:18 And the King of Egypt called the midwives and said to them, "Why have you done this thing?"

וַיִּקְרָא מֶלֶךְ־מִצְרַיִם לַמְיַלְּדֹת וַיֹּאמֶר לָהֶן
lahen vayomer lam'yal'dot Mitzrayim melech vayikra

מַדּוּעַ עֲשִׂיתֶן הַדָּבָר הַזֶּה
hazeh hadavar asiyten madua

Although the word 'obey' - variously translated in the pages of the Tanakh from שָׁמַר, guard or keep, שָׁמַע, hear or listen, or נָצַר, keep or observe - does not appear in the text, obedience is the key to the verses that surround it in the *Torah*. The Hebrew midwives had been commanded by Pharaoh to allow any new-born girls to live, but to kill any Hebrew boys at birth. The *Midrash* goes beyond the biblical narrative by telling us that Pharaoh's astrologers had told him that a boy would be born who would save the Israelites (Shemot Rabbah 1:14). Like King Herod, some thousands of years later (Matthew 2:16), Pharaoh over-reacted and decided to try and kill all the boys rather than miss the one he feared. But the Hebrew midwives simply did not carry out his orders, which brings us to the text. The midwives gave an evasive answer that was enough to show Pharaoh that he couldn't expect them to obey him in this matter, so instead he ordered that the baby boys should be thrown into the Nile.

Saul, the first king of Israel found himself having to decide who to obey when he was sent to obliterate the Amalekites. "Now go and attack Amalek, and completely destroy everything they have. Don't spare them, but kill men and women, children and babies, cows and sheep, camels and donkeys" (1 Samuel 15:3, CJB), *Adonai* instructed him through Samuel the prophet and judge. But pressed by the people who no doubt wanted some spoil or booty from their fighting, Saul kept alive the Amalekite king and the best of the sheep and cattle, later trying to pass this off as if it were an intended sacrifice to the Lord. Samuel has to rebuke Saul with these famous words:

"Does Adonai take as much pleasure in burnt offerings and sacrifices as in obeying what Adonai says? Surely obeying is better than sacrifice, and heeding orders than the fat of rams" (1 Samuel 15:22, CJB). No matter how it is dressed up, our relationship with God requires that we obey Him at all times, no matter what the alternatives might be.

This is a choice that God's people are always having to make: who do we obey? Shortly after being used to heal the lame man in the Yaffa (Beautiful) Gate of the Temple (Acts 3), Peter and John were telling the crowds in the Temple all about Yeshua when they were arrested and hauled before the *Sanhedrin* who were shocked to hear of the miracle and that the issue of Yeshua was not going to go away as they had hoped. Being unable to deny the miracle which many had seen, the *Sanhedrin* ordered the two *shlichim* not to speak or teach in the name of Yeshua again. Peter and John replied, "Whether it is right in the sight of God to give heed to you rather than to God, you be the judge; for we cannot stop speaking what we have seen and heard" (Acts 4:19-20, NASB).

Further Study: 1 Samuel 13:8-14; Acts 16:23-34

Application: When it comes to the crunch, what would you do? How obedient would we be when faced with these sorts of situations? Most of us have to take this sort of decision every day and it is all too easy without even thinking to fall in line with those around us rather than stand out by being obedient to God's word.

שְׁמֹות ׳ג

Shemot - Names - 3

Shemot / Exodus 2:11 - 25

Shemot/Exodus 2:11 And it was, in those days, that Moshe grew up

וַיְהִי | בַּיָּמִים הָהֵם וַיִּגְדַּל מֹשֶׁה

Moshe vayig'dal haheym bayamiym vay'hiy

Rashi asks, "Has the *Torah* not already written 'The boy grew up'?" Indeed, at the start of the previous verse it says וַיִּגְדַּל הַיֶּלֶד, "and the boy grew up". Rashi answers his own question by quoting Rabbi Yehuda the son of Rabbi Ila'i who said that, "the first is in terms of stature and the second is in terms of attainment of rank". In other words, there is growing up and then there is growing up - physical growth in size, stature and strength; and growing into maturity in wisdom, judgement, authority and personality. Jewish tradition has it that Pharaoh appointed Moshe to significant authority and position over his household (Midrash Tanchuma Yashan, Va'eira 17) and this idea is significant because it fits the pattern that we often see repeated in the Scriptures that God calls people out of something that they are already doing in order to serve Him.

For example, we read, "The words of Amos, a sheep-breeder from Tekoa, who prophesied concerning Israel ... I am not a prophet, and I am not a prophet's disciple. I am a cattle breeder and a tender of sycamore figs, but the Lord took me away from following the flock, and the Lord said to me, 'Go, prophesy to Israel'" (Amos 1:1, 7:14-15, JPS). When challenged by the religious authorities in Israel, Amos freely confessed that he had been doing something else, he was something else, until *HaShem* told him to be a prophet to the house of Israel; he already had an established trade, position, livelihood, from which the Lord called him and sent him to be a prophet.

Rav Sha'ul was a tent-maker by profession (Acts 18:3) and a zealous Pharisee with years of rabbinic training (Acts 22:3, Galatians 1:14) actually engaged in persecuting the followers of Yeshua when the Lord met with him on the road to Damascus. Yeshua Himself earned a living and supported his family for possibly 10-15 years as a builder/carpenter in the Nazareth area of the Galil before He started His years of ministry at around the age of 30.

Elisha was ploughing when Elijah threw his cloak over him and called him to be his disciple and successor (1 Kings 19:19). All very ordinary, routine ways of growing up, learning to make a living, being under authority, taking on responsibility and being faithful; yet God wants more for us and from us and He calls us on into more of His service when He knows that we are ready and have served our first apprenticeship.

The man who had been blind from birth but was given his sight by Yeshua could only say: "Once I was blind, but now I see" (John 9:25). He did not know how the change had come about, but he was certain that it had and described the contrast of before and after. Writing to the believers in the *Diaspora*, Peter said that we were called "in order for you to declare the praises of the One who called you out of darkness into His wonderful light" (1 Peter 2:9, CJB). Little wonder, then, that "in those days Moshe grew up" as he realised who he was, which people he belonged to and felt God's call on his life.

Further Study: Philippians 3:4-9; Jeremiah 1:4-10

Application: Have we grown up to hear and feel the call of God on our lives? Not always dramatic, not always a complete change, but often change within the same framework; God calls each and every one of us to grow up, know who we are and who it is we are to serve.

שְׁמוֹת 'ד

Shemot - Names - 4

Shemot / Exodus 3:1 - 15

Shemot/Exodus 3:1 And Moshe was grazing the flock of Yitro, his father-in-law

וּמֹשֶׁה הָיָה רֹעֶה אֶת־צֹאן יִתְרוֹ חֹתְנוֹ
khotno Yitro tzon et ro'eh hayah oo'Moshe

Forty years have now passed since Moshe fled from Egypt after killing an Egyptian overseer who was abusing one of the Israelites. What has he been doing in the meantime? He married Tzipporah, one of the daughters of Yitro/Jethro, the priest of Midian and has been blessed with a son, Gershon. But what has he been doing, this man who was brought up and educated in the palace and household of Pharaoh, king of Egypt? How has he been using his time; how has he occupied the years; what skills has he been developing; how has he advanced his mind? The Scriptures are silent, save for the news of his marriage and son, until we reach this verse: Moshe was grazing the sheep - he was a shepherd. Like Ya'akov and his sons before him, Moshe learnt to walk vast distances, leading the sheep to pasture; he slept rough, out with the sheep, guarding them from predators; he tended to their physical needs and took care of the sick; he picked up the stragglers and kept the flock together. After forty years - which to a keen, intelligent mind like his must have seemed an eternity - *HaShem* called him from shepherding the sheep of his father-in-law Jethro to shepherd the people of Israel out of Egypt - from a hundred or so sheep to a people of two to three million - for another forty years, to the Promised Land.

When King Saul heard what David had been saying about Goliath, the champion of the Philistines, he questioned whether this ruddy youth would be able to fight. David's answer showed how God had been preparing him: "Your servant was tending his father's sheep. When a lion or a bear came and took a lamb from the flock, I went out after him and rescued it from his mouth; and when he rose up against me, I seized him by his beard and struck him and killed him" (1 Samuel 17:34-35, NASB). It could not have been easy, particularly as a youth, being a shepherd in those days before quad-bikes and .22 rifles, defending the sheep from bears and lions, yet David knew that the Lord had been with him and making him ready for the fight with Goliath, as he continued: "The Lord who delivered me from the paw of the lion and from the paw of the bear, He will deliver me from the hand of this Philistine" (1 Samuel 17:37, NASB). Even though he was still many years of further preparation away from being king, David knew that God had His hand on his life and would not let him fall, so that eventually Nathan the prophet could say to David, "Thus says the Lord of Hosts, 'I took you from the pasture, from following the sheep, that you should be ruler over My people Israel. And I have been with you wherever you have gone and have cut off all your enemies from before you'" (2 Samuel 7:8-9, NASB).

Centuries later, another Saul - this time the great rabbi and Jewish theologian, Rav Sha'ul - was to say, "If anyone thinks he has grounds for putting confidence in human qualifications, I have better ground: b'rit milah on the eighth day, an Israeli by birth, from the tribe of Binyamin, a Hebrew speaker, with Hebrew speaking parents, in regard to the Torah a Parush/Pharisee" (Philippians 3:4-5, CJB) and "I am a Jew, born in Tarsus of Cilicia but brought up in this city [Jerusalem] and trained at the feet of Gamli'el in every detail of the Torah of our forefathers" (Acts 22:3, CJB). God had uniquely prepared and placed Rav Sha'ul for the witness he was to bring to both the Jewish and Gentile worlds.

Even Yeshua Himself was born into an artisan family; Joseph was a τέκτων - normally translated 'carpenter' but having more the sense of 'builder' - a craftsman working in stone and wood. Yeshua would have supported both Himself and His family for perhaps 10-15 years before starting His years of ministry. He too learnt and practiced a trade: staying late to finish a job, taking patience and care with sometimes indifferent materials, getting splinters in His fingers and breaking his fingernails; being prepared for the task ahead of Him; a careful and diligent worker as Luke tells us in his gospel: "And Yeshua grew both in wisdom and stature, gaining favour both with other people and with God" (Luke 2:52, CJB).

Further Study: Luke 5:1-11; 1 Corinthians 1:26-30

Application: What are you doing today? What is God teaching you in the daily events of your life? Look around you and see what skills God is developing in you, the people He is using to mould and shape you, and the abilities and gifts that He is building as He prepares you for what is to come. So what are you doing today?

שְׁמוֹת ׳ה

Shemot - Names - 5

Shemot / Exodus 3:16 - 4:17

Shemot/Exodus 3:16 Go and you shall assemble the elders of Israel, and you shall say to them ...

לֵךְ וְאָסַפְתָּ אֶת־זִקְנֵי יִשְׂרָאֵל וְאָמַרְתָּ אֲלֵהֶם
aleyhem v'amar'ta Yisrael zikney et v'asaph'ta leych

This command is part of third cycle of *HaShem* instructing Moshe to go back to Egypt so that He may use Him to set the Israelites free from their bondage and servitude. Notice that the command starts with לֵךְ, an imperative form of the verb הָלַךְ, to go or walk, as *HaShem* tells Moshe: "Go!", and is followed by two more verbs using the Affix form with a *vav*-reversive to make them future in tense: you will or you shall.

Moshe is told to gather the elders of Israel. Who were they? Sarna comments that, "although the elders are frequently mentioned in the Exodus narrative, little information about them is offered." However, in the tribal-patriarchal system, "the council of elders was entrusted with considerable authority, judicial and political." So Moshe's first task is to address and win over the elders of the people; Rashi dryly asks, "How could it be that Moshe would assemble all the myriads of 600,000 people!" Moshe has to have a starting point in bringing *HaShem's* message of redemption to the people and this is the proper way to proceed: Moshe tells the elders, the elders tell the representatives of each tribe and they tell the people.

The process of revelation begins with God Himself: "Behold, the former things have come to pass, now I declare new things; before they spring forth I proclaim them to you" (Isaiah 42:9, NASB). God declares His plans in advance so that when they come to pass we will recognise that God told us about them beforehand and be confirmed in our faith in Him. But what does He do with this revelation - how is it disseminated to the people? The next link in the chain is the prophets: "Adonai, God, does nothing without revealing His plan to His servants the prophets" (Amos 3:7, CJB). God communicates His revelation, His vision, to the prophets who then tell the kings, the leaders of the people. Jeremiah is told at various times, "Stand at the gate of the house of Adonai and proclaim this word" (Jeremiah 7:2, CJB), to all the people in Jerusalem, "Proclaim all these words in the cities of Y'hudah and in the streets of Yerushalayim" (11:6, CJB), to all the people, "to the royal house of Y'hudah say ..." (21:11, CJB), to the king, "then the prophet Yirmeyahu said to the prophet Hananyah in front of the cohanim and all the people standing in Adonai's house ..." (28:5, CJB), to the religious leaders and authorities. This reminds us of the chain of command envisioned by the rabbis when they wrote, "Moshe received the *Torah* from Sinai and transmitted it to Joshua; Joshua to the elders; the elders to the prophets; and the prophets transmitted it to the men of the Great Assembly" (*m.* Pirkei Avot 1:1).

God has defined the proper venues and ways in which He will communicate with people, through prophecy, through teaching, by His word. After all, as Rav Sha'ul writes, "For God is not a God of confusion, but of peace, as in all the churches of the saints" (1 Corinthians 14:33, NASB). How is this to be brought about, for does not God speaks through any or each of us? Rav Sha'ul again: "When you assemble, each one has a psalm, has a teaching, has a revelation, has a tongue, has an interpretation. Let all things be done for edification" (14:26, NASB) so there is an expectation that everyone can contribute. In another letter he writes, "Sing psalms, hymns and spiritual songs to each other; sing to the Lord and make music in your heart to Him" (Ephesians 5:19, CJB), emphasising that this is to be an expression of joy in which every believer is not only expected but urged to participate.

In just the same way that Moshe was told to "Go, assemble the elders of Israel", so God today wants us to share the insights, visions and exhortations that He gives us for His people. We are to share those through the proper channels: the leaders of our congregations, at public meetings or house-groups - whatever opportunities He provides. "Let two or three prophets speak, while the others weigh what is said" (1 Corinthians 14:29, CJB). Unlike Moshe who was called to leadership of the nation and so had the responsibility to insist that God's word was put into action, those of us that are not in leadership can only bring God's word into our fellowships, and the responsibility then transfers to the leadership to implement what God is saying to them through us and the other members of the group. Our job is to communicate what God has laid on our heart and to make sure that we do that effectively.

Further Study: Isaiah 48:3-7; Colossians 3:16-17

Application: Today there is a great need for God's word to be heard in our world and God is calling each of us to participate with Him in sharing His heart with those around us. That includes you! Why not speak to your pastor or minister and ask how you can work with him to bring God's word alive in your congregation?

Shemot - Names - 6

Shemot / Exodus 4:18 - 31

Shemot/Exodus 4:18 And Moshe went and returned to Jethro his
father-in-law

וַיֵּלֶךְ מֹשֶׁה וַיָּשָׁב | אֶל־יֶתֶר חֹתְנוֹ
khotno   Yeter   el   vayashav Moshe vayeylech

The first thing to note in this text is the translation of יֶתֶר as Jethro.
Jethro's identity is quite clear, since he is also described as Moshe's
father-in-law, but how did his name get changed? He is mentioned in
Shemot 3:1 and 18:1, where his name takes the expected form: יִתְרוֹ, but
Rashi tells us that he has seven different names in the Hebrew tradition:
these two and רְעוּאֵל (Shemot 2:18), קֵינִי (Judges 1:16), חוֹבָב (Judges
4:11), חֶבֶר (this name is found in Judges 4:11 as one of the descendants of
Jethro, and is assumed to be one of Jethro's names by tradition) and פּוּטִיאֵל
(deduced from Shemot 6:25). Rashi explains that he was originally called
R'uel, but was given the name Jether - which means "extra" or "more" -
because he caused an extra passage of *Torah* (Shemot 18:21-23, Jethro's
advice as to how the judges should be chosen) to be written; he was called
Jethro by the addition of the final letter ו when he kept the commandments
and went back to his own people as an evangelist of the God of Israel.

The Sages debate why Moshe returned to Jethro, his father-in-law, to
seek his permission before carrying out *HaShem's* instructions to go to
Egypt. After all, if God had told him to go, what was it to do with Jethro? In
a beautiful piece of rabbinic logic, the Sages connected Moshe's suitability
to lead the people of Israel with the commitment Moshe had given Jethro
upon his marriage to one of Jethro's daughters: "Moshe agreed to stay with
the man, and he gave Moses his daughter Zipporah in marriage" (Shemot 2:21,
NRSV). Having given his word to Jethro, Moshe needed to be released
before he could leave for Egypt and lead the people to Mt. Sinai because the
Scripture asks: "Who may ascend into the hill of the Lord? And who may stand
in His holy place?" (Psalm 24:3, NASB). One of the criteria with which the

Psalmist answers that question is: "He who has clean hands and a pure heart, who has not lifted up his soul to falsehood, and has not sworn deceitfully" (v. 4, NASB), so the Sages comment: "this is Moshe; for when he came to Jethro, he swore to him that he would not depart without his knowledge, and when he went on his divine mission, he went to ask Jethro to absolve him of his oath. Hence: "and he returned to Jethro his father-in-law" (Shemot Rabbah 4:1). This is why, writing in the 11th century, Rashi comments: "Moshe would not leave Midian except with Jethro's permission".

It is also constructive to compare the departure of Moshe from his father-in-law with that of Jacob from his. "When Laban had gone to shear his flock ... Jacob deceived Laban the Aramean, by not telling him that he was fleeing. So he fled with all that he had, and he arose and crossed the Euphrates River and set his face toward the hill country of Gilead" (B'resheet 31:19-21, NASB). There then followed a seven-day hot pursuit through the desert between Haran and Canaan and it required divine intervention by way of a dream in the night to prevent Laban and his kinsmen from having a serious and possibly armed disagreement with Jacob. As the conversation in the following verses shows, there was significant disagreement, at least on Laban's part, over the ownership of most of Jacob's family and flocks; there was also the issue of Laban's idols, but Jacob was unaware of this at the time. Whether Laban would, in practice, have kept to his suggestion, "Why did you flee secretly and deceive me, and did not tell me, so that I might have sent you away with joy and with songs, with timbrel and with lyre?" (v. 27, NASB), is open to debate, but the basic assumption - both in that culture and in this - is that simply leaving or running away from a situation implies at best a broken relationship or at worst dishonesty or serious offence.

The words at the end of the verse relate that Jethro responded positively to Moshe's request; more, instead of simply releasing him, Jethro blessed him with peace in his mission. It is only after Moshe's conversation with Jethro that *HaShem* gives Moshe his specific marching orders: "Now the Lord said to Moses in Midian, 'Go back to Egypt, for all the men who were seeking your life are dead'" (Shemot 4:19, NASB). When the release is complete, Moshe can move forward, so then *HaShem* tells Moshe that the time has come to put the plan - outlined in the conversation at the Burning Bush - into practice. There is a time and a place to do everything; Moshe simply had to clear the ground and wait for *HaShem's* instructions. Although not expressed in the text, we know that Jethro was a priest - in fact, the priest of Midian - and it is therefore more than possible that just as *HaShem* gave Laban a dream at night to prevent trouble with Jacob, Jethro also seems to recognise that God is at work; perhaps God had been speaking to him as well. As an older man, with experience in helping people make decisions and sense the will of God in their lives, Jethro had probably been expecting this move for some time and was prepared for Moshe's request so that it didn't come out of the blue. In spite of losing his daughter and grandsons as Moshe left, Jethro was able to bless them with peace because he recognised God's hand at work and may have even done so since Moshe first turned up in Midian after his flight from Egypt.

This brings us to some words in the closing chapter of Hebrews: "Obey your leaders and submit to them, for they keep watch over your lives, as people who will have to render an account. So make it a task of joy for them, not one of groaning; for that is of no advantage to you" (Hebrews 13:17, CJB). Whilst "heavy shepherding" - abuse of the flock by a domineering leadership who control and manipulate those under them - rightly has a bad reputation, this verse tells us something important about the relationship between individuals, their elders/leaders and God. Clearly individuals are presumed to hear for themselves what God is saying to them, how they are intended to conduct their lives, the decisions they are to take, career paths to follow and so on. Each individual has to make those choices for themselves and the people for whom they are accountable. Since that responsibility rests with them, individuals can and should expect to hear from God themselves, in whatever way God speaks to them: through the Scriptures, through prophecy, through circumstances, through things that other people say to them - these are all valid and, provided that they don't contradict the overall balance of the Scriptures, should play a part in determining God's will. At the same time, the spiritual leaders of the congregation or church to which the individual belongs should also expect to hear from God so that they can correctly exercise the ministry of guidance that their job obviously includes. When the various leaders - be they a house-group leader, minister/pastor, elder, counsellor - pray about the individual and listen to their plans, they should expect that God will provide them with some specific way to either encourage or correct the individual, to confirm or question the proposed course of action. Similarly, individuals should expect God to particularly speak to them through their leadership and be prepared to carefully weigh the input that they provide. Of course, each person has to obey their own conscience before God and may end up correctly disregarding an incorrect leadership opinion or suggestion if they are convinced that God has spoken differently to them. But they should not do this lightly or on a repetitive basis.

This framework particularly applies in the area of changing congregation or church membership. Except in the case of abuse, no covenantally committed individual should leave one part of the Body of Messiah without at least discussing the reasons why they want to go elsewhere with their leadership. In most cases, they should follow the advice that their leaders give them. No leadership should accept someone into membership until they have confirmed that a previous leadership have released them or that release is being unreasonably withheld. Those in leadership should listen carefully to their members' explanations and reasons for changing membership and pray with the members, relaying faithfully what they hear from the Lord, not being afraid to admit that they haven't heard anything if that is the case, and being prepared to let people go as the Lord calls them. Only in this way will proper relationship be maintained and will hurt and broken relationship patterns be prevented from spreading within the body of Messiah.

Further Study: 1 Timothy 6:1; 1 Thessalonians 5:12

Application: Are you considering a change of fellowship or are you discontent with your current leadership? Before you do anything, why not talk and pray through the issues with your house-group leader or another leader that you trust to get some more input or see if you can change your position or assignment within the fellowship.

שְׁמוֹת ז׳

Shemot - Names - 7

Shemot / Names 5:1 - 6:1

Shemot/Exodus 5:2 Who is Adonai ... I do not know Adonai and moreover I will not let Israel go.

מִי יהוה ... לֹא יָדַעְתִּי אֶת־יהוה וְגַם
v'gam Adonai et yada'tiy lo ... Adonai miy

אֶת־יִשְׂרָאֵל לֹא אֲשַׁלֵּחַ
ashaleyakh lo Yisra'el et

Moshe and Aharon have returned to Egypt after Moshe's encounter with *HaShem* at the Burning Bush. Following a fairly positive meeting with the Israelite elders, they proceed with their instructions to seek an audience with Pharaoh in order to pass on *HaShem's* invitation to release the Israelites from bondage so that they may worship their God and - although the initial invitation doesn't go quite that far - return to their land, as promised to Avraham, Yitzkhak and Ya'akov. Moshe and Aharon are surprised and hurt by the negativity that they receive at the palace; after all, the Israelites made a valuable contribution to the Egyptian economy and Moshe had hoped for a more sympathetic response. Later, when the Israelites and their elders find out just how badly Pharaoh reacted to *HaShem's* initiative, their ire is turned against their erstwhile redeemers in words of some bitterness.

The word יָדַעְתִּי is a *Qal* affix 1cs form of the root יָדַע - to know. Sarna has noticed that this root "is a key term in the Exodus narrative, occurring over twenty times in the first fourteen chapters." He points out that the biblical idea of knowledge is often significantly different from the modern. Today, knowledge is considered to be largely an intellectual or mental activity; then it was "embedded in the emotions, so that it may encompass such qualities as contact, intimacy, concern, relatedness and mutuality." Not to know - the case in our text above - "is synonymous with dissociation, indifference, alienation and estrangement." Given Sarna's range of meanings, this allows Pharaoh's reply to range from "I do not know

HaShem", "*HaShem* who?", "I've never heard of *HaShem*", "I don't have any relationship with *HaShem*" to "I don't take orders from *HaShem*" or even the deliberate "I refuse to acknowledge *HaShem*".

Targum Onkelos, sensitive to the level of offence or even contempt in the Hebrew text, tones down the unseemly outburst for the sake of God's honour. Replacing it with the rather more pedestrian, "The Name of *HaShem* has not been revealed to me", it also adds the phrase, "that I should accept His *memra*". Drazin & Wagner explain that *memra* is an Aramaic term equivalent to the Greek *logos* and should be translated as "wisdom", "word", "command" or "teaching" as the context may require. Its principle use is to remove anthropomorphisms. However, it also has the effect of revealing the actions of God's Word - His spoken authority and, of course, a New Covenant name for Yeshua, the Word of God - and highlighting His involvement in the day-to-day governance of the world and its affairs, as Rav Sha'ul was later to demonstrate: "He is the visible image of the invisible God. He is supreme over all creation, because in connection with Him were created all things - in heaven and on earth, visible and invisible, whether thrones, lordships, rulers or authorities - they have all been created through Him and for Him. He existed before all things and He holds everything together" (Colossians 1:15-17, CJB).

Richard Elliott Friedman explains that it is only at this time that God starts to become known. Whilst the narrator has told us that God created the world, was responsible for the flood and made promises to Avraham, up until this point He has been known personally only to a few individuals and no nations. Friedman wryly remarks that "Pharaoh's first words to Moshe are 'Who is *HaShem*? - I don't know *HaShem*!'. By the end of the story he knows." The Sforno splits Pharaoh's words into two parts: first, "I know not *HaShem*. I do not know any Being that can bring another into being *ex nihilo* (from nothing)." Pharaoh reduces God to his own level; Pharaoh was supposed to be the incarnation of a god and he knew that he could not create things from nothing, so he arrogantly assumes that *HaShem* cannot do so either. Secondly, "And moreover I will not let Israel go. And even if this be so, that there is such a Being, I will not send forth Israel on this account." Here Pharaoh's arrogance goes up a level: "So what?" the Sforno sees him saying, "What is that to me? I will do exactly as I please."

In previous generations from ours, for hundreds of years, there has been at least a general awareness of God in the general background of our culture. Queen Victoria was a devout Christian; many people went to church on a regular basis, even if only on a social level; the founding fathers of the USA were men of faith - and this pattern was repeated around the world. Men may have chosen not to follow God's standards or have relationship with Him, but - even in spite of what a more educated and enlightened age would regard as great inequality and even abuse in society - God was a part of the basic social fabric; He was taken for granted and if He was mentioned, everyone knew who He was. Most countries in the world have built their justice system around the Judaeo-Christian ethic, based however loosely on the Ten Commandments, and ethical principles such as honesty, charity, compassion and decency were - even if ignored or flouted by a few - widely recognised.

Today, living in a post-modern world, where everyone is right and entitled to their own beliefs, the situation is very different. Many people have no idea who God is; they have not even heard of God. Father Christmas, Sir Winston Churchill, William the Conqueror: yes; but God - who is He? In talking to people, it is not uncommon to encounter genuine incredulity and puzzlement at the suggestion that there is a God or that He has standards and expectations for peoples' behaviour and conduct. The concept of sin is at best regarded as a primitive superstition, at worst a technique for manipulation and the suppression of the individual. Pharaoh's words are being echoed increasingly on every street corner: "I have never heard of God!"

Rampant individualism leads many on a bizarre life of self-determination and self-expression, trying to find themselves in a world where everyone is lost. Many religious leaders emphasise personal autonomy, the right of the individual to pick and choose, to select for themselves what feels right for them out of a pot-pouri of different religious ideas and experiences. Spirituality is exploited to sell books, CDs and DVSs; new-age jewelry and symbols abound. Traders stand on every street corner and website, hawking their wares and proclaiming Pharaoh's words: "Even if there is a God, what is that to you and I? Buy this product and do as you please." The words at the end of the book of Judges are still accurate today: "In those days there was no king in Israel; everyone did what was right in his own eyes" (Judges 21:25, NASB).

Our part, as believers, is exactly the same as that of Moshe and Aharon: to be a witness both to the existence and the power of God. We proclaim before the Pharaohs of the world, "Let My people go!" as we share the gospel with everyone we meet. God works His miracles through and around us to confirm the truth of His word, as people hear about Him and come into the kingdom. The self-motivated and money-driven values of the world are exposed as valueless as we give of our time and money in volunteer projects, mercy ministries and outreach, selflessly giving without expecting any return. Not random acts of kindness but intentional and planned generosity; compassion that touches hearts and lives with the grace and mercy of God: "the light of the knowledge of God's glory shining in the face of the Messiah Yeshua" (2 Corinthians 4:6, CJB). We can even see the progression through the plagues of Egypt being worked out again in our lives and times; the evidence of the lice and boils is all around us! The book of Revelation speaks of fire and hail: "The first [angel] sounded his shofar; and there came hail and fire mingled with blood, and it was thrown down upon the earth. A third of the earth was burned up, a third of the trees were burned up, and all green grass was burned up" (Revelation 8:7, CJB) as the extremes of weather become more pronounced. Even the fabric of the physical world seems to be breaking down: "the whole creation has been groaning as with the pains of childbirth" (Romans 8:22, CJB) as earthquakes, tsunamis and volcanic activity tear up the earth's crust. We can sense the darkness approaching, yet know that it will not be dark in the household of faith; we await the return of Yeshua Himself to lead us out of slavery, for Him to be proclaimed king in Jerusalem.

Further Study: Job 21:7-16; Jeremiah 44:15-19; Romans 8:19-23

Application: As we see the signs of the breakdown of society and the physical world, it is easy to become afraid and fearful; this is what the enemy wants. Instead, we should be looking and waiting, joining with creation on tip-toes, eagerly waiting for Yeshua's return. Ask God to give you that sense of anticipation today!

וָאֵרָא

Va'era - And I appeared

Shemot / Exodus 6:2 - 9:35

רִאשׁוֹן	Aliyah One	Shemot/Exodus 6:2 - 13
שֵׁנִי	Aliyah Two	Shemot/Exodus 6:14 - 28
שְׁלִישִׁי	Aliyah Three	Shemot/Exodus 6:29 - 7:7
רְבִיעִי	Aliyah Four	Shemot/Exodus 7:8 - 8:6
חֲמִשִׁי	Aliyah Five	Shemot/Exodus 8:7 - 18
שִׁשִׁי	Aliyah Six	Shemot/Exodus 8:19 - 9:16
שְׁבִיעִי	Aliyah Seven	Shemot/Exodus 9:17 - 35

וָאֵרָא א׳

Va'era - And I appeared - 1

Shemot / Exodus 6:2 - 13

Shemot/Exodus 6:2 And God spoke to Moshe and He said to him, "I am Adonai".

וַיְדַבֵּר אֱלֹהִים אֶל־מֹשֶׁה וַיֹּאמֶר אֵלָיו אֲנִי

aniy   eylayv vayomeyr Moshe   el   Elohiym vay'dabeyr

יהוה:

Adonai

This portion starts with an unusual combination of words. The verb דִּבֵּר is almost always only used in the *Pi'el* stem, implying an intensified or concentrated effect, and refers to the action of speaking. Used for many adn varied speakers, it would normally be translated, "he spoke". Indeed, the combination וַיְדַבֵּר יהוה is repeated many times in the *Torah* and stresses how *HaShem* spoke to Moshe on a direct face-to-face basis: a close or even intimate conversation. However, here the verb is coupled with the name of God that is associated in classical Jewish thought with the Attribute of Justice - a rare combination - so that it is taken by several commentators to be a harsh or stern rebuke (Gur Aryeh) in response to Moshe's doubts expressed at the end of the previous *parasha* (Shemot 5:22-23).

It seems it is necessary for God to speak strongly even to Moshe, whom He later describes to Aharon and Miryam as, "the only one who is faithful in My entire household. With him I speak face to face and clearly, not in riddles; he sees the image of Adonai" (B'Midbar 12:7-8, CJB). Later, we find King Saul, the anointed king of Israel, being rebuked by the prophet Samuel, "You did a foolish thing. You didn't obey the mitzvah of Adonai, which He gave you" (1 Sam 13:13, CJB), when he disobeyed the Lord's instructions regarding the bringing of a burnt offering. Similarly, we hear a definite tone of rebuke in Yeshua's words to the *P'rushim* in such instances as, "Woe to you hypocritical Torah-teachers and P'rushim! For you are shutting the Kingdom of Heaven in peoples' faces, neither entering yourselves nor allowing those who wish to enter to do so" (Matthew 23:13, CJB).

Some believers make the mistake of assuming that God will only speak to them in gushy words of love and encouragement, dismissing corrective words or scriptures as being for someone else, or simply being wrong or mis-applied. Whilst moments of rebuke may be few, for God does not condemn His children, sometimes He does need to speak more strongly to us when we are not paying attention properly or fall into sin. After all, as the Scriptures tell us, "those whom the Lord loves He disciplines ... as sons; for what son is there whom his father does not discipline" (Hebrews 12:6-7, NASB). God still speaks to us face-to-face, by His Spirit - we must be careful to take seriously whatever He says, be it encouragement or correction and not dismiss those words which we find uncomfortable, for it is just these words that we most need to hear.

Further Study: Job 5:17-18; Proverbs 3:11-12; Revelation 3:19

Application: Has God been speaking to you recently? Have you heard and acknowledged His voice? If not, can you remember the last thing He spoke to you about which perhaps you should be acting upon?

וָאֵרָא 'ב

Va'era - And I appeared - 2

Shemot / Exodus 6:14 - 28

Shemot/Exodus 6:14 These are the heads of their fathers' houses: the sons of Reuven ...

אֵלֶּה רָאשֵׁי בֵית־אֲבֹתָם בְּנֵי רְאוּבֵן

R'uveyn b'ney avotam   veyt   roshey   eyleh

This somewhat truncated genealogical list (it only features the first three of Israel's sons: Reuben, Simeon and Levi) comes at a strange place in the text. In the previous verse (v. 13) *HaShem* starts speaking to Moshe and Aharon, is interrupted by these names and finally resumes in verse 29. Rashi comments that "[the *Torah*] had to set out the genealogy of the tribe of Levi until Moshe and Aharon because of Moshe and Aharon." This doesn't immediately make sense because both Moshe and Aharon have been mentioned before in the narrative without any mention of their lineage - why does the *Torah* have recourse to it at this point? The list has two purposes, one of which is disclosed in verse 27: "this Moshe and Aharon" - in other words, it authenticates which Moshe and Aharon *Hashem* spoke to: these particular ones. The second purpose is to show that Moshe and Aharon are among the leaders of Israel - they are clan or tribe leaders, recognised as such by the community (HaGriz).

In the days following the building of the Second Temple and the rebuilding of Jerusalem after the return from Babylon, Nehemiah conducted a census of the returnees and checked the genealogies of those who were to serve as Priests and Levites in the Temple. He writes that there were those who could not prove their ancestry - even among the *cohanim* - and "these searched their ancestral registration, but it could not be located; therefore they were considered unclean and excluded from the priesthood ... until a priest arose with Urim and Thumim" (Nehemiah 7:64-65, NASB). These priests were not allowed to share in either the obligations or the benefits of the priesthood until it was proven that they really were *cohanim* either by genealogical documents or directly by the Lord.

Perhaps that is why we find two genealogies for Yeshua in the *B'rit*

Hadashah. Although slightly different and starting from different points, Matthew's (Matthew 1) and Luke's (Luke 3) list of Yeshua's ancestors serve those two same purposes: firstly to anchor Him in His people - a true Israelite, a descendant of the fathers: Avraham, Yitz'chak and Ya'akov - and a true man, descended from Adam and Eve. Secondly, it provides His accreditation as a direct descendant of King David, of the tribe of Judah and therefore standing in the prophecy originally given to Ya'akov: "The sceptre shall not pass from Y'hudah ... until He comes to whom [obedience] belongs" (B'resheet 49:10, CJB), confirmed to David: "I will maintain Him in My house and in My kingdom forever; and His throne will be set up for ever" (1 Chronicles 17:14, NASB) and spoken of by the prophets: "Then a shoot will spring forth from the stem of Jesse, and a branch from his roots will bear fruit" (Isaiah 11:1, NASB). This is why, on the day of *Shavuot*, Peter could stand before the people and say: "God has made Him both Lord and Messiah - this Yeshua - who you executed on a stake" (Acts 2:36, CJB).

Further Study: Psalm 2:1-12; Hebrews 1:1-5

Application: Sometimes in our focus on Yeshua as our Friend and Brother (and, indeed, He is both), we can lose sight of the fact that He is the Lion of the tribe of Judah, that He is not only qualified but entitled to be the Messiah, the Anointed One, the Holy One of God and that He is not only to receive our prayers but our worship.

וָאֵרָא *'ג*

Va'era - And I appeared - 3

Shemot / Exodus 6:29 - 7:7

Shemot/Exodus 6:29 I am Adonai! Speak to Pharaoh, king of Egypt

אֲנִי יהוה דַּבֵּר אֶל־פַּרְעֹה מֶלֶךְ מִצְרָיִם
Mitz'rayim melech Par'oh el dabeyr Adonai ani

This verse is nearly a repeat of the text earlier in the chapter: "HaShem spoke to Moshe to say, 'Come, speak to Pharaoh, king of Egypt ...'" (6:10-11) and the commentators say that it is repeated to rejoin the narrative after the interlude of presenting the genealogy of Moshe and Aharon. Nevertheless, there is one important difference, namely the substitution of the phrase אֲנִי יהוה for the word בֹּא. The latter is the imperative form of the verb בּוֹא, to come or enter, and could be taken as an exhortation: "Come along now and speak to Pharaoh ..." The former, on the other hand, might at first glance be thought of as being disconnected from the rest of the sentence - a 1st common singular pronoun and a name or proper noun are often used in this way to present a claim of identity: I am *Adonai* - perhaps identifying who is speaking or a little fanfare to emphasise what *HaShem* said. On closer examination, however, we can see that those two words perform an important function.

Firstly, we know that Moshe is a hesitant and reluctant speaker. Here he is being called to speak for a second time to Pharaoh, the man in whose house he was brought up, over whose household - at least according to Jewish tradition - he had had significant authority, yet who has reacted very badly to Moshe's first visit to request the release of the Israelites. So Moshe could well be feeling considerable inner reluctance to put his head, so to speak, back in the lion's mouth. So here, *Adonai* is reminding Moshe that it is He that is giving the orders and because it is *Adonai* speaking, this is not negotiable on Moshe's part. He will go and speak to Pharaoh because *Adonai* says so.

Secondly, *Rashi* comments bluntly: "I am *Adonai*: I have the wherewithal to send you and to fulfill the words of My mission." Moshe is not simply a man speaking to Pharaoh, however well Pharaoh may know

27

him; he is an accredited ambassador of the Lord. Whether Pharaoh accepts the accreditation or not is irrelevant; Moshe is speaking on behalf of heaven and with the full weight and authority of heaven behind him. Moshe is here being commissioned to go and speak in the name of God Himself and, as we know, God is going to back up what Moshe says and force Egypt to let the people of Israel go.

In the ancient world, great importance was placed when anybody spoke or performed some action; whose name, reputation or authority stood behind the words or action. It was as if the immediate person delivering the message was simply a messenger and that value was only attached to whomever had commissioned or sent him. This is why we find Yeshua being asked: "By what authority are You doing these things, and who gave You this authority?" (Matthew 21:23, NASB) Hence the words of the old chorus: "Go in My name and because you believe, others will know that I live!"

Further Study: Matthew 10:40-42; Zechariah 14:9

Application: Where are you being challenged to speak for the Lord? Make no mistake, God has both called and equipped you to speak for Him somewhere, just as He did with Moshe. Ask Him where that place is and what you are to say today.

וָאֵרָא 'ד

Va'era - And I appeared - 4

Shemot / Exodus 7:8-8:6

Shemot/Exodus 7:9 When Pharaoh speaks to you to say, "Give, for yourselves, a sign ..."

כִּי יְדַבֵּר אֲלֵכֶם פַּרְעֹה לֵאמֹר תְּנוּ לָכֶם מוֹפֵת
mopheyt lachem t'nu leymor Par'oh aleychem y'dabeyr kiy

Abravanel asks, "What made God so sure that Pharaoh would ask them to provide a miracle?" He then goes on to answer the question by pointing out that God knew Pharaoh: "I know the man, he will insist that you perform a miracle to confirm your *bona fides[1].*" Ibn Ezra supports this by adding that God knew that the first time Moshe and Aharon went before Pharaoh he would simply deny knowing *Adonai* - effectively refusing to recognise His existence at all - whereas on this occasion he would demand a marvel, some miraculous sign or attesting supernatural act of power, to prove that they were not just trying to bluff Pharaoh in their own strength. Moshe and Aharon are then limited to performing the specific sign that God has given them - nothing more and nothing less - with no accompanying *shpiel* or justification. Although Pharaoh demanded that Moshe and Aharon prove who they were by performing a sign, they were only allowed to perform the sign that God had given them to prove who He was.

1 Kings 13 tells the story of a nameless prophet who was sent to speak out against the pagan and idolatrous practices of Jereboam, the first king of the northern kingdom, Israel. The prophet came from Judah to Bethel and there spoke out the words that *Adonai* had given him, but when Jereboam (eventually) offered him hospitality and a reward, he refused saying, "So it was commanded me by the word of the Lord, saying, 'You shall eat no bread, nor drink water, nor return by the way which you came'" (1 Kings 13:9, NASB). Yet he was deceived by an old prophet, who lied to him, and returned to eat and drink in his house. So in spite of his previous obedience and boldness in denouncing the religious practices of Jereboam, the word of the Lord came: "Because you have disobeyed the command of the Lord, and

---

1. Latin for "good faith".

have not observed the commandment which the Lord your God commanded you, but have returned and eaten bread and drank water in the place of which He said to you, 'Eat no bread and drink no water'; your body shall not come to the grave of your fathers" (vv. 21-22, NASB); the prophet was killed by a lion on his way home. The prophet's disobedience, even though he was deceived by another prophet who claimed to be speaking from the Lord, cost him his life.

Yeshua faced the same challenge during the time that He was being tempted by the Devil: Prove it! Notice the progression from Matthew's account: "If you are the Son of God, command that these stones become bread" (Matthew 4:4, NASB) or, in other words: prove it to yourself; "If you are the Son of God, throw Yourself down [from the pinnacle of the Temple]" (v. 6, NASB) or: prove it to the world. Yeshua answers each stage of the trial by quoting God's command - in this case not specific commandments to Him personally, but commands from the *Torah* given to Israel. We see Yeshua operating throughout His ministry within the parameters set by His Father and refusing to go outside those limits.

Often we are tempted to exceed our position or authority as believers. We are placed in situations - witnessing to others, counselling friends, frustrated at the world's stupidity and wickedness - when we find ourselves echoing the words of the prophet, "Oh that Thou wouldst rend the heavens and come down, that the mountains might quake at Thy presence - as fire kindles the brushwood, as fire causes water to boil - to make Thy name known to Thine adversaries, that the nations may tremble at Thy presence!" (Isaiah 64:1-2, NASB). Yet God is gracious and deals with things and people in His own way and in His own time and like Moshe and Aharon, we have to work with Him, not the other way around. God's power is most evident when we do exactly what He tells us to do and no more.

Further Study: Isaiah 8:16-18; Romans 8:35-39

Application: If you struggle with other peoples' expectations, or feeling that you have to justify your faith to others, take time this week to relax in the knowledge that you are only to do or say what God has said, not what man expects or seems to require. Make sure that you are there - on the nail - for God and leave Him to deal with everyone else.

וָאֵרָא 'ה

Va'era - And I appeared - 5

Shemot / Exodus 8:7 - 18

Shemot/Exodus 8:7 And the frogs will be removed from you, your servants and from your people

וְסָרוּ הַצְפַרְדְעִים מִמְּךָ וּמִבָּתֶּיךָ

oomibateycha mimcha hatz'far'd'iym v'saru

וּמֵעַמֶּךָ וּמֵעֲבָדֶיךָ

oomey'amecha oomey'avadeycha

The verb וְסָרוּ comes from the root סוּר which can have both an active and a passive meaning: "to depart from" - which is often used in the sense of departing from God and His ways - or "to be removed". In this context, although the active meaning is possible: "the frogs will depart from you ...", the second seems more likely: "the frogs will be removed ..." and also emphasises that God needed to make it happen. Ramban picks up on this when he comments, "Moshe emphasises that as soon as he prays they will all retreat to keep Pharaoh from fearing that that these frogs would die but others would come up from the Nile. The plague will depart entirely, even though frogs remain in the Nile. All of this was to make clear to Pharaoh that the plague was carried out by God."

Ibn Ezra, on the other hand, shows up another concern that the rabbis had with this verse: "The frogs shall retreat - Moshe made the promise without consulting God, confident that He would not embarrass him; Moshe even adds 'and your servants' although Pharaoh had not asked for this (v. 4)". This is a really interesting point, for it touches on the degree of control or free-will that Moshe experienced. When he talked to Pharaoh, was God bound by Moshe's promise? Or did Moshe know enough of God's plans so that he could speak from certainty or guess-work? The text itself gives no help in answering the question - it isn't important to the main flow of the narrative, so we are left to speculate whether Moshe knew that the frogs would be removed or simply that God would bring the plague to an end and assumed or guessed the rest. Was the working relationship between God and

Moshe so tight that Moshe could say things or fill in details that God would then have to execute in addition to the basic plan? Or was it instead that Moshe was so close to God that he just naturally spoke exactly what God had in mind all along?

Hundreds of years later in Jerusalem, at a low point in our people's history, approaching the destruction of Jerusalem itself and the first Temple by King Nebuchadnezzar of Babylon, a prophetic drama was played out in the house of the Lord before the priests and the people. Hananiah, whom the text acknowledges to be a prophet, said, "Thus says the Lord of Hosts, the God of Israel, 'I have broken the yoke of the king of Babylon. Within two years I am going to bring back to this place all the vessels of the Lord's house, which Nebuchadnezzer king of Babylon took away from this place and carried to Babylon ...' declares the Lord, 'for I will break the yoke of the king of Babylon'" (Jeremiah 28:3-4, NASB). Then, despite Jeremiah's warning, Hananiah took the yoke off the neck of Jeremiah and broke it as a symbolic gesture and picture to confirm his words, which he then repeated. Yet the following verses tell us that the Lord then told Jeremiah to go to Hananiah later and rebuke him for speaking falsely in God's name: "Listen now, Hananiah, the Lord has not sent you, and you have made this people trust in a lie ... this year you are going to die, because you have counseled rebellion against the Lord" (Jeremiah 28:15-16, NASB).

What went wrong here? How could a man whom the Tanakh confirms is a prophet get things so desperately wrong that he brings a completely invalid word from God and pays for this offence with his life? The previous chapter gives us the background context to this scene, where God warns King Zedekiah of Judah and the kings of the surrounding nations that they are to serve Nebuchadnezzer and not believe false prophets, diviners, dreamers or soothsayers (27:9,16). Hananiah thought that he was speaking for God, but God said, "No", he was only speaking on his own initiative; God had not sent him. A clue is given in Jeremiah's warning to Hananiah: "The prophets who were before me and before you from ancient times prophesied against many lands and against great kingdoms, of war and of calamity and of pestilence" (28:8, NASB) - Hananiah was speaking out of line with not only the political situation around him, but with the previously spoken words of the Lord through many other prophets. If he had stopped to think, to weigh what he was about to say against what God has already said, then Hananiah might not have fallen prey to saying what the people wanted to hear rather than what God knew they needed to hear.

This makes all the more remarkable the words of Yeshua: "Yes! I tell you that whoever does not doubt in his heart but trusts that what he says will happen can say to this mountain, 'Go and throw yourself into the sea!' and it will be done for him" (Mark 11:23, CJB). This promise of Yeshua can be found at least three more times in similar or slightly different contexts in both

Matthew (17:20, 21:21) and Luke (17:6) so it must have made a significant impact upon the gospel writers and the early church. Yeshua continues, "Therefore, I tell you, whatever you ask for in prayer, trust that you are receiving it, and it will be yours" (Mark 11:24, CJB). When God has already spoken into your heart and told you what to say and what He is about to do, then you can speak out in faith, commanding that action to take place and it will, because you will be speaking in the faith that comes from knowing that you have heard from God.

Further Study: Ezekiel 13:1-3; Luke 11:9-13

Application: If you shrink back from proclaiming what God has laid on your heart, be encouraged today to start taking the first steps to being a little more bold. Find someone whom you trust to share some of these words with, who can pray with you and help to build up your faith and discernment as you develop God's gift, so that God's word for today may be clearly heard by His people.

וָאֵרָא ו'

Va'era - And I appeared - 6

Shemot / Exodus 8:19 - 9:16

Shemot/Exodus 8:19 And I shall place redemption between My people and your people

וְשַׂמְתִּי פְדֻת בֵּין עַמִּי וּבֵין עַמֶּךָ

amecha ooveyn amiy beyn f'dut v'samtiy

The Ba'al HaTurim explains that the *Masoretic* note to the word פְדֻת means that it occurs three times in the Hebrew Scriptures; he lists these occurences as here, with *defectiva* spelling, and at Psalm 111:9 and Psalm 130:7 with *plene* spelling: פְדוּת. Even-Shoshan reports that the word does actually occur a fourth time, in Isaiah 50:2 as מִפְּדוּת, with the preposition מִן - from - as an assimilated prefix. פְדֻת is a feminine noun - usually translated 'redemption' or 'salvation' - from the root פָּדָה - to redeem, ransom, set free, deliver (Davidson). Following the Septuagint and the Vulgate, albeit with a footnote that the Hebrew text is translated 'redemption', most English versions (for example, NASB, NIV, ESV, RSV, NRSV) change their translation here to 'distinction', possibly because they are theologically uncomfortable with the idea of salvation or redemption being available before Yeshua. Although 'distinction' is also supported by some of the Jewish commentators, Nahum Sarna underlines this inconsistency by stating that "פְדֻת is otherwise invariably translated as rescue or redemption". *Targum Onkelos* explicitly uses the Aramaic word פּוּרְקָן and paraphrases the verse to read, "I will bring redemption to My people and I will bring a plague upon your people".

The Ba'al HaTurim goes on to explain that the use of פְדֻת in Psalm 111 - "He has sent redemption to His people; He has ordained His covenant forever; Holy and awesome is His name" (v. 9, NASB) - shows that the redemption provided from Egypt was only a partial redemption, but that the use in Psalm 130 - "Isra'el, put your hope in Adonai! For grace is found with Adonai, and with him is unlimited redemption" (v. 7, CJB) - shows that the future redemption will be full and complete. Rashi, after pointing out in his commentary for the previous verse that when *HaShem* says "I will distinguish" means "I will set apart", comments that the redemption "will distinguish between My people and your people"; that is to say, that the redemption is the means by which the two people groups will be separated: the Israelites will be saved or redeemed, the Egyptians will not. The Ramban produces a cross-reference to the verse "For I am the Lord your God, The Holy One of Israel, your Savior; I have given Egypt as your ransom, Cush and Seba in your place" (Isaiah 43:3, NASB), to show that *HaShem* is in the redemption business, giving other nations and peoples as a ransom for Israel.

An early anonymous Christian apologetic from the 2nd century describes the separation that existed between the believers of his time and the rest of the Roman world:

For Christians are not distinguished from the rest of humanity by country, language or custom. For nowhere do they live in cities of their own, nor do they speak some unusual dialect, nor do they practice an eccentric way of life. This teaching of theirs has not been discovered by the thought and reflection of ingenious people, nor do they promote any human doctrine, as some do. But while they live in both Greek and barbarian cities, as each one's lot was cast, and follow the local customs in dress and food and other aspects of life, at the same time they demonstrate the remarkable and admittedly unusual character of their own citizenship. They live in their own countries, but only as non-residents; they participate in everything as citizens, and endure everything as foreigners. Every foreign country is their fatherland, and every fatherland is foreign. They marry like everyone else, and have children, but they do not expose their offspring. They share their food but not their wives. They are in the flesh, but they do not live according to the flesh. They live on earth, but their citizenship is in heaven. They obey the established laws; indeed in their private lives they transcend the laws. They love everyone, and by everyone they are persecuted. They are unknown, yet they are condemned; they are put to death, yet they are brought to life. They are poor, yet they make rich; they are in need of everything, yet they abound in everything. They are dishonoured, yet they are glorified in their dishonour; they are slandered, yet they are vindicated. They are cursed, yet they bless; they are insulted, yet they offer respect. When they do good, they are punished as evildoers; when they are punished, they rejoice as though brought to life. By the Jews they are assaulted as foreigners, and by the Greeks they are persecuted, yet those who hate them are unable to give a reason for their hostility.(*Epistle to Diognetus 5:1-17*; The Apostolic Fathers, trans. Michael W. Holmes)

We hear the probably deliberate echoes of the gospel texts and the letters of Rav Sha'ul running through this description but nevertheless it shows what a distinct and set apart people these believers were. We may regret the way in which they were rejected by the Jews of their time, just as believers - particularly Messianic Jews - are rejected today by mainstream Orthodox Jewry, but their lives were a testimony to the hope and faith they had in Yeshua as their Messiah and the redemption that they experienced in their lives despite the hostility of the people and environment in which they lived. Put another way, there was no mistaking these people - although just like everyone else around them, they stuck out like sore thumbs - the salvation that they had separated them from everyone else. Although their neighbours could not identify anything wrong with the believers or any reason to dislike them, their redemption set them apart from those who did not have a relationship with the One True God.

In his vision of the end times, John saw, "a great white throne and the One sitting on it. Earth and heaven fled from His presence, and no place was found for them" (Revelation 20:11, CJB). The text goes on to tell us that all the people who ever lived were standing before that throne and were judged according to their actions in this life. The single question that divided those who would spend eternity in heaven and those who would not is clearly explained: "And if anyone's name was not found written in the book of life, he was thrown into the lake of fire" (v. 15, CJB). How does one's name become written in the Book of Life? In the next chapter, this book is described as "The Lamb's Book of Life" (21:27, CJB) and Yeshua is the one who erases peoples' names from the book (Revelation 3:5). The Psalmist knows of the book, for he begs God concerning the wicked, "May they be blotted out of the book of life, and may they not be recorded with the righteous" (Psalm 69:28, NASB). So it is the righteous whose names are written in the book, those who are in covenant relationship with God and those whose lives witness to their separation from the world around them. Yeshua describes their situation: "I have given them Thy word; and the world has hated them, because they are not of the world, even as I am not of the world" (John 17:11, NASB). Those who belong to Yeshua and are called by His name are those who are the separate ones, those who possess God's salvation, the ones who have experienced His redemption.

Further Study: Isaiah 56:3-7; Ephesians 2:11-13

Application: Do you know God's redemption in your life? If you were arrested and charged with being a believer, would there be enough evidence to convict you? It is time to seek God as to how you are to be separate and distinct - without being weird or whacky - from the world around you so that there may be a difference and a witness in your life.

וָאֵרָא 'ז

Va'era - And I appeared - 7

Shemot / Exodus 9:17-35

Shemot/Exodus 9:17 "Still you are trampling on My people and do not let them go."

עוֹדְךָ מִסְתּוֹלֵל בְּעַמִּי לְבִלְתִּי שַׁלְּחָם:
shalkham   l'viltiy   b'amiy   mis'toleyl   od'cha

The verb מִסְתּוֹלֵל, a *hapax legomenon* in this form and from a root סָלַל that is only used eleven times in the Hebrew Bible, has caused some excitement among the commentators. This is a *Hitpa'el* participle, in infix rather than prefix form - the ת, rather than appearing before the root consonants, has been inserted between the first and second root letter[2]. The *Hitpa'el* stem implies a meaning that is either reflexive - the action is done to oneself - or iterative - the action is carried out repeatedly - sometimes both may apply. The root appears to have the meaning "to raise up, cast up; to prepare or make a way" (Davidson). Rashi connects the verb with the noun מְסִלָּה in B'Midbar 20:19 - "We will keep to the beaten track" (JPS), the Israelites said to the people of Edom when asking permission to cross their land during their journey into *Eretz Yisrael - Targum Onkelos* translates it there as "a well trodden road". The same word also occurs in "And there will be a highway from Assyria ..." (Isaiah 11:16, NASB). On that basis, Rashi translates the first two words as "Still you are treading My people". In this verse, *Targum Onkelos* switches to the Aramaic verb כְּבֵישַׁת, translated as 'suppress': "You continue to suppress My people". Following the *Rashbam*, the NJPS version translates the verb as 'thwart', while Ibn Ezra follows the opinion of Ibn Janah and suggests "You extol yourself against My people" as found in "Sing to God, chant hymns to His name; extol Him who rides the clouds" (Psalm 68:5, JPS).

Abuse - treading down other people, ignoring their feelings and wishes

---

2. This process is known as *metathesis*, where a *tav* and a sibilant letter (*samech, shin, sin*) swap places to avoid an overlap with the 'ts' sound of the *tsadi*. See Jouon, Muraoka, *A Grammar of Biblical Hebrew*, page 74, §17b

- can be both reflexive and iterative. People may abuse themselves and others; abuse is often a cyclic or repetitive pattern. During the days when the Tabernacle rested at Shiloh, when Eli was the priest, his sons abused both those who brought offerings and the Lord to whom the offerings were brought. By insisting on taking raw meat that they could roast, before the fat had been burnt and the meat boiled, they invalidated the offering to the Lord and abused their positions as priests. "Thus the sin of the young men was very great before the Lord, for the men despised the offering of the Lord" (1 Samuel 2:17, NASB). Although Eli challenged his sons about their behaviour, "Why do you do such things, the evil things that I hear from all these people? No, my sons; for the report is not good which I hear the Lord's people circulating" (vv. 23-24, NASB), they ignored him. A prophet came to Eli, bringing him a rebuke from the Lord: "Why, then, do you maliciously trample upon the sacrifices and offerings that I have commanded? ... And this shall be a sign for you: the fate of your two sons Hophni and Phinehas -- they shall both die on the same day" (vv. 29,34, JPS). Eli's sons were unwilling or unable to break the pattern of abuse which had developed in their lives and so they died.

During the years of the kings, when Israel and Judah often served the gods of the surrounding nations, God sent the prophets to challenge the people: "'What need have I of all your sacrifices?' says the Lord. 'I am sated with burnt offerings of rams, and suet of fatlings, and blood of bulls; and I have no delight in lambs and he-goats. That you come to appear before Me - who asked that of you? Trample My courts no more; bringing oblations is futile, incense is offensive to Me. New moon and sabbath, proclaiming of solemnities, assemblies with iniquity, I cannot abide.'" (Isaiah 1:11-13, JPS). The people had not only turned away from God, they were repeatedly abusing the weaker members of society, the orphans and the widows, those who could not defend themselves. Relationship with God was impossible for a society that practiced abuse on a significant scale.

Even in Second Temple times, after the shock of the First Temple's destruction and the Babylonian exile, Yeshua nevertheless spoke about the religious leaders of His day: "'The Torah-teachers and the P'rushim,' He said, 'sit in the seat of Moshe . So whatever they tell you, take care to do it. But don't do what they do, because they talk but don't act! They tie heavy loads onto people's shoulders but won't lift a finger to help carry them. Everything they do is done to be seen by others; for they make their t'fillin broad and their tzitziyot long, they love the place of honour at banquets and the best seats in the synagogues'" (Matthew 23:2-6, CJB). Here the abuse worked all ways: the leaders abused the people, their positions as leaders and teachers,and themselves; they had adopted routine patterns of behaviour that were obvious to Yeshua.

We know today from many studies that those who abuse their partners in marriage or those who abuse children usually come from an abusive home themselves, and that this kind of behaviour is deeply patterned and habitual. Even periods of time in prison and many hours of counselling and therapy often fail to break the hold that the abusive cycles have built up in their lives; once they are unsupervised, the old habits take over and the abuse begins again. That is not to say, of course, that today's abusers are simply themselves victims and unable to take choices to avoid or prevent abuse - they are and remain responsible for their actions - but the pattern is so strong that most fail to break it or even realise that they have a choice.

Each generation, however, does have a choice. *Qohelet* warned the people about guarding their relationship with God: "Guard your steps as you go to the house of God, and draw near to listen rather than to offer the sacrifice of fools; for they do not know they are doing evil" (Ecclesiastes 5:1, NASB). The people should not compound their abuse towards people by pretending that their relationship with God was still alright. The people in Isaiah's time were offered that choice very clearly: "'Come, let us reach an understanding - says the Lord. Be your sins like crimson, they can turn snow-white; be they red as dyed wool, they can become like fleece'" (Isaiah 1:18, JPS). The abused people of Eli's days were offered a prophetic ray of hope, pointing the way forward: "But I will raise up for Myself a faithful priest who will do according to what is in My heart and in My soul; and I will build him an enduring house, and he will walk before My Anointed always" (1 Samuel 2:35, NASB). God wants to break the patterns of abuse and set people free from abusive addictions. God is in the ransom business: ransoming souls from abusive behaviour to spouses or children, from abusive addictions to alcohol, pornography and drugs, from self-abusive lifestyles such as prostitution, homosexuality and the sex industry. The answer to abuse is found in Yeshua, who suffered the ultimate abuse - being crucified on the stake although innocent of any crime or offence - so that He might bear the pain and punishment for our abuse in His physical body, that we might be forgiven and set free.

Each of us has a choice today. We can continue with our abusive behaviour, along that well-beaten path - be that as simple as continually arguing with our spouse, or as complex as the most serious cases of criminal abuse - or we can invite Yeshua to break the pattern of abuse in our lives. We should not allow the enemy of our souls to have the final word; we must not become like Pharaoh, whose heart was hardened by his continual rejection of *HaShem*. Instead, let us soften our hearts to each other and to God and "along with those who call on the Lord from a pure heart, pursue righteousness, faithfulness, love and peace" (2 Timothy 2:22, CJB).

Further Study: 1 Corinthians 6:18, Ecclesiastes 11:9-10; 3 John 11

Application: The signs of abuse are often well hidden in our lives. Do you still suppress or oppress members of your family or are you perhaps the victim of another's abuse? If so, then you need to hear Yeshua's words of freedom and release today: "Come to me, all of you who are struggling and burdened, and I will give you rest" (Matthew 11:28, CJB). They are real and they are for you.

בֹּא

Bo - Come

Shemot / Exodus 10:1 - 13:16

רִאשׁוֹן	Aliyah One	Shemot/Exodus 10:1 - 11
שֵׁנִי	Aliyah Two	Shemot/Exodus 10:12 - 23
שְׁלִישִׁי	Aliyah Three	Shemot/Exodus 10:24 - 11:3
רְבִיעִי	Aliyah Four	Shemot/Exodus 11:4 - 12:20
חֲמִשִׁי	Aliyah Five	Shemot/Exodus 12:21 - 28
שִׁשִּׁי	Aliyah Six	Shemot/Exodus 12:29 - 51
שְׁבִיעִי	Aliyah Seven	Shemot/Exodus 13:1 - 16

Bo - Come - 1

Shemot / Exodus 10:1 - 11

Shemot/Exodus 10:1 And the Lord said to Moshe, "Come to Pharaoh"

וַיֹּאמֶר יהוה אֶל־מֹשֶׁה בֹּא אֶל־פַּרְעֹה

Par'oh el bo Moshe el Adonai vay'omer

Why did the Lord have to tell Moshe to come to Pharaoh at this time? There had already been seven plagues, each following the same formula: Moshe and Aharon re-present the Lord's demand to Pharaoh that he should let the people of Israel go, he refuses and they announce the next plague which then duly happens. After the seventh plague, Pharaoh at last admits his sin against God - "This time I have sinned; the Lord is in the right, and I and my people are in the wrong" (Shemot 9:27, ESV), then hardens his heart once the hail and rain stop, just as Moshe said he would. Perhaps Moshe was starting to feel like the prophet Jonah was to feel some hundreds of years later when sent by God to the city of Nineveh - that he didn't want to go because he knew what was going to happen.

Rashi tells us that Moshe was commanded to warn Pharaoh of the judgement that was still to come. Pharaoh himself had hardened his own heart after the lifting of the last plague, so it was not yet a foregone conclusion that the full series of plagues and the death of the first-born would have to happen; there was still an option for Pharaoh to come round and be obedient to God's demands. Yet we read that after this point, in this week's *parasha*, in the conversations in and around the last three plagues, *Adonai* hardened Pharaoh's heart. It is as if, once past a certain point, instead of Pharaoh doing the hardening, the Lord took over so as to complete the process not only of rescuing our people from Egypt, but defeating the Egyptian gods and demonstrating His power to Egyptian and Hebrew alike.

This resonates with what the New Covenant Scriptures tell us, "The Lord is not slow in keeping His promise, as some people think of slowness; on the contrary, He is patient with you; for it is not His purpose that anyone should be destroyed, but that everyone should turn from his sins. However, the Day of the Lord will come, 'like a thief'" (2 Peter 3:9-10, CJB). God is patient, giving each of us many opportunities to come to know Him, to obey Him in various ways, both in starting out on our walk with Him and along the way while He is fashioning us into the image of His Son. But a day does come when it is too late; a time is reached when God's purposes cannot be held back any longer - then God's plan rolls forward and those who are obstructing it are cast in their (own, chosen) roles as obstructors and detractors, although God continues to use them in those roles to accomplish His purposes.

That is why Rav Sha'ul wrote to the Corinthians, "Working together with Him, we also urge you not to receive the grace of God in vain - for He says, 'At the acceptable time I listened to you, and on the day of salvation I helped you'; behold, now is the acceptable time; behold, now is the day of salvation" (2 Corinthians 6:1-2, NASB).

Further Study: Luke 12:16-21

Application: Each of us needs to be certain that we are not resisting the purposes of God in our lives. We need to know Him and move forward with Him every day. Consult your heart and ask God to confirm where you stand with Him today.

Bo - Come - 2

Shemot / Exodus 10:12 - 23

Shemot/Exodus 10:12 Stretch out your hand over the land of Egypt for the locusts

נְטֵה יָדְךָ עַל־אֶרֶץ מִצְרַיִם בָּאַרְבֶּה

ba'ar'beh Mitz'rayim eretz al yad'cha n'teh

HaShem told Moshe to stretch out his hand so that the locust storm might come upon Egypt. Ramban debates at length with Rashi over the size of the storm (cf. verse 14) and both compare it to that mentioned in Joel 2:2 "there was never one like it". Was it Moshe's hand or Moshe himself that brought all those locusts to Egypt, so that neither before or after was there a storm like it? The command נְטֵה, stretch out, comes from the root נָטָה, which means "to stretch out, extend, as the hand" and "to stretch, spread out, expand, as a tent"; neither definition seems to mention locusts! No, this sounds like one of the four great "I will" promises that *HaShem* gave Moshe that we remember each year in the Haggadah: "I will redeem you with an outstretched arm and with great judgements" (Shemot 6:6, CJB). It was God's arm that brought the locusts in on the easterly wind, but it was the sweep of Moshe's arm before Pharaoh and his court that was the signal that the plague was about to start and marked the all-encompassing nature of the invasion: every corner of Egypt - throughout their entire territory - was engulfed.

Early in Mark's gospel another hand is being stretched out: that of the man with the paralysed hand. "So [Yeshua] told the man with the paralysed hand, 'Stand in the centre of the synagogue.' Then He asked them, 'Is it right to do good or to do evil on the day of worship, to give a person back his health or to let him die?' But they were silent. Yeshua was angry as He looked at them. He was deeply hurt because their minds were closed. Then He told the man, 'Hold out your hand.' The man held it out, and his hand became normal again" (Mark 3:3-5, GWT). Again, it is obvious that the man didn't heal himself by stretching out his hand - his obedience and faith in Yeshua was the signal that God healed the man's hand. And again on this occasion, the signal was given in the face of unbelief and opposition, and God's arm was outstretched to bring healing.

God also promises to do the same for us: "'As I live,' declared the Lord God, 'surely with a mighty hand and with an outstretched arm and with wrath poured out, I shall be King over you. And I shall bring you out from the peoples and gather you from the land where you are scattered with a mighty hand and with an outstretched arm and with wrath poured out'" (Ezekiel 20:33-34, NASB). This is not something that we can do for ourselves; this is not something that we can organise, negotiate, fund and manage - this will be the hand of God moving in a sovereign way upon Israel and upon all the nations of the world; a great sign, performed on the public stage for all to see and know that there is a God in heaven.

Further Study: Jeremiah 32:16-22; Acts 4:23-31

Application: It is easy to fall into the idea of thinking that God is no longer willing or able to stretch out His arm and that if anything is to happen, we have to do it for ourselves. But His promise and power are just as effective and available today as they ever have been. Why not review God's promises to you?

Bo - Come - 3

Shemot / Exodus 10:24 - 11:3

Shemot/Exodus 10:24 "Go - serve the Lord: except your flock and your herd, he shall be left"

לְכוּ עִבְדוּ אֶת־יהוה רַק צֹאנְכֶם וּבְקַרְכֶם יֻצָּג
yutzag oov'kar'chem tzon'chem rak Adonai et iv'du l'chu

Rashi comments, lest any should doubt, that the verb יֻצָּג, which can mean to set in place, here means to be set in the same place: to be left behind. Here we see Pharaoh's third attempt at partial capitulation. The first comes after the plague of insects, when Pharaoh says, "Go and sacrifice to your God here in the land ... only you are not to go very far away" (Shemot 8:21,24, CJB). The second attempt comes three plagues later, in the negotiations before the plague of locusts: "Adonai certainly will be with you if I ever let you go with your children ... Just the men among you may go and worship Adonai" (Shemot 10:10-11, CJB). This, the final effort, comes after the plague of darkness and just before the final plague, the death of the firstborn. Almost completely broken, Pharaoh concedes that all the people may go but he tries to retain one last vestige of control over the people by insisting that the flocks and herds remain. What is the man trying to do? Does he know that the people won't come back, so is trying to exact a financial penalty for the exit visas? Does he really think that the flocks and herds will be a sufficient inducement for the people to return, having tasted freedom? Or is he simply trying to save face and not give them everything they asked for, so that he can claim that he drove a hard bargain?

After Saul had been anointed king over Israel, he is told to attack and destroy the Amalekites - to punish them for the way they treated Israel during the Exodus from Egypt. Samuel's instructions to Saul are clear: "Now go and strike Amalek and utterly destroy all that he has, and do not spare him; but put to death both man and woman, child and infant, ox and sheep, camel and donkey" (1 Samuel 15:3, NASB). Saul is successful in battle but keeps the Amalekite king and the best of the sheep and cattle alive, because he and the people could not bear to destroy them. When called to account for his disobedience, Saul tries to bluff his way out by claiming that he had been obedient in most of the instructions, but that the people had brought some of the best sheep, cattle and spoil to sacrifice to the Lord at Gilgal. Samuel puts the issue firmly into focus by telling Saul: "Has the Lord as much delight in burnt offerings and sacrifices as in obeying the voice of the Lord? Behold! To obey is better than sacrifice, to heed than the fat of rams" (1 Samuel 15:22, NASB). It didn't matter how Saul attempted to wriggle or justify his position - he had disobeyed God and so was rejected as king.

Yeshua calls us to the same level of obedience and consistency in serving in the Kingdom of God today. At the end of a group of teachings about the cost of discipleship, He says: "No-one who puts his hand to the plough and keeps looking back is fit to serve in the Kingdom of God" (Luke 9:62, CJB). If we are to serve God then it must be wholeheartedly, with everything we have and without holding back or half-measures.

Further Study: D'varim 6:4-9; Luke 9:57-62

Application: How has your service been this last week? Have you served God with everything you have: lock, stock and barrel, or have you been holding something back: time, money, heart, attitude? Conduct a spiritual inventory and see if your accounts need some adjustments.

Bo - Come - 4

Shemot / Exodus 11:4 - 12:20

Shemot/Exodus 11:4 At midnight I Myself will go out in the midst of Egypt

כַּחֲצֹת הַלַּיְלָה אֲנִי יוֹצֵא בְּתוֹךְ מִצְרָיִם:
Mitzrayim b'toch yotzey Aniy halaylah kakhatzot

There is great debate among the commentators over the meaning of the word כַּחֲצֹת, led by Rashi who states that this is literally "at midnight" or "when the night is divided", taking the word as a verb form. On the other hand, he apologetically explains, the Sages have interpreted it as if it was a noun, preferring the translation "at about midnight", lest Pharaoh's astrologers err in their calculation of the precise midpoint of the night and so call Moshe - and of course, by inference, *HaShem* - a liar. After having his say on this controversy and coming down in favour of the "about" translation, Ibn Ezra makes a short comment that might pass unseen if it were not so important. He says, "I will go out: by means of an agent - My decree will go forth."

A modern commentator, Richard Friedman, takes strident issue with this: "Later Jewish tradition, presumably unable to bear the thought of God personally passing through Egypt and causing the deaths, introduced the horrible concept of the 'Angel of Death'. But there is no such thing as an Angel of Death in the Bible. The text is explicit that God personally passes through Egypt". In the Maggid section of the *Pesach Haggadah* each year we affirm, "'HaShem brought us out of Egypt' - not through an angel, not through a seraph and not through a messenger, but the Holy One, Blessed be He, He alone, in His glory", echoing the use of the personal pronoun אֲנִי in the text.

This is important for it speaks of the way in which God deals with each of us. On the one hand, we must not lose sight of the corporate nature of our people's relationship with God: Israel is a nation, a people before God and there are certain things that happen because of that corporate identity, both to us and because of our actions as a whole; similarly, all those who believe in Messiah Yeshua are part of the Body of Messiah, an identifiable whole that the Scriptures tell is is being prepared as a bride for Yeshua Himself. On the other hand, God deals with us, speaks to us, knows each one of us personally, by name, on a one-to-one basis. He doesn't relate to us indirectly, through a proxy or an intermediary. Rav Sha'ul was quite explicit: "For God is One; and there is but one Mediator between God and humanity, Yeshua the Messiah" (1 Timothy 2:5, CJB). It is God Himself, through the person of Yeshua, who teaches us, who receives our worship and prayer, who provides for us and - ultimately - made it possible for us to have relationship with Him at all.

In the same way, we must not lose sight of the fact that discipline and correction come from God. Don Francisco, a popular Christian singer of a few years back, has a little song where he puts the following words in the mouth of the Devil: "Here's a package of suffering from God - He always sends me when there's dirty work to do"[3] as though Satan is somehow active in our relationship with God. But the writer to the Hebrews is definite that it is God who is responsible: "Regard your endurance as discipline; God is dealing with you as sons. For what son goes undisciplined by his father?" (Hebrews 12:6-7, CJB).

It is easy to slip into a kind of dualism, thinking that good things come from God and bad things from the enemy, as they battle for control of our lives, alternately bribing us and assaulting us to try and modify or influence our behaviour. This is simply not true! Although God certainly allows us to experience the consequences of sin and allows us to be challenged in many ways, He alone is in control of the process; He alone has authority over our lives and this world; as Yeshua said: "Aren't sparrows sold for next to nothing, two for an assarion? Yet not one of them will fall to the ground without your Father's consent" (Matthew 10:29, CJB).

Further Study: Micah 2:12-13; John 10:14-18

Application: If you are in a place of receiving challenge or discipline from the Father, don't be tempted to simply suffer and get depressed, thinking that the world and the enemy are grinding you down. Instead, lift up your head and be aware that God is working in your life; respond to the challenges and lessons so that you may grow and become more like Yeshua.

---

3. Don Francisco, The Package, New Pax Music Press/ASCAP

בֹּא ה'

Bo - Come - 5

Shemot / Exodus 12:21 - 28

Shemot/Exodus 12:22 And you shall touch the lintel and the two doorposts from the blood that is in [the] basin

וְהִגַּעְתֶּם אֶל־הַמַּשְׁקוֹף וְאֶל־שְׁתֵּי הַמְּזוּזֹת
v'higatem   el   hamashkof   v'el   sh'tey   hamzuzot

מִן־הַדָּם אֲשֶׁר בַּסַּף
hadam min   asher   basaf

Taking the blood - or as Rashi explains, receiving the blood - is the second of the four steps involved in bringing an animal offering to the Lord. The first two - "slaughtering" the animal and then "receiving" or catching the blood into a vessel after slaughter - are performed here as part of the Exodus Passover ritual, the second two - "bringing" the blood in the vessel to the altar and then "sprinkling" or dashing the blood against the altar - are here replaced by daubing the blood against the doorposts and the lintels of the houses where the Israelites lived and are to eat the *Pesach* offering during the night before they set out from Eygpt.

Some of the commentators differ in their understanding of where this action was to take place. Rashbam states that the lintel is "the upper threshold that is visible to all at the entrance of the house", working from B'resheet 26:8 where "Abimelech King of the Philistines looked out, (וַיַּשְׁקֵף) of the window" to see Yitz'chak and Rivka. Ibn Ezra, drawing on his experience of Middle Eastern architecture, connects the lintel to 1 Kings 6:4 where Solomon "made narrow windows (שְׁקֻפִים) for the Temple" - these windows were wider on the outside than on the inside to let the outside world benefit from the light of the Temple. Ibn Ezra points out that houses in Egypt are built around a courtyard, with each house having its own door, doorposts and lintel, and the courtyard having an outer gate or door; he suggests that the blood was put only on the inner doors of each house, in secret, after the outer gates were closed, at evening, so that no-one should see.

According to verses 13 and 23, the blood is to be a sign to the Destroyer, who is to pass through the land of Egypt at midnight. Nahum Sarna explains that "the lintels and doorposts form the demarcation between the sacred Israelite interior and the profane world outside" and stresses that there is no suggestion that the blood itself had any magical properties; "the deliverance of Israel is ascribed solely to divine decision." Another example can be seen in the Vision of Slaughter seen by the prophet Ezekiel: the man clothed in linen is told to "Go through the midst of Jerusalem, and put a mark on the foreheads of the men who sigh and groan over all the abominations which are being committed in its midst" (Ezekiel 9:4, NASB), while other men, referred to as the "executioners of the city" (v. 1, NASB) are told to "Go through the city after him and strike ... utterly slay ... but do not touch any man on whom is the mark" (vv. 5-6, NASB). The same imagery crops up again in the book of Revelation where the beast "causes all ... to be given a mark on their right hand, on their forehead, and ... no-one should be able to buy or to sell except the one who has the mark" (Revelation 13:16-17, NASB); those who do receive the mark "will also drink of the wine of the wrath of God ... and will be tormented with fire and brimstone" (14:9-10, NASB). The idea of the sign, then, as a powerful token of ownership and allegiance is strong and consistent throughout the Scriptures.

Standing on Mt. Arbel at the western side of the Sea of Galilee and looking north you can see a large town or city crowning the hilltops past the northern end of the Kinneret. Visible from Tiberias, Migdal and all the towns and biblical sites round to Capernaum and Bethsaida, this is Safed - Tz'fat in Hebrew - the town where many well known rabbis gathered in the 16th century and known today as one of the holy cities of Israel. The city was unmistakable in Yeshua's day, in that prominent position overlooking the towns and villages where Yeshua spent much of His ministry time, and commentators suggest that it was the model for Yeshua's striking remark in the Sermon on the Mount. You can imagine Him pausing, turning away from the people listening to Him and pointing away up the hill as He said, "You are light for the world. A town built on a hill cannot be hidden" (Matthew 5:14, CJB). Funnily enough, one of the things that Safed is known for today is its candles; beautiful, hand-made, dipped and crafted candles, in many shades and colours, can be bought everywhere in Israel and are exported all over the world: *Shabbat* candles, Hanukkah candles - candles for decoration and pleasure.

So from the blood on the lintel, a sign to the Destroyer, which whether done in public or private nevertheless played a key part in the redemption of our people from Egypt, to a mark on the forehead that protected a man from execution, to a mark that enables trade but brings the wrath of God, to Safed - the city on a hill - we can see how important and powerful signs and symbols can be. God intends that each of us should be a sign, both to the people around us and to the powers and authorities in the heavenly realms, of His kingdom and authority in the world!

Further Study: Joshua 2:17-21; Ephesians 4:30

Application: How are you doing on the sign scale? Whether out in public or in a more private setting, God has chosen you so that you may be a sign for Him in what many see as a dark world. Wherever you are, do what you can to shine today. God's light will never be extinguished, but we each have to play our part to let the light shine out brightly.

בֹּא 'ו

Bo - Come - 6

Shemot / Exodus 12:29 - 51

Shemot/Exodus 12:30 And Pharaoh arose at night, he and all his servants and all Egypt

וַיָּקָם פַּרְעֹה לַיְלָה הוּא וְכָל־עֲבָדָיו

avadayv v'chol hu laylah Par'oh vayakam

וְכָל־מִצְרַיִם

Mitzrayim v'chol

The verb וַיָּקָם - from the root קוּם - when used by itself (i.e. not followed by another verb, in which case it usually denotes purpose) most often means to rise up from a sitting or lying position. Rashi comments: "Pharaoh arose: from his bed" to show that this was rising from sleep, not simply that he stood up at some point during the hours of darkness. Moreover, he did not just get up to use the bathroom; the Mekhilta explains that "in the night" shows that this is not according to the customs of kings, since kings don't usually arise before the third hour, 9am! Neither was he woken by his family or servants; the Mekhilta says: "the passage 'he and all his servants and all the Egyptians' tells us that it was Pharaoh who went around to the houses of all his servants and to the houses of all the Egyptians and aroused every one from his place." This was a major event of great significance, that Pharaoh suddenly had to wake up and experience - it was not something that the Egyptians just found out about the next morning when they woke up as usual.

Once again, the Ba'al HaTurim points to a *Masoretic* note that tells us something important about the text. The note, attached to verse 29, tells us that the Hebrew phrase בַּחֲצִי הַלַּיְלָה - at midnight - is used only three times in the Hebrew Bible; here and in two other places. In the story of Ruth and Boaz, it occurs during the night when Ruth has gone down to the threshing floor and slept at Boaz's feet: "In the middle of the night the man was startled and turned over, and - there was a woman lying at his feet!" (Ruth 3:8, CJB). When Boaz wakes, the Tur suggests, he is startled or frightened; so when the Egyptians awoke, they were greatly frightened. The phrase's other use is during the story of Samson, where the text records: "And Samson lay till midnight, and arose at midnight, and took the doors of the gate of the city, and the two posts, and went away with them, bar and all, and put them upon his shoulders, and carried them up to the top of an hill that is before Hebron" (Judges 16:3, NASB). From here, the Tur comments, "this indicates that God performs miracles for the righteous at midnight."

What seems clear here is that Pharaoh and the Egyptians didn't take God seriously. Even after the nine previous miracles, culminating in the "darkness over the land of Egypt, even a darkness which may be felt" (Exodus 10:21, NASB), still Egypt didn't believe that God could and would act again in order to free His people from slavery, to validate His command and to fulfill His word. They were not ready, they didn't think it would happen, they had simply lost the plot and taken their eye off the ball so that when God did act, they were taken aback by both the timing and the sheer scale of God's next move: the death of all the firstborn as God had said, "all the first-born in the land of Egypt shall die" (Exodus 11:5, NASB).

Yeshua uses another image - that of a surprise burglary - to extend the idea of being ready for God to act: "no house-owner would let his house be broken into if he knew when the thief was coming" (Luke 12:39, CJB). No-one goes out for the evening, knowing that a burglar is going to burgle their house before they return. It is necessary to take sensible precautions; the police post public notices in car-parks where there has been a lot of car break-ins and theft, to warn people not to leave valuables in their cars and to make sure that they lock the cars properly.

Rav Sha'ul picks up the same image when he writes to the early believers about the day of the Lord's return: "For you yourselves know full well that the day of the Lord will come just like a thief in the night" (1 Thessalonians 5:2, NASB) and Peter echoes him: "However, the Day of the Lord will come 'like a thief'. On that Day the heavens will disappear with a roar, the elements will melt and disintegrate, and the earth and everything in it will be burned up" (2 Peter 3:10, CJB). As Yeshua Himself said, we don't know the exact moment of His return and to many people it will come just like a thief: a totally unexpected and unwanted interruption in their daily routines. So why do Sha'ul and Peter make such a point of telling the early believers this? If we don't and aren't supposed to know when the Day of the Lord is, why is it so important?

There are two things here that we need to consider. The first is the surprise factor and the unexpected but certain nature of the event. Yeshua told the story of a slave who had been left in charge of the master's household, to look after everyone else until the master's return. The slave must keep attending to his duties and not abuse his position because "the master of that slave will come on a day when he does not expect him and at an hour which he does not know" (Matthew 24:50, NASB). The master will reward the slave according to how well he has obeyed the master's instructions and kept his trust. The master will return; there is no question about that - the only open issue is exactly when. Of one thing we can be certain: each day that passes is another day less until Yeshua does return. Many feel that it cannot be much longer, that the signs of the times are now pointing to a date that is sooner rather than later, but Yeshua is quite explicit that even for believers there will be an element of surprise.

The second factor that we need to keep in mind is the time at which redemption will happen. Our people were redeemed from Egypt in the middle of the night; Boaz pledged to act on Ruth's behalf in the middle of the night; Samson was enabled to perform miracles in the middle of the night. The night is the period of darkness, when the light is least present, and represents the spiritual state of the world. The book of Revelation paints quite graphic and frightening pictures of the way that life on earth will deteriorate in the last few minutes (relatively speaking) before the Day of the Lord, when He will appear to rescue us from the darkness and crush the powers of evil finally and for ever. As we see various issues becoming more noticeable in our day: the promotion of the homosexual and pro-choice agendas, the widening of the gap between rich and poor, the exploitation of minorities and persecution of the household of faith, these should all alert us to the closeness of the Lord's return. There is, of course, a large harvest yet to be gathered for the Kingdom of God and much work that can be done, but we should recognise that it is nearly time to close the door!

Speaking nearly 600 years before Yeshua came, the prophet Isaiah spoke out with an expression of the peoples' frustrations and anxieties during the times of the kings: "Oh, that Thou wouldst rend the heavens and come down, that the mountains might quake at Thy presence - as fire kindles the brushwood, as fire causes water to boil - to make Thy name known to Thine adversaries, that the nations may tremble at Thy presence! When Thou didst awesome things which we did not expect, Thou didst come down, the mountains quaked at Thy presence. For from of old they have not heard nor perceived by ear, neither has the eye seen a God besides Thee, who acts in behalf of the one who waits for Him" (Isaiah 64:1-4, NASB). When God acted, it surprised the people who - within their lifetimes, or in the generations past - had no expectation or understanding of God who acts on behalf of His people, who are waiting for Him. No matter what has happened in recent time, we are now approaching days that are "just like the days of Noah. For as in those days which were before the flood they were eating and drinking, they were marrying and giving in marriage, until the day that Noah entered the ark, and they did not understand until the flood came and took them all away; so shall the coming of the Son of Man be. Then there shall be two men in the field; one will be taken, and one will be left" (Matthew 24:37-40, NASB). Make sure you aren't left behind!

Further Study: Zechariah 12:10-11; Habakkuk 2:3-6

Application: Do you believe that the Day of the Lord is going to happen? Do you sense the urgency to prepare and be ready so that you are not taken by surprise? What can you do to increase your own level of expectation and raise hope in those around you?

Bo - Come - 7

Shemot / Exodus 13:1 - 16

Shemot/Exodus 13:2 Sanctify to Me every firstborn, the opening of each womb ...

קַדֶּשׁ־לִי כָל־בְּכוֹר פֶּטֶר כָּל־רֶחֶם

rekhem kol peter b'chor chol liy kadesh

פֶּטֶר is a noun from the root פָּטַר - to burst open, let out, let go, or dismiss (Davidson) - with the meaning "a breaking forth, an opening". Rashi illustrates this with the verse, "Like one who makes water burst forth from a hole in a dam, is one who starts a dispute" (Proverbs 17:14). The imagery speaks of more than a forceful process to bring the first child into physical life; it is also the bursting forth of a new family and the start of a new generation. More, although the birth of any child is a unique and special moment, it is also a new spiritual phase in the life of the parents who now have to raise, disciple and encourage their growing family. They will truly never be the same again.

Nahum Sarna comments that "the first-born belongs to God solely by reason of an act of divine will decreed at the time of the Exodus and not on account of any inherent sanctity." That is: God said so! On the other hand, he continues, "It is explicitly related in B'Midbar 3:12 'Now, behold, I have taken the Levites from among the sons of Israel instead of every first-born, the first issue of the womb among the sons of Israel' (NASB) and 8:16 'for they are wholly given to Me from among the sons of Israel. I have taken them for Myself instead of every first issue of the womb, the first-born of all the sons of Israel' (NASB) that ... the Levites supplanted the first-born in assuming priestly and ritual functions." That being so, Sarna claims "it may safely be inferred that Moshe is here installing the first-born to fulfill priestly duties" and cites the Sages of the Mishnah: "Before the tabernacle was set up, the high places were permitted and the service was done by the first-born. When the tabernacle was set up, the high places were prohibited and the service was done by the priests" (*m. Zevachim* 14:4). Sarna is supported by the Rashbam who said, "Before the priests were consecrated, it was the first-born who performed God's service."

Obadiah Sforno adds another piece to the picture with his comment about the roles of sacred and secular: "They are all obligated to be redeemed similar to all other consecrated objects, in order that they be permitted to do secular work, for without redemption they are prohibited to occupy themselves with secular work, similar to 'you shall not work with the first-born of your herd, nor shear the first-born of your flock' (D'varim 15:19, NASB)." Release from the exclusivity of the sacred realm, so that the first-born can also perform secular work in order to keep himself and his family, is achieved only through redemption, otherwise the first-born is dedicated completely to God.

Rabbi Hirsch brings these thoughts another step forward when he writes, "In order that the one thought of their common mission that unites them all about the One God should remain vivid and vital in all of them, God appointed living representatives of this thought within the families and homes ... in the midst of the family, the first-born son as His representative, to be the bearer, cultivator and defender of His will; and in the herd, the first-born as the expression of the family possessions belonging to, and being given up to, this will. By the efficacy of the first-born sons and by the consecration of all first-born, the homes and families are to be kept conscious of the holy common mission of the nation." This comes so close to God's plan and purpose, but just fails to make the final connection to Yeshua as God's first-born Son who fulfilled the role of both the first-born son and the first-born of the herd, being given up in consecration to God.

So we find God Himself declaring Yeshua to be His Son at His moment of consecration: "As soon as Yeshua had been immersed, He came up out of the water. At that moment heaven was opened, He saw the Spirit of God coming down upon Him like a dove, and a voice from heaven said, 'This is My Son, whom I love; I am well pleased with Him'" (Matthew 3:16-17, CJB). Then Rav Sha'ul explains how God gave Him up, "He who did not spare even His own Son, but gave Him up on behalf of us all" (Romans 8:32, CJB). God Himself kept the *Torah*, knowing that His own Son had to be the one single exception from the rule that all first-born sons must be redeemed, so that He might be the means of redeeming all of us who believe in Him and in that faith find forgiveness for our sins and reconciliation with God. But the text continues to speak of Yeshua as the first-born: "He is the beginning, the firstborn from the dead" (Colossians 1:18, CJB). Uniquely raised from death never to die again, "the Messiah has been raised from the dead, the firstfruits of those who have died" (1 Corinthians 15:20, CJB) so that He might be "the first-born among many brothers" (Romans 8:29, CJB).

In the same way, just as the Levites were set apart following the incident with the Golden Calf to take the place of the first-born in each family, so Yeshua has been set apart to perform the service of worship in the heavenly tabernacle before God. We should notice that this is not a matter of replacement or supersession in the same role, for Yeshua does not offer sacrifices at the Temple in Jerusalem. Instead, just as the Psalmist foretold: "The Lord has sworn and will not change His mind, 'You are a priest forever according to the order of Melchizedek'" (Psalm 110:4, NASB). Although by earthly descent from the tribe of Judah, Yeshua's priesthood is of a different order or category than the Aaronic priests, who served God first in the tabernacle and then in the Temple. Moreover, this was not something that Yeshua chose or took for Himself but was both a part of who He is and God's calling on Him: "And no one takes this honor upon himself, rather, he is called by God, just as Aharon was. So neither did the Messiah glorify Himself to become cohen gadol; rather, it was the One who said to Him, 'You are my Son; today I have become Your Father.' Also, as He says in another place, 'You are a cohen forever, to be compared with Malki-Tzedek'" (Hebrews 5:4-6, CJB).

We read about Melchizedek in the *Torah* just after Abram (as he was still, then) had defeated the kings who had captured his nephew Lot from Sodom. "And Melchizedek king of Salem brought out bread and wine; now he was a priest of God Most High. And he blessed him and said, 'Blessed be Abram of God Most High, Possessor of heaven and earth; and blessed be God Most High, Who has delivered your enemies into your hand.' And he gave him a tenth of all" (B'resheet 14:18-20, NASB). The author of Hebrews explains that Melchizedek simply is; he has no record of birth, parentage, life or death outside this one appearance, yet he is both a king of righteousness (his name) and a priest of God Most High. Since Yitz'khak and Ya'akov had not yet been born, the tribe of Levi did not at that time exist, yet in form all the tribes of Israel including Levi - and so the Aaronic priests - acknowledged and submitted to the priesthood of Melchizedek; a different order to their own, although both called of God. The Hebrews author makes it plain that Melchizedek was greater than our father Abram: "he blessed Avraham, the man who received God's promises; and it is beyond all dispute that the one who blesses has higher status than the one who receives the blessing" (Hebrews 7:6-7, CJB) and that Levi was included: "Levi, who himself receives tenths, paid a tenth through Avraham; inasmuch as he was still in his ancestor Avraham's body when Malki-Tzedek met him" (vv. 9-10, CJB). Notice the use of the present tense in that verse; the Levitical priests were still receiving tithes at the time the letter was written (cf. Acts 6:7), so that Yeshua's priesthood did not terminate the Aaronic priesthood - God simply suspended the majority of their functions by removing the Temple, although the Aaronic benediction is still pronounced during *Shabbat* services and at the *Kotel* at the *regalim* feasts three times each year - Yeshua is a priest of a different order, without beginning or end and serves in the heavenly tabernacle rather than the earthly one.

Yeshua, then, is the first-born Son of God. He was given up - that is, sanctified solely to God, without being redeemed - so that He might fulfill all the promises that God had revealed through the prophets and be the permanent presence of God in both the house of Israel and the hearts of believers from all the nations. By His obedience and sacrifice, He has redeemed the many. He is both the King of Israel and the High Priest of Israel; it is He who takes our prayers and service before the Father in the heavenly tabernacle; He who brings about our sanctification.

Further Study: Hebrews 7:1-10

Application: Do you sometimes doubt that your prayers and petitions are reaching the Father? Yeshua was perfectly serious when He said: "I am the Way, the Truth and the Life" (John 14:6). He is our perfect conduit and channel to the Father and we find our peace in Him.

בְּשַׁלַּח

B'shalach - When letting go

Shemot / Exodus 13:17 - 17:16

רִאשׁוֹן	Aliyah One	Shemot/Exodus 13:17 - 14:8
שֵׁנִי	Aliyah Two	Shemot/Exodus 14:9 - 14
שְׁלִישִׁי	Aliyah Three	Shemot/Exodus 14:15 - 25
רְבִיעִי	Aliyah Four	Shemot/Exodus 14:26 - 15:26
חֲמִשִׁי	Aliyah Five	Shemot/Exodus 15:27 - 16:10
שִׁשִּׁי	Aliyah Six	Shemot/Exodus 16:11 - 36
שְׁבִיעִי	Aliyah Seven	Shemot/Exodus 17:1 - 16

בְּשַׁלַּח א׳

B'shalach - When letting go - 1

Shemot / Exodus 13:17 - 14:8

Shemot/Exodus 13:17 After Pharaoh had let the people go, God did not guide them to the highway that goes through the land of the P'lishtim

וַיְהִי בְּשַׁלַּח פַּרְעֹה אֶת־הָעָם וְלֹא־נָחָם
nakham v'lo ha'am et Par'oh b'shalakh vay'hiy

אֱלֹהִים דֶּרֶךְ אֶרֶץ פְּלִשְׁתִּים
P'lishtim eretz derech Elohiym

Why didn't *HaShem* lead our people straight out to the Land by the shortest and most direct route? The text goes on to answer the question: God thought that the people would be frightened by having to fight so soon and might change their minds and try to return to Egypt. Looking at our progress through the desert and the number of times we disobeyed, rebelled and grumbled, God's concern looks right on target.

Have you ever noticed that God doesn't go about things the way we would? Sometimes, what seems to us to be the obvious way forward is simply passed over in favour of something that we think much less attractive. But we shouldn't be surprised for God tells us that, "'My thoughts are not your thoughts, neither are your ways My ways,' declares the Lord. 'For as the heavens are higher than the earth, so are My ways higher than your ways, and My thoughts than your thoughts'" (Isaiah 55:8-9, NASB). God encourages us to seek His ways, "Stand by the ways and see and ask for the ancient paths, where the good way is, and walk in it; and you shall find rest for your souls" (Jeremiah 6:16, NASB). The prophet Hosea adds, "For the ways of the Lord are right, and the righteous walk in them" (Hosea 14:9, NASB). Micah speaks of the nations who will say, "Come and let us go up to the mountain of the Lord and to the house of the God of Ya'akov, that He may teach us His ways and that we may walk in His paths" (Micah 4:2, NASB).

Yet we don't seem to be very good at hearing that message. When our people came back to the Land after the exile in Babylon, we set about building our own houses while the house of the Lord was still in ruins, so that the prophet Haggai said, "Thus says the Lord of Hosts, 'Consider your ways!'" (Haggai 1:5, 7, NASB). God even had to criticise the Levites before the people because, "you are not keeping My ways, but are showing partiality in the Torah" (Malachi 2:9, NASB).

In fact, the Bible records that, "God, after He spoke long ago to the fathers in the prophets in many portions and in many ways, in these last days has spoken to us in His Son" (Hebrews 1:1-2, NASB). God spoke to people of His ways in many ways, calling them to leave their ways and follow His ways. When Yeshua came, He made quite a remarkable statement: "I am the Way, the Truth and the Life" (John 14:6). So God's way is Yeshua; those who follow Yeshua exactly are sure to be walking in God's way. In the years that followed the Resurrection, the followers of Yeshua became known as followers of The Way (Acts 9:2) as they put into practice His teaching and lived according to His *Torah*. They no longer followed the *derech eretz*, the way of the land, but the *derech Yeshua*, the *derech Adonai*.

Further Study: Psalm 25:4-7; Lamentations 3:39-40; Luke 10:2-9

Application: Which way are we walking on? Are we following the broad, smooth way that leads to destruction or are we on the narrow way, the way of faith, following the footsteps of the Master who is the way?

בְּשַׁלַּח ׳ב

B'shalach - When letting go - 2

Shemot / Exodus 14:9 - 14

Shemot/Exodus 14:9 And the Egyptians pursued them and overtook them, encamped at the sea

וַיִּרְדְּפוּ מִצְרַיִם אַחֲרֵיהֶם וַיַּשִּׂיגוּ אוֹתָם חֹנִים
khoniym   otam   vayasiygu akhareyhem mitzrayim vayir'd'fu

עַל־הַיָּם
hayam al

Nachmanides (also known as The Ramban) points out that this was towards the end of the sixth day of our freedom from Egypt. Hirsch adds that although it took the Israelites six days to accomplish this journey because of the flocks and herds with them, the Egyptians had covered the same ground in only two days because they were travelling in chariots with fast horses (cf. v. 6). The physical proximity of their so-recently ex-captors caused our people to panic so that they cried out to God and gave Moshe his first chewing out - the honeymoon was over! The word the *Torah* uses וַיַּשִּׂיגוּ, from the root נשׂג, which has a range of meanings from the simple "to reach", through "overtake, go beyond", as far as "acquire or obtain", shows how real the threat seemed - as our people saw the Egyptian chariots bearing down on them, they felt their precious new freedom evaporate like the dawn mist on a hot day - an ignominious return to slavery back in Egypt seemed to be beckoning only too clearly.

During a time of war between Aram and Israel (the northern kingdom), "the king of Aram sent a great army with many chariots and horses" (2 Kings 6:14, NLT) in order to capture the prophet Elisha. "When the servant of the man of God got up early the next morning and went outside, there were troops, horses and chariots everywhere. 'Ah, my lord, what will we do now?' he cried out" (v. 15, NLT). Elisha's servant thought that the game was up: that he and his master would be captured and killed; he couldn't see any way out. But "'Don't be afraid!' Elisha told him. 'For there are more on our side than on theirs.' Then Elisha prayed, 'O Lord, open his eyes and let him see!' The Lord opened his servant's eyes, and when he looked up, he saw that the hillside around Elisha was filled with horses and chariots of fire" (vv. 16-17, NLT). The servant couldn't see things from the same perspective as Elisha until the Lord opened his eyes.

John the *Shaliach* wrote, "You, children, are from God and have overcome the false prophets, because He who is in you is greater than he who is in the world" (1 John 4:4, CJB). God's *Ruach*, the Spirit of Yeshua who lives in us, is greater than the Adversary and all the forces of evil in the world. We simply need to be reminded of it, so that we continue to look at things from the right perspective.

The writer to the Hebrews adds, "Therefore, since we have so great a cloud of witnesses surrounding us, let us also lay aside every encumbrance, and the sin which so easily entangles us, and let us run with endurance the race that is set before us" (Hebrews 12:1, NASB). Those who have gone before, from *Avraham Avinu* (our father Avraham) to the current day, are not only examples of seeing the world through God's eyes of faith, but also encouraging us (though unheard on earth) from the spiritual realms to press on and know that God is in control.

Further Study: Luke 16:27-28; John 3:31-36

Application: Which perspective have you been using to view your life and the situations and circumstances you find yourself in? Find the time today to ask God to help you see the world afresh through His eyes.

בְּשַׁלַּח ג׳

B'shalach - When letting go - 3

Shemot / Exodus 14:15 - 25

Shemot/Exodus 14:15 Why do you cry out to Me? Speak to the children of Israel they they should break camp.

מַה־תִּצְעַק אֵלָי דַּבֵּר אֶל־בְּנֵי־יִשְׂרָאֵל וְיִסָּעוּ:

v'yisa'u Yisra'el b'ney el dabeyr eylay titz'ak mah

Do you detect a hint of irritation here on God's part? Is *HaShem* showing just a little frustration at the behaviour of the people? Rashi provides us with two ideas: the first suggests that "Moshe was standing and praying. The Holy One, blessed be He, said to him, 'Now is not the time for long prayer, for Israel is in distress'", implying that Moshe should stop praying and do something. Alternatively, Rashi suggests that *HaShem's* question implies, "the matter is for Me and not for you" as God later chides the prophets for murmuring about Israel's difficulties as if God hadn't taken enough trouble Himself (Isaiah 45:9-12). After all, Israel has only to break camp and move forward to walk into what God has planned and set up before them.

Sforno, on the other hand, suggests that Moshe was complaining to *Adonai* about the leaders of the people who had just been moaning about being brought out into the desert to die (v. 11), and that He is rebuking Moshe for speaking disrespectfully about the leaders of God's people; in effect, "stop complaining and move out!" God is reassuring Moshe's doubts as to whether the people can be trusted by telling him that he only has to give the order and they will go forward - they will not disobey him.

So perhaps the issue here is with Moshe, rather than with God. Moshe is having a leadership crisis and is not certain that he has what it takes to lead the people through their fears and doubts. Did the people have a problem? Certainly, you only have to read their conversation in the previous verses (vv. 11-12) to know that they had effectively lost the plot. Although Moshe makes the right response (vv. 13-14) pointing to God's promises and abilities to deliver the people, his own faith is sufficiently shaken that *HaShem* has to take a firm line to snap Moshe out of his self-doubt and get him back on track; the people have gone to pieces and God can't allow His leader to go the same way. So although neither Moshe nor the people are directly recorded as crying out to God, He steps in and gives Moshe a fairly sharp set of instructions about what he is to do and what God is about to do.

There comes a time in each of our lives when prevarication and delay, the so-called "waiting upon the Lord", is not only damaging to us and those around us, but contrary to God's will. Elijah the prophet challenged the people of Israel on Mt. Carmel: "How long are you going to jump back and forth between two positions?" (1 Kings 18:21, CJB); in the letter to the community in Laodicea, Yeshua said, "You are neither cold nor hot. How I wish you were either one or the other!" (Revelation 3:15, CJB). James in his letter sums it up: "If any of you lacks wisdom, let him ask God ... but let him ask in trust, doubting nothing, for the doubter ... should not think that he will receive anything from the Lord, for he is double minded, unstable in all his ways" (James 1:5-8, CJB). Having asked, do it!

Further Study: Proverbs 3:5-7; Romans 14:22-23

Application: Are you debating a big decision at the moment and seeking the Lord as to what you should do? When you have taken counsel and advice from trustworthy people, you must act. You cannot delay indefinitely, waiting for one more confirmation - you just have to do it.

בְּשַׁלַּח

B'shalach - When letting go - 4

Shemot / Exodus 14:26 - 15:26

Shemot/Exodus 14:26 Stretch out your hand over the sea and the waters will return upon Egypt ...

נְטֵה אֶת־יָדְךָ עַל־הַיָּם וְיָשֻׁבוּ הַמַּיִם

hamayim v'yashuvu hayam al yadcha et n'teyh

עַל־מִצְרַיִם

Mitzrayim al

The Mekhilta comments to this verse that the Egyptians are to receive due and appropriate punishment for their actions against Israel. "For with the same device with which they planned to destroy Israel I am going to punish them" is placed in God's mouth. As the Egyptians had decreed that all the male Israelite babies should be drowned in the Nile, so God is about to drown all the armies of Egypt - chariots, horsemen and warriors - in the water of the Sea of Reeds. The wisdom books in the Bible are full of pithy sayings that illustrate the principle: "He has dug a pit and hollowed it out, and has fallen into the hole that he made" (Psalm 7:15, NASB); "He who digs a pit will fall into it, and he who rolls a stone, it will come back on him" (Proverbs 26:27, NASB); "He who digs a pit may fall into it, and a serpent may bite him who breaks through a wall" (Ecclesiastes 10:8, NASB).

The prophets paint a picture that is more deliberate and less a matter of simple consequence: "According to their deeds, so He will repay" (Isaiah 59:18, NASB); "Because they have burned incense on the mountains and scorned Me on the hills, therefore I will measure their former work into their bosom" (Isaiah 65:7, NASB); even to the point of direct proportionality: "giving to everyone according to his ways and according to the fruit of his deeds" (Jeremiah 32:19, NASB); "Repay her according to her work; according to all that she has done, so do to her" (Jeremiah 50:29, NASB); "For they sow the wind, and they reap the whirlwind" (Hosea 8:7, NASB).

This all serves to illustrate the principle of sowing and reaping which can be found throughout the Scripture. We are inescapably involved in this process whether we like it or not, simply as a part of living and interacting with the people around us, but we are encouraged to be active participants: "Send out your bread upon the waters, for after many days you will get it back" (Ecclesiastes 11:1, NRSV). Yeshua tells the parable of the talents (Matthew 25:14-30) where a master leaves his servants various amounts of capital for them to invest and 'work' while he is away; from the master's responses upon his return - congratulating and rewarding the two servants who have doubled his investment - it is clear that their industry, even taking some risks as all trading must entail, is an important part of kingdom life. However, the third servant who returns his capital untouched, without gain or loss, is rebuked for not at least depositing it in the bank so that there might be interest added to the original sum.

The question is how, with what and where do we sow or invest to reap the harvest that God requires of us. Writing to the Corinthians, Rav Sha'ul uses the farming metaphor to describe how he and Apollos had shared the gospel with them, how they had taught and encouraged the new believers and started the messianic community there: "I planted the seed, and Apollos watered it, but it was God who made it grow" (1 Corinthians 3:6, CJB). He goes on to talk about what had been planted: "we have sown spiritual seed among you" (1 Corinthians 9:11, CJB); they have preached Yeshua crucified and taught the truth of the Kingdom of God to these people; they have shared their lives with them, working and living alongside them on a practical level. As the prophet Hosea said: "If you sow righteousness for yourselves, you will reap according to grace. Break up unused ground for yourselves, because it is time to seek Adonai, till He comes and rains down righteousness upon you" (Hosea 10:12, CJB). We are to be active in finding unproductive or fallow areas in our lives and then sowing good seed in them, so that we may harvest a crop of righteous deeds and words for the Kingdom of Heaven; more, we are to invest of ourselves in the lives of others that both we and they may yield a return for God.

Further Study: D'varim 15:7-11; Romans 1:8-15

Application: Where are you sowing your time and interests? What sort of return is God making on your life? Look around today and see if there are fallow areas in your life that God wants to plant with His seeds of righteousness.

בְּשַׁלַּח ה'

B'shalach - When letting go - 5

Shemot / Exodus 15:27 - 16:10

Shemot/Exodus 15:27 And they came to Elim; and there were twelve springs of water and seventy date-palms

וַיָּבֹאוּ אֵלִמָה וְשָׁם שְׁתֵּים עֶשְׂרֵה עֵינֹת מַיִם
mayim eynot esreyh sh'teym v'sham eylimah vayavo'u

וְשִׁבְעִים תְּמָרִים
t'mariym v'shiv'iym

    Also mentioned as one of the way-stations in the journey from Egypt in B'Midbar 33:9, Elim was a wooded fresh-water oasis, generally identified with Wadi Gharandel; this is near to the plain of el-Markhah, a convenient camp site[4]. After the bitter waters at Marah, the Israelites could enjoy not only sweet water but natural shade from the heat of the sun as they relaxed before moving on to the Wilderness of Sin. The Mekhilta suggests that they stayed for only three nights, while Ibn Ezra's opinion is that they encamped at Elim "beside the water" for 20 days or more. Quoting Rabbi Eleazar of Modi'im in the Mekhilta, "On the very day when the Holy One, blessed be He, created His world, He created there twelve springs corresponding to the twelve tribes of Israel, and seventy palm-trees, corresponding to the seventy elders", Nachmanides explains that the text tells us about the springs and palm-trees so that we should know that each tribe camped at its own spring, and the elders sat in the shade of their own trees, and so we should marvel at the detailed provision that God had made beforehand for this time.

    Throughout Israel's history, as recorded both in the pages of the Bible and in the rabbinic writings, the hand of God can be seen at work preparing things in advance or making amazing provision in the most incredible circumstances. King David knew how this worked as he wrote the poems, prayers and songs that make up many of the psalms. David describes the way in which God provided for him during his challenging wilderness years:

---

4. J. Simons, *The Geographical and Topographical Texts of the Old Testament* (Leiden: Brill, 1959), sec 428, pp. 252f.

"You prepare a table before me in the presence of my enemies; You have anointed my head with oil; my cup overflows" (Psalm 23:5, NASB). He knew too God's constant presence and comfort even in the most extreme of circumstances: "Even though I walk through the valley of the shadow of death, I fear no evil, for You are with me; Your rod and Your staff, they comfort me" (Psalm 23:4, NASB).

The same thoughts and feelings obviously passed through the minds of the prophets so that Isaiah could write: "When you pass through the waters, I will be with you, and through the rivers, they will not overflow you" (Isaiah 43:2, NASB). Though this latter promise is, of course, given to Israel, it is symbolic of the way God cares for and looks after those who belong to Him; its nearest recorded outworking at a personal level being very close to the literal words of the promise: "The satraps, the prefects, the governors and [King Nebuchadnezzar's] high officials gathered round and saw in regard to [Shadrach, Meshach and Abed-nego] that the fire had no effect on the bodies of these men nor was the hair of their head singed, nor were their trousers damaged, nor had the smell of fire even come upon them" (Daniel 3:27, NASB).

During Yeshua's ministry there were many instances where *HaShem* had prepared people and situations beforehand so that Yeshua could demonstrate the power of God and His status as Messiah through the miracles that He performed. Apart from the over-arching destination of His crucifixion and resurrection, a number of examples stand out: firstly, at Yeshua's baptism, John tries to protest because He - the Messiah - is coming to be baptised by him - the fore-runner or herald - but Yeshua calmly brushes that away by saying, "Let it be this way now, because we should do everything righteousness requires" (Matthew 3:15, CJB); in other words, this is a divine appointment, part of God's plan, and we need to do this. Secondly, when the paralysed man was lowered through the roof by his friends so that Yeshua might heal him, Yeshua first forgives his sins and then when the watching scribes and Pharisees began to murmur about only God forgiving sin, Yeshua responds, "I will prove to you that the Son of Man has authority on earth to forgive sins - I say to you, pick up your mattress and go home!" (Luke 5:24, CJB). After Lazarus the brother of Mary and Martha dies, Yeshua having stayed away in spite of being summoned, He then tells the disciples, "E'lazar has died. And for your sakes, I am glad that I wasn't there, so that you may come to trust" (John 11:14-15, CJB). Another divine appointment where Yeshua not only shows no surprise but demonstrates that He knew of the situation beforehand that He might show God's power and glory to people.

Rav Sha'ul applies the same logic to believers in Messiah when he writes to the Ephesians: "For we are His workmanship, created in Messiah Yeshua for good works, which God prepared before hand, that we should walk in them" (Ephesians 2:10, NASB). We need to know that in no less way than that God engineered circumstances in the lives of the patriarchs, the prophets and His Son Yeshua, He similarly designs and orchestrates situations where we are to obey Him and show the glory of God in the good works that we do, the constructive words that we say or the good attitudes that we display - quite possibly against normal human expectation - for His praise and glory! Knowing that, we should be on the look-out and always be ready to fulfil the purpose of God in our lives.

Further Study: 2 Kings 6:15-17; Ephesians 1:3-4

Application: How good are you at sensing those God-moments when He has set you up to say or do something for Him? Ask Him to help you be more attuned today and to provide an opportunity to put this into practice. You won't be disappointed, for He longs to use us to touch the people around us each day!

בְּשַׁלַּח ו'

B'shalach - When letting go - 6

Shemot / Exodus 16:11 - 36

Shemot/Exodus 16:12 I have heard the complaints of the sons of Israel

שָׁמַעְתִּי אֶת־תְּלוּנֹת בְּנֵי יִשְׂרָאֵל

Yisra'el b'ney t'lunot et shamatiy

Following the general rule that "nouns with a prefixed ת usually denote the action of the verbal root from which they are derived"[5], the noun here translated 'complaints' - תְּלוּנֹת is derived from the root לוּן, "to complain or murmur". Davidson gives the noun the meanings "a murmuring or complaining", while the JPS prefers "grumbling". Even though the noun is plural, *Targum Onkelos* makes it singular - murmuring - and paraphrases away the anthropomorphism by making the verb passive: "The murmuring of the sons of Israel has been heard before Me" (Drazin & Wagner). This softens the Israelites offence by suggesting that they were not complaining directly against *HaShem*, but only against His words or commands; more, *HaShem* doesn't actually hear the complaint, rather He is aware of it. The Mekhilta seems to disagree, putting these words in the mouth of *HaShem*: "You have asked for bread; since it is impossible for human beings to live without bread, I have given it to you. Now you turn round and, out of a full stomach, you ask for meat!", clearly feeling that the request for meat is an affront to *HaShem*, as if the Israelites are questioning His ability to feed them properly.

The Ramban, looking back to the complaint itself - "If only we had died by the hand of the Lord in the land of Egypt, when we sat by the fleshpots, when we ate our fill of bread!" (16:3, JPS) - explains that our text "makes clear that the manna is not an act of God's freely given love, nor something that they deserved (which it was originally intended to be), but a response to the sin of complaining." The Israelites sinned because they did not believe in God's ability to carry out His promises to provide for them and bring them

---

5. Andrew E. Steinmann, "Intermediate Hebrew Grammar" (Virtualbookwork.com, 2004), 1-58939-611-1

into the Land; the grumbling was an open expression of their unbelief, so although *HaShem* had to feed them in order that they would physically survive through the desert, the *Ramban* suggests that this becomes a matter of duty or necessity rather than the bestowal of love and relationship that God had wanted it to be. Confirming some of the *Ramban's* feelings, Sarna - while providing an excuse "that livestock is the most valuable possession of the pastoralist, who can seldom be induced to part with an animal" and that other animals may already have been lost on the journey - comments that "the cry for bread was reasonable; the craving for meat was not." The people would not feed themselves from their own flocks and herds and were insisting that God should provide both bread and meat; effectively they were calling Him on His promise and demanding service!

How often do we find or place ourselves in the same wrong position before God? He graciously provides the air we breathe, the food that we eat, the money that we earn, our very life comes from Him. Yet either because we do not like where we are, are not satisfied with what we have, or think that it is time to move on, we adopt an attitude of complaint, grumbling against God, reviewing what we consider to be His promises to us before Him in an accusing tone of voice as if we have the right to challenge His wisdom and authority. Clearly there is a balance to be struck here, for Isaiah prophetically speaks to all generations when he says, "You who call upon Adonai, give yourselves no rest; and give Him no rest until He restores Yerushalayim and makes it a praise on earth" (Isaiah 62:6-7, CJB). Yeshua taught the *talmidim* about persistence in prayer by using the illustration of the widow allowing the corrupt judge no peace until he granted her justice: "Because this widow bothers me, I will give her legal protection, lest by continually coming she wear me out" (Luke 18:5, NASB). On the other hand, Rav Sha'ul tellingly reminds us, "Nor let us try the Lord, as some of them did, and were destroyed by the serpents. Nor grumble, as some of them did, and were destroyed by the destroyer. Now these things happened to them as an example, and they were written for our instruction, upon whom the ends of the ages have come. Therefore let him who thinks he stands take heed lest he fall" (1 Corinthians 10:9-12, NASB).

Nechama Leibowitz sees the provision of the manna as a test that God was using to challenge our people during the years of the desert experience. She suggests that in one of two ways, either by the monotony of the diet and their inability to provide an alternative, or in the potential idleness with nothing else to do, God was challenging the people over their relationship with Him. By forcing them to be totally dependent - over and over, every day for forty years - God was testing their hearts: "that I may prove them, whether they will walk in My law or not" (Shemot 16:4). In Egypt, although forced by a taskmaster to work, make bricks, finish their allotted tasks, they nevertheless imagined that they had some responsibility for their own destiny, their own livelyhoods, even if that boiled down to choosing what they ate for supper. Now that they were free, the people were discovering that they were totally dependent on God - as in fact they always had been, although they had not realised it - and they did not like it. "The trial then consists of living in continual expectation, in outright dependence on God." This same trial is ours today; to acknowledge our dependence on God, feeling and gratefully receiving His grace in our lives, or to struggle to produce our own bread from the ground, the while complaining to God because we don't have everything we think we should.

Further Study: Lamentations 4:9; 1 Thessalonians 5:14-18

Application: Ask yourself whether you are a grumbler or a beseecher. Are you protecting your rights or seeking the advancement of the kingdom, often through or for someone else? The response to our prayer is often conditioned upon our attitude as much as our motives and we need to remember who we are!

בְּשַׁלַח ז׳

B'shalach - When letting go - 7

Shemot / Exodus 17:1 - 16

Shemot/Exodus 17:2 And Moshe said to them, "Why are you contending with me? Why are you testing Adonai?"

וַיֹּאמֶר לָהֶם מֹשֶׁה מַה־תְּרִיבוּן עִמָּדִי מַה־תְּנַסּוּן

t'nasoon mah imadiy   t'riyvoon mah Moshe lahem vayomer

אֶת־יְהוה:

Adonai   et

Now out of Egypt and heading towards Mt. Sinai for their appointment with *HaShem*, our people reach Rephidim to find that there is no water to drink. As usual, the people turn to Moshe and berate him for bringing them out to die of thirst in the wilderness. This is Moshe's reply to the people. The particle מָה is usually translated 'what' but is here more accurately rendered 'why'. The first question he asks, with the verb תְּרִיבוּן - a *Qal* 2mp prefix form of the root רִיב with a paragogic *nun*[6] - has legal overtones; although the verb means "to contend, strive or quarrel", it can also mean "to plead or defend a cause" (Davidson) and one noun derived from it - רָב - is a defender, while another - יָרִיב - is an adversary. The people have addressed their suit to the wrong party; they should be addressing their complaints to *HaShem* - it is He who has brought them out into the desert, Moshe is only following His instructions. The Sforno comments on this by supplying an amplification of what Moshe might have said: "Why do you strive with me? You certainly know that I am but commanded (by God) and perform (His will)." The Ba'al HaTurim points out that a *Masoretic* note to the verb shows that it is used three times in the Hebrew Scriptures: here, in the challenge of Joash (Gideon's father) when asked to surrender his son for

---

6. We do not know the exact reason for the use of the paragogic *nun*, but it is thought to be an aid to pronunciation, so that the ו it follows is known to be an 'oo' sound (וּ) rather than the 'oh' (וֹ) sound that might otherwise be possible in the unpointed text if the *nun* were not present.

destroying the altar of Ba'al and the Asherah pole that stood beside it: "Will you contend for Ba'al" (Judges 6:31), and in Job's response to Zophar the Naamathite: "Will you contend for God?" (Job 13:8) meaning, "Will you be His advocate?" The Ba'al HaTurim concludes that "this is to teach you that one who contends with his *Torah* teacher is considered as if he is contending with the Holy One, Blessed be He."

In his second question, as Rashi points out, Moshe gets to the point of what the people are really doing: they are testing - תְּנַסּוּן, a *Pi'el* 2mp prefix from the root נָסָה, again with a paragogic *nun* - HaShem. This verb can mean "to try, prove or tempt" but is also used for "to try or assay", suggesting that the people might be putting *HaShem* to the test to see if He is up to providing for their needs. The Sforno again suggests that Moshe is counselling the people that "this testing is fraught with great danger, for if He is angered He will show His deeds to destroy you, and this test will result in dire consequences for you." Richard Friedman points out that "in each of the two chapters that precede this, God is described as testing the people (15:25, 16:4). Now the people dare to test God and Moshe asks them why they do that. It is a rhetorical question: the point is that there is no reason to test God. It is presumptuous, because God can be counted upon."

The event clearly struck a chord in our collective memory and conscience. Later in the *Torah*, God Himself complains about the way that the Israelites have made it a habit to grumble about and test Him: "all the men who have seen My glory and My signs, which I performed in Egypt and in the wilderness, yet have put Me to the test these ten times and have not listened to My voice" (B'Midbar 14:22, NASB) and Moshe, in his recapitulation to the next generation on the Plains of Moab, later uses this specific incident as the principle example of this: "You shall not put the Lord your God to the test, as you tested Him at Massah" (D'varim 6:16, NASB). The Psalmist picks it up again when urging the people of his day not to be hard-hearted towards God "Do not harden your hearts, as at Meribah, as in the day of Massah in the wilderness; when your fathers tested Me, they tried Me, though they had seen My work" (Psalm 95:8-9, NASB).

The Ramban explains that when the people quarreled with Moshe, "it means that they complained about their situation: 'What shall we do? What shall we eat? What shall we drink?'". These are very familiar words for believers, who hear Yeshua chiding the people of His day for their concern about material things: "So don't be anxious, asking, 'What will we eat?,' 'What will we drink?' or 'How will we be clothed?'" (Matthew 6:31, CJB). Yeshua dryly comments, "For it is the pagans who set their hearts on all these things" (v. 32a, CJB); the people of Israel should not be concerned because they are in relationship with God, they have seen His works, they know what He can do: "Your heavenly Father knows you need them all" (v. 32b, CJB). All those who have been invited to participate in the Kingdom of God are covered by this provision; all those who are called to be a part of the Body of Messiah are included. We are to recognise the Kingdom priority and trust God to provide for our material needs without putting Him to the test: "But seek first His Kingdom and His righteousness, and all these things will be given to you as well" (v. 33, CJB).

Now of course in our modern world, people have largely been freed of the existential day-to-day worries of food, drink and clothing. Our welfare states provide benefit systems so that no-one should ever be lacking a roof over their head and certain basic essentials of life unless they choose to put themselves outside the scope of that support. Whether employed or unemployed, all of us should be free to concentrate on Yeshua's words and forge ahead with the work of the kingdom, trusting Him to provide for our basic life necessities, even if that is through such mundane activities as having a job and working to earn money.

Strangely, that doesn't seem to be the case. So much so that only a few years after Yeshua's time, during those early formative years of the church, before any of the splits and schisms that were later to divide the church between Jew and Gentile and then into multiple denominations as the results of that original tearing apart bore fruit in successive generations right down to the present age, the writer to the Hebrews warned his audience in no uncertain terms: "Watch out, brothers, so that there will not be in any one of you an evil heart lacking trust, which could lead you to apostatize from the living God! Instead, keep exhorting each other every day, as long as it is called Today, so that none of you will become hardened by the deceit of sin. For we have become sharers in the Messiah, provided, however, that we hold firmly to the conviction we began with, right through until the goal is reached" (Hebrews 3:12-14, CJB).

Many believers today are still absorbed in keeping up with their neighbours, with having as much as their work colleagues. Sometimes, in a strange inverted way, it is seen as a sign of their faith in God that they should have more than everyone else around them, to show that they are blessed by being Christians. The Jewish people, of course, are not immune to these pressures; just ask any Jewish mother! Oftentimes, it is our lack of faith in God's basic promises, our own prideful (read: sinful) do-it-yourself attitude that prevents God from being able to bless us with the basic things of life and more, while we waste kingdom time and opportunities fighting to make what we see as 'enough' money for ourselves. In so doing, we forfeit the right to enter into God's rest. When we insist on doing everything for ourselves, we prevent ourselves being "sharers in the Messiah", because we have abandoned our convictions and have not endured through to the end. Yeshua said that "the one who endures to the end, he shall be saved" (Mark 13:13, NASB). Let us not be caught in this trap but instead resolve, while balancing our responsibility to provide for our immediate families and contribute to the household of faith, to put God and His priorities first in our lives and not put Him to the test!

Further Study: Colossians 2:8; Ephesians 4:22

Application: Perhaps it is time to take an inventory of where you stand before God. Are you trusting in His provision and faithfully working through whatever that entails, or are you sacrificing the Kingdom of God for the sake of existence today? Take a hard look and be sure!

יִתְרוֹ

Yitro - Jethro

Shemot / Exodus 18:1 - 23:26

רִאשׁוֹן	Aliyah One	Shemot/Exodus 18:1 - 12
שֵׁנִי	Aliyah Two	Shemot/Exodus 18:13 - 23
שְׁלִישִׁי	Aliyah Three	Shemot/Exodus 18:24 - 27
רְבִיעִי	Aliyah Four	Shemot/Exodus 19:1 - 6
חֲמִשִׁי	Aliyah Five	Shemot/Exodus 19:7 - 19
שִׁשִּׁי	Aliyah Six	Shemot/Exodus 19:20 - 20:14
שְׁבִיעִי	Aliyah Seven	Shemot/Exodus 20:15 - 23:26

יִתְרוֹ א'

Yitro - Jethro - 1

Shemot / Exodus 18:1 - 12

Shemot/Exodus 18:1 And Yitro, the priest of Midyan, Moshe's
father-in-law, heard

וַיִּשְׁמַע יִתְרוֹ כֹהֵן מִדְיָן חֹתֵן מֹשֶׁה
Moshe khoteyn Midyan coheyn   Yitro vayish'ma

What could it have been that Yitro heard that made him come out to
Moshe and the people in the desert and, at least according to tradition, be
prepared to convert to Judaism? *Rashi* points out that *Chazal* say it was two
things: the parting of the *Yam Suf* (Sea of Reeds) and the war with Amalek
(*b.* Zevachim 116*a*). The battle with Amalek is assumed, as it is the last
thing the *Torah* tells us about in the previous *parasha* (Shemot 17:8-15) and
the parting of the Sea because it was a miracle that Moshe had prophesied
that the whole (known) world would hear about: "The peoples have heard,
and they tremble ... all those living in Kena'an are melted away" (Shemot
15:14-15, CJB). Forty years later, the inn-keeper Rahab tells Joshua's spies,
"Fear of you has fallen on us ... we've heard how Adonai dried up the water in
the Yam Suf ahead of you, when you left Egypt" (Joshua 2:9-10, CJB); the
Canaanites were still talking about it.

Hundreds of years on, Isaiah reminds our people of the same thing,
"Who divided the waters before them ... Who led them through the depths"
(Isaiah 63:12-13, NASB), and Stephen alludes to it in his testimony before
the *Sanhedrin*, "wonders and signs in the land of Egypt and in the Red Sea"
(Acts 7:36, NASB). Rav Sha'ul uses it in his letter to the Corinthians (1
Corinthians 10:1-2); the writer to the Hebrews cites it as an example of faith
(Hebrews 11:29) and it is still in synagogue currency to this day! Here is an
event which has captured the heart and imagination of not only our people
but generations of believers, notwithstanding the sceptics who would try to
tell us of freak tidal waves or of a crossing further north in the shallows of
the Delta. God moved in history, over 3000 years ago, and people the world
over are still talking about it today.

At the beginning of Matthew's gospel we read about some other travellers who said, "Where is He who has been born King of the Jews? For we saw His star in the east, and have come to worship Him" (Matthew 2:2, NASB). Here were magi, wise men, possibly astrologers, who had heard of what God was doing and, just like Yitro, came from a distance to find out what was going on. Once again, God had broken through into this world and it was already impacting peoples' lives so that they had to respond in some way. And, just as our people are still talking about the way *HaShem* parted the *Yam Suf* so that we could walk through on dry land, so people the world over are still talking about the Baby who was born in Bethlehem 2000 years ago and 33 years later died on the cross to bring atonement not just for our people, but for the sins of the world.

Further Study: Isaiah 40:7-8; Matthew 24:32-35

Application: Jethro and the Magi had to leave where they were and what they were doing to travel some distance in order to respond to what they had heard, but did not hesitate or delay. How have you responded to the news that you have heard about Yeshua?

יִתְרוֹ ב׳

Yitro - Jethro - 2

Shemot / Exodus 18:13 - 23

Shemot/Exodus 18:13 Moshe sat to judge the people and the people stood

וַיֵּשֶׁב מֹשֶׁה לִשְׁפֹּט אֶת־הָעָם וַיַּעֲמֹד הָעָם
ha'am vaya'amod ha'am et lish'pot Moshe vayeyshev

Rashi tells us that Moshe's father-in-law, Jethro, was disturbed by this, for he felt that Moshe was belittling the honour of Israel by making them stand while he sat, like a king among them, dispensing justice. The Mechilta even goes as far as to turn Jethro's question in the next verse into a rebuke: "Why do you alone sit, while all those stand?" The practicalities of the situation suggest, since Moshe spent all day teaching the people in this way, "from morning to evening" (v. 13), whereas they would each bring their question or case in turn, that if he didn't sit down then he would soon be exhausted. It is also customary to accord a measure of honour to those who teach and judge disputes - in courts to this day it is common practice for all the people to rise when the judge enters or leaves the court and only re-seat themselves when the judge is seated.

Some time later, "Deborah, a prophetess, the wife of Lappidoth, was judging Israel at that time. And she used to sit under the palm tree of Deborah between Ramah and Bethel in the hill country of Ephraim; and the sons of Israel came up to her for judgement" (Judges 4:4-5, NASB). Whether Jethro liked it or not, it was becoming established that teaching and judgement - which would often amount to arbitration or determination of principle rather than the criminal justice element so prevalent today - was undertaken by someone who was seated as a sign of their authority. As Israel developed fortified cities, archaeologists point to the gate chambers where the judges of the city would sit to hear cases and disputes not only for the city with its traders and merchants, but also for those in the neighbouring countryside so that Moshe's instructions came true: "So you shall come to the Levitical priest or the judge who is in office in those days, and you shall enquire of them, and they will declare to you the verdict in the case" (D'varim 17:9, NASB). Later, in the time of the kings, the husband of the *Eyshet Chayil*, the Woman of Valour, "is known in the gates, when he sits among the elders of the land" (Proverbs 31:23, JPS).

Yeshua recognised the position of the Scribes and Pharisees: "'The Torah-teachers and P'rushim', He said, 'sit in the seat of Moshe. So whatever they tell you, take care to do it!'" (Matthew 23:2-3a, CJB) Although in His next breath He warned that they didn't do it themselves, He nevertheless affirmed their right and responsibility to be in that position and exercise that authority.

Today, when talk of authority and submission to leaders is not very popular, it is important to realise that God still appoints leaders over congregations, schools and colleges for the purpose of teaching and judging; for exercising godly authority over those in their charge. So the words of the writer to the Hebrews are true for us: "Obey your leaders and submit to them, for they keep watch over your lives, as people who will have to give an account" (Hebrews 13:17, CJB).

Further Study: Isaiah 62:6; Acts 20:28; 1 Thessalonians 5:12-13

Application: Everyone in the Kingdom of God, from the highest to the lowest, has been placed under authority or made accountable; it is a kingdom principle. Why not pray today for your leaders, that they may exercise their role faithfully and be able to take joy in serving the people of God.

יִתְרוֹ ג׳

Yitro - Jethro - 3

Shemot / Exodus 18:24 - 27

Shemot/Exodus 18:25 Moshe chose men of valour from all Israel

וַיִּבְחַר מֹשֶׁה אַנְשֵׁי־חַיִל מִכָּל־יִשְׂרָאֵל

Yisra'el mikol khayil an'shey Moshe vayiv'khar

These words describe how Moshe followed the advice of Jethro his father-in-law. A few verses earlier Jethro had said, "But you must seek out from among all the people capable, God-fearing men - men of truth, who hate injustice" (Shemot 18:21, Living Torah). Sforno suggests that Moshe sought to find men who possessed all the qualities mentioned by Jethro, but not being able to find anyone who had them all, he chose capable or able men because they would at least have the skill to understand cases and render correct judgements. Our Sages said, "Even if a scholar is vengeful and bears malice like a serpent, gird him on your loins; whereas even if an *am ha'aretz* (literally,"a man of the earth", meaning an ignoramus) is pious, do not dwell in his vicinity" (*b. Shabbat 63a*).

But is that true in either respect? The Hebrew word חַיִל, translated here as 'valour', in the quote from verse 21 as 'capable', has a wide range of meanings. It is used to describe the Woman of Valour in Proverbs 31, to describe Bo'az (Ruth 2:1) and by Bo'az to describe Ruth (Ruth 3:11). It can mean 'competent' or 'resourceful' (Hirsch), 'leadership qualities' or 'efficient' (Ramban), 'strong' (Ibn Janach), 'strong-hearted' or 'confident' (Ralbag), 'wealthy' (Rashi), or simply 'status' (Rashbam). This is a collection of qualities that describe someone who not only has scholarship skills but is wealthy enough to be above a bribe or financial influence, who is a natural and resourceful leader, who has the strength of character to be both compassionate and fair, who can be respected by the community as of excellent reputation and integrity. So perhaps Moshe summed his choice up in one word rather than six!

Rav Sha'ul wrote to his friend and disciple Timothy about the qualities he should encourage in the people of God, that "when the men pray, no matter where, they should lift up hands that are holy - they should not become angry or get into arguments" (1 Timothy 2:8, CJB). There is an echo of Psalm 24 here: "clean hands and a pure heart", as Sha'ul stresses the spiritual and behavioural characteristics of one who worships God. "Likewise, the women, when they pray, should be dressed modestly and sensibly in respectable attire" (1 Timothy 2:9, CJB). Nothing outlandish here, no unreasonable restrictions, just a simple focus on being quiet, normal, decent people behaving sensibly towards each other. The following verses go on to list the qualities that mark out leaders and officers/servants within the community - qualities that seem very reasonable for all of us - and Sha'ul sums up by saying, "I am writing these things so that ... you may know how someone should behave in the household of God" (1 Timothy 3:14-15, CJB) thus establishing a pattern for all of us to live and share our lives together in the body of Messiah.

Further Study: 1 Timothy 3:1-13; Titus 2:1-10

Application: Are you living your life in a way that is consistent with Scripture? In the modern world, where competitiveness and a certain ruthless drive to succeed and to stand out from the crowd are considered *de rigeur*, we are called to be different, to show those qualities that God values. Think about your lifestyle today!

יִתְרוֹ ד׳

Yitro - Jethro - 4

Shemot / Exodus 19:1 - 6

Shemot/Exodus 19:1 In the third month of the Exodus of the Children of Israel from Egypt ...

בַּחֹדֶשׁ הַשְׁלִישִׁי לְצֵאת בְּנֵי־יִשְׂרָאֵל מֵאֶרֶץ
mey'eretz Yisrael b'ney l'tzeyt hashliyshiy bakhodesh

מִצְרָיִם
Mitzrayim

The Ba'al HaTurim points out that the phrase בַּחֹדֶשׁ הַשְׁלִישִׁי, in the third month, is an illustration of the dictum established by the Sages that a female captive, a female convert and an emancipated maid-servant may not marry until three months have elapsed (*b.* Yevamot 35*a*, *b.* Ketubot 37*a*, based on among others D'varim 21:13), so that the patrimony of any child would be clear. "For the Israelites went free from the Egyptian captivity, and He waited for them three months[7] until the day of the giving of the *Torah*, which established their marriage bond with God."

This theme is picked up by the Psalmist who, in a psalm written to celebrate the king's marriage, urges the bride to "Listen, O daughter, give attention and incline your ear; forget your people and your father's house; then the King will desire your beauty; because He is your Lord, bow down to Him" (Psalm 45:10-11, NASB). Like the captive woman, the bride is to make a clean break, a separation between her family, position and status as her father's daughter and instead focus on being her husband's wife. As the *Torah* says, echoed by Yeshua: "Therefore a man leaves his father and his mother and cleaves to his wife and they become one flesh" (B'resheet 2:24, RSV), this time using the man to describe how the married couple are a separate entity, no longer a part of their parents' households.

This in turn is a powerful image of how our lives are supposed to

---

7. While strictly the time between *Pesach* and *Shavuot* is only seven weeks and one day, the Exodus started started on the 14th day of Aviv, the first month of the year (Shemot 12) and Israel came to Sinai in the third month (Shemot 19)

change when we come to know God in Messiah Yeshua: we turn from sin to God, we put off the old and put on the new, we abandon our old, sinful ways and habits to walk before God in righteousness and truth. As Rav Sha'ul put it: "Therefore, if anyone is united with the Messiah, he is a new creation - the old has passed; look, what has come is fresh and new!" (2 Corinthians 5:17, CJB). Just, therefore, as God didn't give the *Torah* to our people immediately after we left Egypt, but waited until the third month for us to experience His provision and guidance as we trekked across the desert from the Sea of Reeds to Mt. Sinai, Yeshua makes it plain that following Him is a radical departure from what has gone before: "Don't think I've come to make life cozy. I've come to cut - make a sharp knife-cut - between son and father, daughter and mother, bride and mother-in-law - cut through these cozy domestic arrangements and free you for God ... if you prefer father or mother over Me, you don't deserve Me" (Matthew 10:34-37, Message). Take note that elsewhere Yeshua speaks about honouring father and mother and providing for parents, so He isn't advocating neglecting parents; He is describing the high level of commitment we are to have for Him, over and above the normal love, care and concern we have for family members.

It took time for our people to shake off enough of the life of slavery and bondage in Egypt before they could make that confession of faith and obedience, "Everything that Adonai has spoken, we will do and obey" (Shemot 24:7, CJB), but *HaShem* needed to give them that time so that they would recognise the degree of change required. In the days of the Early Church, when confessing the name of Messiah was all too often a guarantee of an appearance in the arena - and not as a spectator - believers had to be very sure of what they believed and why, because they could frequently be called to account for it with their lives. A complete change and an absolute conviction of faith was needed to face that end.

Further Study: Song of Songs 2:10-13; Isaiah 55:1-3; Philippians 3:7-9

Application: Do you wonder sometimes about your faith, asking yourself just exactly why it is that you believe in Yeshua or, indeed, if you really believe in Him at all? Do you look back in your life and see no change point, no moment of transition from one lifestyle to another? Now is the time to ask God to show you the reality of the cross and to call you into a deep and meaningful relationship with Him.

יִתְרוֹ ה׳

Yitro - Jethro - 5

Shemot / Exodus 19:7 - 19

Shemot/Exodus 19:7 And he put before them all these words that Adonai had commanded him

וַיָּשֶׂם לִפְנֵיהֶם אֵת כָּל־הַדְּבָרִים הָאֵלֶּה אֲשֶׁר
asher ha'eyleh hadvariym kol eyt lifneyhem vayasem

צִוָּהוּ יְהוָה׃
Adonai tzivahu

    This phrase relates Moshe's obedience to the instructions he had been given in the previous verse: "These are the words you shall speak to the Children of Israel" (v. 6). Rashi dryly comments there: "These are the words: no more and no less" to emphasise that *HaShem* is not giving Moshe any licence to explain, amplify or modify the explicit and exact words that He has spoken for the Israelites to hear. From this we may deduce that on other occasions Moshe was allowed to explain, paraphrase, repeat or even translate *HaShem's* words so that the people would be able to clearly understand and relate to what God was saying. The Mekhilta agrees with Rashi, adding the comment, "The first first and the last last" to suggest that Moshe didn't even alter the ordering or arrangement of the words, he simply repeated what God had said, verbatim.

    The Mekhilta goes on to offer another thought on the next phrase, which we might not have obviously seen: "Which *Adonai* commanded him: also what was said for the women." The first part of this verse tells us that Moshe spoke to the elders, all of whom were men, but the next verse is going to say that all the people answered "as one", together, so the women must have been involved so that as a 50% part of "all the people", they too had heard from God. It is also possible that this comment implies a criticism of some rabbis and teachers at the time the Mekhilta was written, who may have excluded women from classes or discussions, treating them much less equally than the *Torah* requires; by suggesting that Moshe had particular things to say to the women[8] (at Sinai) this comment is a reminder that the women were an active part of the Sinai covenant process and that God not only can but does and has always spoken to and through women as well as through men.

The verb at the start of the phrase, וַיָּשֶׂם, variously translated "set or put before, explained, related" comes from the root שׂום which has a wide usage and range of meanings: set, put, place, establish, set or lay (as a fire), lay up or preserve. Sa'adia Gaon compares it to D'varim 31:19, "put in their mouths", with the idea of teaching; Ibn Ezra explains that the verb can be used of both speech and writing, suggesting that this might refer to the Oral *Torah* rather than the Written *Torah*. Nachmanides, on the other hand, insists that Moshe is explaining and setting a choice before the people: "Let them say whether they choose to accept upon themselves the obligation to perform the *mitzvot*". This is not primarily a teaching venue - that will come later, if the people accept the basic obligation - but a moment of choice or decision: are you in or not?

In order for people to be able to accept a foundational truth, it has to be explained and presented to them in a clear and understandable way; if this is not done, then their understanding of and therefore their commitment to it will be weak. To ensure that the message is properly received and comprehended, that those hearing are able to fully engage with it and appreciate not only the benefits but the costs involved in acceptance, it is necessary to do two things: to simplify the content by reducing or distilling it to a small number of critical facts or points that convey the kernel or essence of the proposal; to communicate the message in clear and unambiguous language so that there should be no confusion or distraction. Once the presentation is complete, it is crucial to bring the hearers to a decision by asking them to respond; all too often a good presentation is wasted - for both the presenter and the hearers - by not asking for a decision. Although neither this nor the following verse record Moshe's question, the narrative clearly shows that the people answered and that Moshe reported that answer to God.

At the start of the Gospels, we find John the Baptist and Yeshua presenting a very simple call to the people to whom they spoke: "Repent, for the kingdom of heaven is at hand" (Matthew 3:2, 4:17, NASB). Throughout His ministry, Yeshua teaches using parables, a format that almost always explicitly or implicitly demands a response from the hearers. After telling the parable of the Good Samaritan, Yeshua asks, "Which of these three do you think proved to be a neighbour to the man who fell into the robbers' hands?" (Luke 10:36, NASB) so that the lawyer who has triggered the story (v. 25) had to respond. At the conclusion of the story of the widow and the

---

8. For example, perhaps the laws of family purity were intended for the women first

unjust judge, Yeshua asks, "When the Son of Man comes, will He find faith in the earth?" (Luke 18:8, NASB) to force His hearers to ask themselves where they stood.

Writing to Timothy, Rav Sha'ul urges him to, "preach the word; be ready in season and out of season; reprove, rebuke, exhort, with great patience and instruction" (2 Timothy 4:2, NASB) that he might engage with the people amongst whom he was working; no stand-off sermons from high pulpits here but down-to-earth grappling and challenge using the words of the Bible. Similarly, Peter encourages the Jewish believers in the *Diaspora*, "always be ready to make a defence to everyone who asks you to give an account for the hope that is in you, yet with gentleness and reverence" (1 Peter 3:15, NASB); not a hit-and-run style, quoting a Bible verse at someone and then rushing away before they have a chance to respond or refusing to debate or explain. No, God requires more of us than that - we must not only engage with people where they are, but be prepared to participate in, if necessary, robust argument and discussion, before asking for a decision and challenging people to respond to what God has said to them.

Further Study: Matthew 17:24-27; Matthew 21:28-32

Application: Are you a hit-and-run evangelist, dropping a bomb and then running for cover, or are you fearful of even speaking a few words, frightened of the flak and attention it might provoke? Either extreme falls short of what God requires of us by denying our hearers - whom God wants to reach - an opportunity to reasonably hear and respond to the message of salvation. How will you prepare for and meet that challenge today?

יִתְרוֹ '

Yitro - Jethro - 6

Shemot / Exodus 19:20 - 20:14

Shemot/Exodus 19:20 Adonai came down upon Mt. Sinai, to the top of the mountain

וַיֵּרֶד יהוה עַל־הַר סִינַי אֶל־רֹאשׁ הָהָר

ha'har rosh el Siynay har al Adonai vayeyred

The authors of the Mekhilta are puzzled about the apparent contradiction between this verse and 20:19 where *HaShem* reminds Moshe and the people that "You yourselves have seen that I have spoken to you from heaven" (CJB): did *HaShem* speak from heaven or the top of the mountain? They answer by suggesting that *HaShem* somehow bent or squashed the heavens, like a mattress on a bed, to enable Him to speak to Moshe at the top of the mountain without leaving the heavens. After using the verse "The heavens are the heavens of the Lord; but the earth He has given to the sons of men" (Psalm 115:16, NASB) to show that heaven and earth cannot mix, "Rabbi Jose stated, Neither did the Shechinah ever descend to earth, nor did Moses or Elijah ever ascend to Heaven" (*b. Sukkah 5a*), the Sages of the Talmud are very precise, asserting that the heavens came to a distance of ten handbreadths of the summit of the mountain; they also link this to the verse "in that day His feet will stand on the Mount of Olives" (Zechariah 14:4, NASB), claiming that the Lord's feet will also rest ten handbreadths above the ground. Scholars suggest that this claim is probably an attempt to counter the idea of Yeshua's ascension to heaven as described in Acts 1.

Ibn Ezra is indignant that the readers should imagine *HaShem* actually being on the mountain. He says, "The Lord came down: The spirit, which is not a body cannot be said to 'come down' or 'go up'. How much less so the Lord, who is God of the spirits of all flesh! The text is speaking of the Presence of God, the Shechinah". *Targum Onkelos* shares the same concerns, paraphrasing the text to read, "The Lord was revealed upon the mountain of Sinai on the top of the mountain." Nachmanides adds, "If you gain enlightenment about this passage, you will understand that His great name came down upon the mountain and dwelt there in fire, and it was this that spoke with Moshe." All these commentators are trying to avoid the plain meaning of the text that God Himself was actually present, in some kind of physical manifestation, on the mountain, talking with Moshe. Scholars suggest that this way of interpreting this verse and similar passages that refer to God as if He might have human form, is a deliberate choice made by Rabbinic Judaism in order to distance themselves from believers in Yeshua.

In the twelfth century, Maimonedes proposed thirteen principles of Jewish faith which include as the third: "אֲנִי מַאֲמִין בֶּאֱמוּנָה שְׁלֵמָה", I believe with perfect faith that the Creator, blessed be His name, is not physical, that no physical attributes can be applied to Him, and that there is nothing whatsoever to compare to Him." (Authorised Daily Prayer). Although the principles were originally widely resisted and have never been totally accepted by the whole of world Jewry, still being contested by many academics today, they have gained a significant position within Jewish orthodoxy. They are present at the start of the *Shacharit* prayer service in the poem known as the *Yigdal*, יְגְדַּל, containing the words, "He has neither bodily form nor substance" and are recited by some at the end of the service after the Ten Commandments.

By contrast, it is a cornerstone of our faith that Yeshua the Messiah of Israel came not only as a human being, but communicated God's message of love and righteousness in a unique and final form: "Long ago, at many times and in many ways, God spoke to our fathers by the prophets, but in these last days He has spoken to us by His Son, whom He appointed the heir of all things, through whom also He created the world" (Hebrews 1:1-2, ESV). The Psalmist prophesies that "Sacrifice and burnt offerings You did not desire, but a body You have prepared for Me" (Psalm 40:6, Septuagint) and "For You will not abandon My soul to Sheol, or let Your holy one see corruption" (Psalm 16:10, ESV) seems not only to apply to a physical body but cannot apply to David, to whom the psalm is attributed, since David clearly died and was buried.

However strange it may seem, or however strongly resisted by others, we have in the pages of the Scriptures the classic three-step pattern used today by teachers, educators, consultants and marketing people the world over: tell them what you are going to tell them, tell them, tell them what you have just told them.

In a consistent thread, from the very earliest chapters of the *Torah*, through Israel's history and the words of the prophets, God made sure to tell our people what He was about to do. For example, the Servant Songs - four passages in the book of Isaiah (42:1-9, 49:1-13, 50:4-9, 52:13-53:12[9]) -

---

9. Some scholars also suggest Isaiah 61:1-3, although the word 'servant' is not actually present in the text

portray the mission and life of God's Messiah, the one who was to come to save not just Israel but all who would acknowledge Him. Although the texts had an immediate application and meaning to the original hearers of Isaiah's words in his time, successive generations recognised that the text had an enduring meaning yet to come. The Midrash Tanchuma from the ninth century and the later Yalqut Shimeoni say that "this is the King, the Messiah, who will rise and be greatly exalted, higher than Abraham, greater than Moses, above the worshipping angels."

The Gospels then tell us the first-hand, eyewitness accounts[10] of Yeshua's life and earthly ministry. They recount the many miracles that He performed, demonstrating the power of the Kingdom of God breaking through into the world of His time: "We know that God doesn't listen to sinners; but if anyone fears God and does His will, God does listen to him. In all history no one has ever heard of someone's opening the eyes of a man born blind. If this man were not from God, He couldn't do a thing!" (John 9:31-33, CJB). They record the way that He taught with authority - "They were amazed at the way He taught, because His word carried the ring of authority" (Luke 4:32, CJB) - and maintained and interpreted the *Torah* and the prophets "Don't think that I have come to abolish the Torah or the Prophets. I have come not to abolish but to complete. Yes indeed! I tell you that until heaven and earth pass away, not so much as a yud or a stroke will pass from the Torah- not until everything that must happen has happened" (Matthew 5:17-18, CJB). They relate the way even His Roman executioners saw him: "And when the centurion, who stood facing him, saw that in this way He breathed His last, he said, 'Truly this man was the Son of God!'" (Mark 15:39, ESV).

Acts and the letters then report how the news of Yeshua was received and spread around the Jewish communities in the *Diaspora*, to the God-fearers and then into the surrounding Gentile population. We hear the words of the twelve disciples: "This man was arrested in accordance with God's predetermined plan and foreknowledge; and, through the agency of persons not bound by the Torah, you nailed Him up on a stake and killed Him! But God has raised Him up and freed Him from the suffering of death; it was impossible that death could keep its hold on Him" (Acts 2:23-24, CJB), the words of Rav Sha'ul: "I have been crucified with Christ; and it is no longer I who live, but Christ lives in me; and the life which I now live in the flesh I live by faith in the Son of God, who loved me, and delivered Himself up for me" (Galatians 2:20, NASB), and the vision of John whose eyes saw that which is yet still to come: "And I saw heaven opened; and behold, a white horse, and

---

10. See particularly "Jesus and the Eyewitnesses: the Gospels as Eyewitness Testimony", Richard Bauckham, Eerdmans 2006, 0802831621 for an outstanding and contemporary presentation of the case for the Gospels being authentic eye-witness accounts and documents.

He who sat upon it is called Faithful and True; and in righteousness He judges and wages war. And His eyes are a flame of fire, and upon His head are many diadems; and He has a name written upon Him which no one knows except Himself. And He is clothed with a robe dipped in blood; and His name is called The Word of God. And the armies which are in heaven, clothed in fine linen, white and clean, were following Him on white horses. And from His mouth comes a sharp sword, so that with it He may smite the nations; and He will rule them with a rod of iron; and He treads the wine press of the fierce wrath of God, the Almighty. And on His robe and on His thigh He has a name written, 'KING OF KINGS, AND LORD OF LORDS'" (Revelation 19:11-16, NASB).

Should we be surprised, then, at the statement in the original text: God came down upon the mountain? No, for Yeshua - the Son of God - came in the flesh and shared our life and the human experience, so that He might uniquely bridge the gap between God and man, reconciling man to God. Truly this was fire on the mountain.

Further Study: Nehemiah 9:13-15; 1 John 4:2-3

Application: Are you ever taken in by those who try to tell you that Yeshua was just a man, or that He just swooned on the cross? Don't let the enemy steal this key part of our faith; pick up your Bible today and start re-reading one of the Gospels and see afresh what God has done for us!

יִתְרוֹ ז׳

Yitro - Jethro - 7

Shemot / Exodus 20:15 - 23:26

Shemot/Exodus 20:15 And all the people saw the thunder and the flames and the sound of the shofar and the smoking mountain ...

וְכָל־הָעָם רֹאִים אֶת־הַקּוֹלֹת וְאֶת־הַלַּפִּידִם

halapiydim   v'et   hakolot   et   ro'iym   ha'am v'chol

וְאֶת קוֹל הַשֹּׁפָר וְאֶת־הָהָר עָשֵׁן

asheyn ha'har v'et hashofar kol v'eyt

We seem to have a sensory paradox here. The verb רֹאִים - a masculine plural participle from the root רָאָה, most often "to see", sometimes "to look at" or "to perceive" - is applied to two audible objects and two visible objects; a clash of senses. The same noun is used in the plural for voices - הַקּוֹלֹת - usually translated "thunder" (see, for example, JPS, NASB, NIV) and in the singular for voice - קוֹל - usually translated "sound", for what are clearly aural events. Yet the flames and the smoking mountain are equally clearly visual events. Nahum Sarna says, "The figurative language indicates the profound awareness among the assembled throng of the overpowering majesty and mystery of God's self-manifestation. It is an experience that cannot be adequately described by the ordinary language of the senses." Rashi comments that "they were seeing that which is audible, which is impossible to see elsewhere". The Mekhilta adds, "Rabbi Akiva says: They saw and heard that which was visible. They saw the fiery word coming out from the mouth of the Almighty as it was struck upon the tablets, as it is said, 'The voice of the Lord hewed out flames of fire' (Psalm 29:7)".

The Ba'al HaTurim connects the overwhelming sensory experience with the Jewish habit of movement during prayer and study: "The nation saw and they trembled: The reasoning behind the custom of swaying back and forth while studying *Torah* is that the *Torah* was given with 'awe, trembling and quaking' (*b. Yoma 4b*)." The Ramban also suggests sensory overload when he says that "Our Sages understood this as 'trembled', as it means in 'The earth is swaying like a drunkard; it is rocking to and fro like a hut ' (Isaiah 24:20, JPS)". The theophany that the people saw caused bodily disturbance because it exceeded the limits that the human neural system was designed to handle and process; shaking, trembling, fear and awe were the symptoms. The experience was so great that it made a lasting memory in the minds not only of the people that were there at the time, but in the collective memory of our people right down to this day. How do we know that our people are in covenant with God and that He gave us His *Torah*? Because we were all there and saw it with all our senses. This event was seen and heard by over two million people - men, women and children - and the truth of the narrative is confirmed because it has been consistently passed down from generation to generation; no-one stood up and said, "I don't remember that", because everyone did remember that! It was an experience and an encounter that no-one could forget.

Hirsch makes another important point. "The conviction that a word has been spoken by any special person can only be accomplished by the simultaneous realisation of eye and ear. With closed eyes we can fix the general direction from which a sound proceeds but we cannot fix the exact point from which a sound that reaches our ear emanates. So here too, the people saw the sounds addressed to them simultaneously with the flash of lightening." In order to perceive and register the significance of the moment, it was necessary that the people should both see and hear at the same time. This was not just the creation of an overwhelming sensory event, it was the positive and deliberate communication of truth and reality concerning God's choice of Israel as His covenant people and the way in which they were to relate to Him and depend on Him. To be more than just a blast of noise, light and fire, to have lasting understanding, the content had to engage with both the primary sight and sound mechanisms so that the people would know what they had seen and why.

John's gospel records another major event: "The Word became a human being and lived with us, and we saw his Shechinah, the Shechinah of the Father's only Son, full of grace and truth" (John 1:14, CJB). We know that this was an even greater revelation than the Sinai experience because the writer to the Hebrews tells us, "In days gone by, God spoke in many and varied ways to the Fathers through the prophets. But now, in the acharit hayamim, He has spoken to us through His Son, to whom He has given ownership of everything and through whom He created the universe. This Son is the radiance of the Shechhinah, the very expression of God's essence" (Hebrews 1:1-3, CJB). We should therefore expect this revelation to be accompanied by a similar multi-sensory engagement so as to create a lasting memory and understanding among those who saw and experienced it. The Bible records that exactly that did occur; first to those in the immediate vicinity: "In the countryside nearby were some shepherds spending the night in the fields, guarding their flocks, when an angel of Adonai appeared to them, and the Shechinah of Adonai shone around them. They were terrified; but the angel said to them, 'Don't be afraid ...' Suddenly, along with the angel was a vast army from heaven praising God: 'In the highest heaven, glory to God! And on earth, peace among people of good will!'" (Luke 2:8-14, CJB). Secondly, there was revelation also to those from afar (both physically and spiritually): "After Yeshua was born in Bethlehem in the land of Judah during the time when Herod was king, Magi from the east came to Yerushalayim and asked, 'Where is the newborn King of the Jews? For we saw His star in the east and have come to worship Him'" (Matthew 2:1-2, CJB).

But more was necessary. So that the experience might fully resonate with people, they needed to engage more than just two senses in what was going on. Back to John again: "The Word, which gives life! He existed from the beginning. We have heard Him, we have seen Him with our eyes, we have contemplated Him, we have touched Him with our hands!" (1 John 1:1, CJB); the result of three years of cheek-by-jowl ministry with Yeshua. When Yeshua had ascended and the disciples waited in Jerusalem for the *Ruach* to be poured out, then followed the last part of the theophany. Closely following the account of Sinai itself, we read: "The festival of Shavu'ot arrived, and the believers all gathered together in one place. Suddenly there came a sound from the sky like the roar of a violent wind, and it filled the whole house where they were sitting. Then they saw what looked like tongues of fire, which separated and came to rest on each one of them. They were all filled with the Ruach HaKodesh and began to talk in different languages, as the Spirit enabled them to speak" (Acts 2:1-4, CJB). Here we have the sound from heaven and the fire that rested - instead of on the mountain - on each of them. Just as Jewish tradition records that the *Torah* was given at Sinai in all the seventy languages of the nations (*b.* Shabbat 88*b*), so now the disciples speak out the glory of God in the languages of the nations so that their hearers too are witnesses to what is going on: "Totally amazed, they asked, 'How is this possible? Aren't all these people who are speaking from the Galil? How is it that we hear them speaking in our native languages? We are Parthians, Medes, Elamites; residents of Mesopotamia, Judah, Cappadocia, Pontus, Asia, Phrygia, Pamphylia, Egypt, the parts of Libya near Cyrene; visitors from Rome; Jews by birth and proselytes; Jews from Crete and from Arabia! How is it that we hear them speaking in our own languages about the great things God has done?'" (vv. 7-11, CJB).

When God wants everyone to sit up and take notice, He manufactures an event that will not only engage with all our senses, but will also create a memory and understanding within us that will last. In three remarkable events, the revelation of the *Torah* at Mt. Sinai, the birth of the Messiah and the outpouring of the *Ruach*, He coordinated sight and sound so that those who witnessed the event should know exactly what they had heard and why, in a way that they could accept and understand, passing a reliable witness on to us in this day. We need to be sure that our relationship with God is founded on nothing less - a personal encounter with God that has engaged all of our senses so that we know that we know that we know!

Further Study: Acts 4:19-22; Isaiah 66:18-19

Application: Do you know? Do you really know? In these days of uncertainty, now is the time to make sure that you are firm and solid in your relationship with God. Study the texts in your Bible and ask God to confirm your relationship with Him - not necessarily with a physical manifestation, although He may graciously do that, but inwardly by the witness of the *Ruach* within you - so that you may stand firm in the rip tides of modern life and give a reliable witness for Him.

מִשְׁפָּטִים

Mishpatim - Judgements

Shemot / Exodus 21:1 - 24:18

רִאשׁוֹן	Aliyah One	Shemot/Exodus 21:1 - 19
שֵׁנִי	Aliyah Two	Shemot/Exodus 21:20 - 22:3
שְׁלִישִׁי	Aliyah Three	Shemot/Exodus 22:4 - 26
רְבִיעִי	Aliyah Four	Shemot/Exodus 22:27 - 23:5
חֲמִשִׁי	Aliyah Five	Shemot/Exodus 23:6 - 19
שִׁשִׁי	Aliyah Six	Shemot/Exodus 23:20 - 25
שְׁבִיעִי	Aliyah Seven	Shemot/Exodus 23:26 - 24:18

מִשְׁפָּטִים א'

Mishpatim - Judgements - 1

Shemot / Exodus 21:1 - 19

Shemot/Exodus 21:1 These are the rulings you are to present to them

וְאֵלֶּה הַמִּשְׁפָּטִים אֲשֶׁר תָּשִׂים לִפְנֵיהֶם:

lif'neyhem   tasiym   asher hamish'patiym v'eyleh

In the Talmud (*b*. Eruvin 54*b*) the Sages debate the meaning of the word תָּשִׂים. While its possible meanings start from "to put, set or place", they extend to "establish, stand erect or appoint". But the Sages go further and suggest that here it means teach: God was telling Moshe to teach His rulings/judgements to the people. The Sages add that it is not be rote learning, just so that the words can be repeated, but learned with understanding so that they can be applied. The analogy is made between raw and cooked food: if the food is raw then it is unpalatable and difficult to digest, whereas properly cooked, it is not only pleasant to eat but can be easily digested and used by the body.

The prophet Jeremiah talks about the new covenant that God is to make with the house of Israel and the house of Judah, "For this is the covenant I will make with the house of Israel after those days ... I will put My Torah within them and write it on their hearts" (Jeremiah 31:32, CJB). At that time, God is saying, the nature of the covenant will change so that instead of being an external thing, learned and explained, the *Torah* will be inside our hearts. "No longer will any of them teach his fellow community member or his brother, 'Know Adonai'; for all will know Me, from the least of them to the greatest" (Jeremiah 31:33, CJB). We will not need a teacher like Moshe, for each of us will know God personally.

Rav Sha'ul picks up the same theme, "you are a letter ... written not with ink but by the Spirit of the Living God, not on stone tablets but on human hearts" (2 Corinthians 3:3, CJB), when he tells the believers at Corinth that they and their lives are much more than ink on stone - an external representation - they they are the embodiment of Jeremiah's prophecy. He goes on to describe the new covenant, "the essence of which is not a written text but the Spirit. For the written text brings death, but the Spirit gives life" (v.

6, CJB). Is he saying that the *Torah* brings death? No, the *Torah* brings life; it is the medium and our attitude to it that causes the problem! *Torah* is for living, not for beating up others. When we see it as a set of fixed rules to be meticulously obeyed to win God's favour, rather than a worked example of how believers live holy lives, truly 'in the Spirit', then we kill our relationship with God because we become focused on our observance of the *Torah* rather than Him.

This is why Yeshua said, "The time is coming ... when the true worshippers will worship the Father spiritually and truly" (John 4:23, CJB). Yeshua is not condemning the sacrificial system itself, for that was ordained by God in the *Torah*; He is lifting the focus from legalistic mechanical rule-keeping to seeing that the things we do are to worship God and must be done in the *Ruach HaKodesh*.

Further Study: Isaiah 12:2-4; John 4:13-24

Application: It is easy to slip into mechanical learning and study so that we become focused on the acquisition of knowledge and techniques rather than using them as guides to a personal relationship with God. Ask God today where the focus of your spiritual eyes is.

מִשְׁפָּטִים ׳ב

Mishpatim - Judgements - 2

Shemot / Exodus 21:20 - 22:3

Shemot/Exodus 21:20 And if a man strikes his slave or slave-girl with the rod and he dies ...

וְכִי־יַכֶּה אִישׁ אֶת־עַבְדּוֹ אוֹ אֶת־אֲמָתוֹ בַּשֵּׁבֶט

basheyvet amato et o av'do et iysh yakeh v'chiy

וָמֵת

oomeyt

This text introduces an exception to the commandment in Shemot 21:12 that "he who strikes a man so that he dies shall surely be put to death". The Hebrew word עֶבֶד (here as עַבְדּוֹ with a 3ms 'his' possessive pronoun suffix) can mean servant or slave, but the next verse makes it clear that this text uses it as 'slave' for it comments that the slave is "his property". Rashi uses the same evidence to deduce further that it must be referring to a Canaanite slave, for a Hebrew slave is not 'property' or a possession, as he only has a limited time of service. The Ramban notes that it is the custom of a ruler or master to keep in his hand a rod of correction (Proverbs 22:15) but that God warns rulers, using the King of Babylon as an example, not to strike without restraint or without ceasing (Isaiah 14:6).

This treatment of slaves seems rather foreign to Rav Sha'ul who, in the same breath as urging submission and love between husbands and wives (Ephesians 5:22, 25) and instructing children to obey their parents while simultaneously telling fathers not to provoke their children but to bring them up in the Lord (6:1), goes on to address the relationship between masters and slaves. Having previously told the Galatians that "there is neither ... slave nor free man ... for you are all one in Messiah Yeshua" (Galatians 3:28, NASB) - that like Jews and Gentiles, men and women, both slaves and their masters have equal status as believers before God in the Messiah - Rav Sha'ul provides instructions for slaves and masters: "Slaves be obedient to those who are your masters according to the flesh ... with good will render service, as to the Lord and not to men ... and masters, do the same things to them ...

knowing that both their Master and yours is in heaven, and there is no partiality with Him" (Ephesians 6:5-9, NASB).

The Greek word for slave, δοῦλος, most frequently translated 'slave', is also the word used to refer to Yeshua Himself in the piece of early Church liturgy encapsulated by Rav Sha'ul's letter to the Philippians: "Messiah Yeshua ... emptied Himself, taking the form of a bond-servant, being made in the likeness of men ... He humbled Himself by becoming obedient to the point of death, even death on a cross" (Philippians 2:5-8, NASB). Our Master Himself modelled the behaviour of the perfect slave by His ultimate obedience to Father God in submitting to bearing the punishment for our sin on the tree.

Even though we have been redeemed - that is, paid for as bought - God does not treat us as harshly as slaves. Yeshua said, "I no longer call you slaves, because a slave doesn't know what his master is about; but I have called you friends, because everything I have heard from My Father I have made known to you" (John 15:15, CJB). How much do these words apply to us - "Whatever work you do, put yourself into it, as those who are serving not merely other people but the Lord" (Colossians 3:23, CJB).

Further Study: Luke 17:7-10; 1 Timothy 6:1-2; Titus 2:9-10

Application: In the work place, in particular, our witness and obedience is challenged, both by those around us and the enemy. What is the standard of our service - do we match up to the model set us by Yeshua Himself?

מִשְׁפָּטִים ג'

Mishpatim - Judgements - 3

Shemot / Exodus 22:4 - 26

Shemot/Exodus 22:4 When a man consumes a field or a vineyard and he releases his livestock

כִּי יַבְעֶר־אִישׁ שָׂדֶה אוֹ־כֶרֶם וְשִׁלַּח אֶת־בְּעִירֹה
b'iyro et v'shilakh kerem o sadeh iysh yav'er kiy

The Hebrew root בָּעַר has a number of different meanings; in this verse it is usually translated 'graze' (NASB, NIV, CJB, JPS). Sarna comments that the root "most frequently means 'to set fire, burn' as in verse 5. But it can also mean 'to ravage' which is the action of a beast" and points out that the same word is used in Isaiah 5:5 "Now I am going to tell you / What I will do to My vineyard / I will remove its hedge / That it may be ravaged". The Septuagint also translates the word here as 'grazed over'. Rashi suggests the word 'consume' which is also listed in Brown, Driver and Briggs as a meaning that the verb can have in the *Hif'il* stem.

It is interesting to see the two meanings juxtaposed in Shemot 22:4-5: "If a man causes a field or vineyard to be grazed over ...he shall make restitution from the best in his own field ... If fire breaks out ... he who started the fire shall make full restitution", bringing together the idea of burning and grazing. In both cases, whether deliberate or accidental, damage is done to a third party so restitution is to be made from the best of the responsible man's crops, equivalent acreage of land or value in money, because the victim's ground and produce has been consumed as if passed over by fire.

King David became very animated and angry one day when Nathan the prophet came to him with a report of injustice in his kingdom. Instead of mere crop damage, a rich man - with flocks and herds of his own - had stolen his poor neighbour's only lamb - a family pet - to feed a travelling guest. "Then David's anger burned greatly against the [rich] man and he said to Nathan, 'As the Lord lives, surely the man who has done this deserves to die. And he must make restitution for the lamb fourfold, because he did this and had no compassion'" (2 Samuel 12:5-6, NASB). When Nathan pointed out that the story was really about him, David confessed his sin for he had consumed the wife of Uriah the Hittite. Although David could not make restitution, he nevertheless committed his heart to God and Psalm 51 recounts David's repentance: "You don't want sacrifices or I would give them - my sacrifice to God is a broken spirit" (Psalm 51:18-19, CJB).

When Yeshua saw the multitudes that came to Him, "He felt compassion for them, because they were distressed and downcast like sheep without a shepherd" (Matthew 9:36, NASB). He could see that the people had been ravaged, consumed, even burnt, so He made restitution: "I am the Good Shepherd. The Good Shepherd lays down His life for the sheep" (John 10:11, CJB). God gave of His best - His only Son - to make restitution for us and to make recompense for the destruction and burning in our lives. As the Lord said, "I will pasture My sheep and I will let them rest ... I will seek the lost, bring back the outcasts, bandage the broken, and strengthen the sick" (Ezekiel 34:13-16, CJB). God Himself will be our shepherd if we let Him.

Further Study: Psalm 51; Joel 2:21-27

Application: God is in the restoration and restitution business. He wants to rescue those who have been consumed and ravaged by the world and bring them into His kingdom. Are you in need of rescuing, or does your heart long to work with Him? Then sign up today and join the greatest reclamation project of all time!

מִשְׁפָּטִים 'ד

Mishpatim - Judgements - 4

Shemot / Exodus 22:27 - 23:5

Shemot/Exodus 22:27 You shall not revile judges, nor curse a leader of your people

אֱלֹהִים לֹא תְקַלֵּל וְנָשִׂיא בְעַמְּךָ לֹא תָאֹר:

ta'or   lo   v'amcha v'nasiy t'kaleyl   lo   elohim

Who is אֱלֹהִים - is this God, or are they judges? *Targum Onkelos* translates it as דַיָּנָא, a judge, but the Mekhilta records the words of Rabbi Akiva connecting this verse to the punishment decreed for someone who curses *HaShem*, "Moreover, the one who blasphemes the name of the Lord shall surely be put to death" (Vayikra 24:16, NASB), on the grounds that the *Torah* would not give a punishment for something that had not already been forbidden. Rabbi Ishmael, on the other hand, reads this as "judges", relating it to the verse earlier in the same chapter, "the owner of the house shall appear before the judges" (Shemot 22:8, NASB). The later commentators appear equally split with Rashi and Nachmanides opting for "God", while the Rashbam and Ibn Ezra choose "judges". The Rashbam comments that "since kings and judges deal with court cases, both civil and criminal, people regularly curse them." We see this pattern of behaviour around us in society every day: almost anyone in authority, but particularly judges, probation officers and the police - anyone involved in the criminal justice system - is roundly lambasted and cursed by a significant proportion of the population. This, of course, includes those who have been involved in some form of criminality that has taken them through that system, but also features a wide range of others in society, whether young or old, who curse the system for its efficiency, its inefficiency or simply because it represents a threat or restraint to their impulses.

During Job's trials at the hand of Satan, "his wife said to him, 'Do you still hold fast your integrity? Curse God [אֱלֹהִים, Elohim] and die!'" (Job 2:9, NASB). She acknowledges the penalty and also the command and offence, but seems to imply that Job could hardly be worse off than he was and would at least feel better if he vented his spleen at God. Job, however, keeps his self-control and simply replies, "You speak as one of the foolish women speaks. Shall we accept good from God and not accept adversity?" (v. 10a, NASB). Job recognises - and goes on in the following chapters to explain to his three so-called comforters - that God is perfectly just; it would be incompatible with His nature and character to be anything other than just; so that it is necessary to accept whatever God allows into his life as being appropriate, be that a blessing or a test or a challenge. The text comments that, "In all this, Job did not sin with his lips" (v. 10b, NASB). Job kept himself from sin by keeping control over what came out of his mouth. Perhaps we could all learn a lesson from that.

Yeshua pointed out that our mouths are simply an output device for our hearts: "The good person produces good things form the store of good in his heart, while the evil person produces evil things from the store of evil in his heart. For his mouth speaks what overflows from his heart" (Luke 6:45, CJB). This implies that however important it is to avoid speaking curses upon people, it is more important not to think in that way about someone. While the original command directly applies to judges and leaders, it should certainly apply to those who have authority in the body of Messiah: pastors, home-group leaders, worship leaders and so on - in fact, as believers, we should not curse anyone. The book of James tells us that it is incompatible for the same mouth that praises God to curse a fellow man or woman (James chapter 3).

However, Yeshua goes on to say something that most people in the world would find quite shocking: "whoever calls his brother 'Good-for-nothing!' will be brought before the Sanhedrin; whoever says 'Fool!' incurs the penalty of burning in the fire of Gei Hinnom (Gehennna, hell)!" (Matthew 5:22, CJB). This is so easy to do and many of us have been brought up in a culture where young people routinely "mouth off" about their elders or peers, so that to say of someone: "He's a bit of an idiot", is really very mild yet still crosses the line that Yeshua so clearly draws. If we are to be serious about guarding our mouths and speech so that we do not even inadvertently speak a curse over someone, then perhaps we all have some work to do.

Further Study: Lamentations 3:37-40; James 3:6-10

Application: Have you found yourself speaking a curse over someone recently, calling them "stupid", "lazy", "ignorant" or worse? Perhaps a child or a family member will receive those words as truth and maybe struggle for years to overcome them? If so, then act before it is too late to recant those words, to apologise and make amends, to repent before God and ask Him to show you how to repair the damage.

מִשְׁפָּטִים 'ה

Mishpatim - Judgements - 5

Shemot / Exodus 23:6 - 19

Shemot/Exodus 23:6 You shall not pervert the justice of your poor in his dispute

לֹא תַטֶּה מִשְׁפַּט אֶבְיֹנְךָ בְּרִיבוֹ:

b'riyvo evyoncha mishpat tateh lo

The word translated 'poor', variously "needy poor" or "destitute person", אֶבְיֹנְךָ, comes from the root אָבָה, which has the meaning to desire or long for something. Rashi therefore comments, "This is an expression of longing for he is detached from any possessions and longs for all that is good," and introduces the idea that there are different types of poor people. The *Midrash* (Vayikra Rabbah 34:6) reports that there are eight designations for the poor that are used in the Hebrew Scripture, each one with a different shade of meaning: עָנִי, afflicted (Shemot 22:24); אֶבְיוֹן, one who longs (our verse); מִסְכֵּן, despised (Ecclesiastes 4:13); רָשׁ, impoverished (1 Samuel 18:23), דַּל, detached [from his ancestral property] (Shemot 23:3); דָּךְ, oppressed (Psalm 9:10); מָךְ, trampled upon (Vayikra 27:8); הֵלֶךְ, vagrant (2 Samuel 12:4). Some of these terms reflect the state of the poor person and how he comes to be in that situation, while others describe the attitude of other people to him. In some cases, the poverty may be of the individual's own making, while in others, he could be an innocent victim of war or circumstances - either of another party's deliberate instigation or by happenstance.

The Mekhilta asks, "Why is this said? Because it says: 'Neither shall you favour a poor man in his cause' (Shemot 23:3) from which I know only about the poor. But what about the needy poor? It says here: 'You shall not pervert the judgement for the needy in his case'". The verb תַטֶּה comes from the root נָטָה[11], which can mean both "to stretch out or extend and "to decline or pervert". The Mekhilta is pointing out that justice may not be

---

11. See also *parasha Bo, aliyah 2*

altered in either direction: not in favour of the poor man because he is needy, so whoever is bringing a case against him must be oppressing or persecuting him unjustly; not against the poor man because in his desperation or sheer wickedness he must have done something wrong. No matter what the status of the plaintiff or the defendant, justice requires that the evidence be examined fully and impartially and that a judgement or verdict be handed down strictly on the basis of that evidence and the applicable law, regardless of the parties involved.

While the poor feature in both stories and teaching in the Gospels, Yeshua said three things things in particular about the poor that bear investigation. Gospel texts in Hebrew today are all modern translations and they universally choose the word הָעֲנָיִּים or עֲנָיֵּי to translate 'poor', which clouds any possible differences that might have been present in Yeshua's actual words. However, we have no extant Hebrew originals for either complete or partial gospels, with the possible exception of the Shem Tov Matthean text, so we have to assume that the word we have is a generic word, covering the other possible meanings.

When Yeshua was anointed with an expensive perfume and His *talmidim* complained that the perfume could have been sold and the money given to the poor, Yeshua replied, "the poor you will always have with you" (Matthew 26:11, Mark 14:7, John 12:8). Whom did Yeshua have in view? Was He talking about people who choose to be poor, the homeless by choice, about those who have fallen on hard times and become poor as it were by accident, or about those who have been persecuted or made poor as a result of human action? Perhaps all three; although the earth could produce enough food to feed everyone on the planet, poverty seems to be one of life's bottomless pits: no matter how much resource is put in - by individuals, by companies or by governments - there are still hungry people and no sign of the problem getting any smaller.

The passage known as the Beatitudes starts, "Blessed are the poor in spirit" (Matthew 5:3, Luke 6:20) and surely addresses a different class of 'poor'. Yeshua here is not talking about the physically poor, or even the afflicted or persecuted, but those who have become separated or have separated themselves from the power of money or their ancestral holdings in order to serve God and focus on kingdom values and priorities. It may also speak of those who are despised or derided by the rest of the world because of their dedication and commitment to God.

Finally, when Yeshua is approached by the disciples of John the Immerser who are seeking confirmation that Yeshua really is the one who was expected, the Messiah whom John had announced, Yeshua replies by quoting from one of the prophetic passages that foretold His ministry: "the poor have the good news proclaimed to them" (Matthew 11:5, quoting Isaiah

61:1). This time, all eight categories of 'poor' are surely intended, for all those who are poor in any way need to hear the Good News. In its direct meaning, this would obviously apply to the financially poor, the disadvantaged and disenfranchised, the outcasts, widows and orphans; indirectly, it must include those who are isolated from God or their communities and long for relationship, or have been separated from their ancestral holding, the assurance of being a part of God's chosen people; reaching further out, even those who have chosen to be vagrant, those who live lives of rebellion, deliberately wandering far from the ways of God - even these get to hear the good news of salvation and reconciliation with God. Why? Because God Himself observes the sense of the commandment in Shemot: "you shall not stretch out or withhold the justice of your needy poor in his conflict".

Further Study: D'varim 16:19-20; Isaiah 10:1-2; 1 John 3:17

Application: Whether you are the poor - in need of hearing of God's redemptive justice - or whether you are now rich because you have received God's grace, know that it is God's purpose to share His good news with everyone - no matter who or where they are.

מִשְׁפָּטִים י׳

Mishpatim - Judgements - 6

Shemot / Exodus 23:20 - 25

Shemot/Exodus 23:20 Behold, I am sending a messenger before you to guard you in the way

הִנֵּה אָנֹכִי שֹׁלֵחַ מַלְאָךְ לְפָנֶיךָ לִשְׁמָרְךָ

lishmar'cha l'faneycha malach sholeyakh anochiy hineh

בַּדָּרֶךְ

baderech

The commentators are broadly split here over the identity of the messenger; the word מַלְאָךְ is translated as both 'angel' and 'messenger'. From a textual point of view, scholars suspect that the word מַלְאָךְ here - a messenger - should perhaps be מַלְאָכִי - My messenger - as it is in just three verses later in the same speech: "For My angel will go before you..." (v. 23, NASB), but the presence of a possessive suffix - as found in the Samaritan Pentateuch, the Septuagint and Vulgate - would not alter the debate over identity. One group agrees that the messenger is divine; one of these is the Ramban, who identifies this messenger with the Angel of the Lord who appears to Joshua once Moshe is dead and the people have entered the Land. Asked by Joshua, "Are you for us or for our adversaries?" (Joshua 5:13, NASB), the messenger somewhat enigmatically replies, "No, rather I come now as captain of the host of the Lord" (v. 14, NASB). The Ramban takes the 'now' to show that this was the messenger who had been promised before but had not actually been sent until Moshe died.

The other group of commentators argue that the messenger was human. The most obvious candidate, in spite of the difficulty of this passage, where *HaShem* is talking to Moshe about sending a messenger, is Moshe himself. Hirsch, connecting this text to very similar words sent by Moshe to the King of Edom some forty years later: "But when we cried out to the Lord, He heard our voice and sent an angel and brought us out from Egypt" (B'Midbar 20:16, NASB), comments, "so we must ... take it that Moshe is specifically to be understood by this term." Hirsch explains that since Moshe was clearly - with hindsight - the agent by whom *HaShem* led the people and through whom He had done the miracles that brought us out of Egypt and kept us alive in the desert, he must have been the person being spoken of in this text. Hirsch must have been well aware of the christological view taken by the church as to the identity of the Angel of the Lord and is perhaps keen to deny any supernatural involvement here except God Himself.

Taking a different tack altogether, Friedman points out that not only is this language to be repeated twice more (32:34 and 33:2), it is also a recurrence of language used in the accounts of the patriarchs: "Abraham told his servant that God 'will send His angel ahead of you'" when the servant goes to find a wife for Yitz'chak (B'resheet 24:7). "That," Friedman says, "is now a reminder that the proceeding angel on a journey is an assurance and protection." This matches the text closely, identifying that the purpose of the messenger is to guard or protect the people in their way. We can see a hint here of the famous verse: "And your ears will hear a word behind you, 'This is the way, walk in it,' whenever you turn to the right or to the left'" (Isaiah 30:21, NASB).

Rav Sha'ul is very clear about the identity of God's messenger in the wilderness time; he infers that all the people ate and drank supernaturally, "For they drank from a Spirit-sent Rock which followed them, and that Rock was the Messiah" (1 Corinthians 10:4, CJB). Sha'ul doesn't want us to lose sight of the fact that just as it was God who provided for our people during the Exodus, and that the means of the provision was Messiah, it is always Messiah who provides the interface between God and man. "He is supreme over all creation, because in connection with Him were created all things ... they have all been created, through Him and for Him. He existed before all things, and He holds everything together" (Colossians 1:15-17, CJB).

In these modern days when everyone has a position and a title - chief assistant to the assistant chief - and the world is full of replacement parts and man-made alternatives to the natural materials or products that used to be the only choice, when the cost of the real thing often forces us to accept a cheaper substitute in the hope that no-one - often including ourselves - will notice the difference, we need to be careful that we don't set up or accept a substitute for God. Rav Sha'ul reminds us that, "there is but one Mediator between God and humanity, Yeshua the Messiah" (1 Timothy 2:5, CJB); there is no-one else who makes peace for us with God, no-one else who brings the comfort and presence of God into our lives. No matter how hard we look - and there are plenty of people who who are looking very hard - we will not find any substitute for Yeshua. Yeshua's own words - often seen as deeply offensive by those who think they have found another way, or are trying to pretend that they don't need a way - are very clear: "I AM the way - and the

Truth and the Life; no-one comes to the Father except through Me" (John 14:6, CJB). As a modern advertising slogan expresses it: Accept no alternative, insist on the real thing!

Further Study: Acts 4:12

Application: Have you set up or accepted a substitute for God? Has your relationship with God dwindled as you have been beguiled by a plausible alternative for spending time with Him? Has the cost and commitment been so high that you have opted for an easier way that is not so demanding? Now is the time to reconsider that there is no alternative and no other way. Come back to God now and resolve never to accept a substitute for Yeshua again. He's waiting for you.

מִשְׁפָּטִים ז׳

Mishpatim - Judgements - 7

Shemot / Exodus 23:26 - 24:18

Shemot/Exodus 23:26 I shall fill the number of your days.

אֶת־מִסְפַּר יָמֶיךָ אֲמַלֵּא:
amaley yameycha mis'par et

Given the context of this promise - that there shall be no miscarriages, stillbirths or barren women in the land - these words are referring to the length of life rather than the content of each day. As well as the people, the land is also to be blessed with fruitfulness. The Ba'al HaTurim comments that the *gematria* of the word אֲמַלֵּא is 72, which excluding the year of birth and the year of death, cross-references to the verse "The span of our life is seventy years" (Psalm 90:10, JPS). The Talmud records a debate between Rabbi Akiva - who taught that only a righteous person would live to this full age, life being shortened in proportion to a person's shortcomings - and the other Sages who held that the "seventy years" was an average, being exceeded by the righteous whose merit granted them extra years, not being reached by the wicked whose deeds cost them years (*b*. Yevamot 49*b*-50*a*). The Rashbam points to "You will come to the grave in ripe old age" (Job 5:26), while Ibn Ezra supports the view of the Sages by citing "The fear of the Lord prolongs life, while the years of the wicked will be shortened" (Proverbs 10:27, JPS). The Ramban produces an example of Barzillai, an ally and staunch supporter of King David who exceeded the 70 years: he "... was very old, eighty years of age" (2 Samuel 19:33, JPS).

In a lengthy comment, the Sforno sums up some of these ideas and points us to an important relationship. "You will live to the measure of oil that is in your lamp [alluding to 'The spirit of man is the lamp of the Lord' (Proverbs 20:27, NASB)], rooted from birth." In other words, it is God who decides the length of a person's life and its limit is set by Him; God provides resources and strength for that number of days. "The reverse of this occurs when man dies of illness before his basic vitality has ceased. This occurs due to wrong choices"; so the choices that we make, some of which will be dietary or lifestyle (e.g. food versus exercise, alcohol) and some of which will involve sin (e.g. sexually transmitted diseases, pornography, drugs). When we step outside God's will, this may shorten our life both as a result of our sin and sometimes as protection for others. "Now when a man's number of days are fulfilled he will in most cases see children born to his children and be able to teach them, as it says, 'make them known to your sons and your grandsons' (D'varim 4:9, NASB)". Without even speaking, our lives teach a message to the next generations, like it or not, good or bad! When we live rightly before God, we have the opportunity to teach our children and grandchildren a consistent message about Him; if we don't live that way, the Sforno hints that we won't get that opportunity.

In the Disney film "Pollyanna", based on the book of the same name by Eleanor H. Porter[12], the minister (Reverend Ford) preaches a sermon on the text "Death comes unexpectedly", which is not to be found in the Bible. It is perhaps meant to be a parody of Jonathan Edward's famous sermon "Sinners in the Hands of an Angry God", preached at Enfield, Connecticut on July 8, 1741, based on the (real) text "Their foot shall slide in due time" (D'varim 32:35). Although a startling example of the old-fashioned "fire and brimstone" sermon, it has more than a hint of Yeshua's parable about the man who tore down his barns and built newer, bigger ones, so that he might store up food for years to come. The parable concludes with God saying to the man, "This very night your soul is required of you; and now who will own what you have prepared?" (Luke 12:20, NASB). This in turn echoes the verse spoken by Job: "For what is the hope of the godless when God cuts him off, when God takes away his life?" (Job 27:8, ESV).

More positively, Yeshua asks the disciples the question, "Which of you by being anxious can add a single cubit to his life's span?" (Matthew 6:27, NASB) in order to focus their attention on God's provision for both the natural world and therefore also for those who labour in the kingdom of God. Length of life is not an issue that the disciples can change or should be concerned about. God has already determined the time when we are born and the time when we return our souls to our Maker. Our priority is to make sure that we take choices to make best use of that time in two ways: firstly, by the choices we take with regard to food, lifestyle and righteousness; secondly by making sure that we occupy ourselves with the work of the kingdom so that we may share in its benefits. Working with Yeshua (1 Corinthians 3:9), being a partner in His work (1 Thessalonians 3:2), being yoked with Him (Matthew 11:28-30) are all expressions that the Bible uses to show how we participate with God in advancing the kingdom. As we involve ourselves in the affairs of the kingdom, its blessings - length of days, fruitfulness, provision - devolve on to us as well. Rav Sha'ul urges

---

12. The incident in question is only present in the film, not in the original book, although it is based on the characters in the book

Timothy to "Be diligent to present yourself approved to God as a workman" (2 Timothy 2:15, NASB) and uses his own lifestyle as an example to others: "Therefore I run in such a way, as not without aim; I box in such a way, as not beating the air; but I buffet my body and make it my slave, lest possibly, after I have preached to others, I myself should be disqualified" (1 Corinthians 9:26-27, NASB).

We are to seriously engage with God across the board of our lives, putting everything on the table and holding nothing back so that He can adjust and tune our priorities, our finances, our desires and even our families and our possessions. Only as we do this can we experience the thrill and exhilaration of living a totally fulfilled life - a life not aimlessly racing at full throttle, but a life well-lived that returns the maximum possible miles to the gallon and accomplishes the will of God. Although not guaranteed to be the easiest or most comfortable journey, we will know that we have done what we were designed to do and can expect to hear Yeshua's words, "Well done, good and faithful servant!" (Matthew 25:21, NASB).

Further Study: Ecclesiastes 7:15-18; Mark 8:34-38

Application: Are you eking out an existence, just managing to keep your head above water, worried about whether tomorrow will come; or do you live in the fullness of the kingdom, knowing the call and purpose of the Master, trusting Him for the fullness of your days? Why not put in a call to Headquarters today to make sure you're running on the right program.

תְּרוּמָה

Terumah - Offering

Shemot / Exodus 25:1 - 27:19

רִאשׁוֹן	Aliyah One	Shemot/Exodus 25:1 - 16
שֵׁנִי	Aliyah Two	Shemot/Exodus 25:17 - 37
שְׁלִישִׁי	Aliyah Three	Shemot/Exodus 26:1 - 14
רְבִיעִי	Aliyah Four	Shemot/Exodus 26:15 - 30
חֲמִשִׁי	Aliyah Five	Shemot/Exodus 26:31 - 37
שִׁשִׁי	Aliyah Six	Shemot/Exodus 27:1 - 8
שְׁבִיעִי	Aliyah Seven	Shemot/Exodus 27:9 - 19

תְּרוּמָה ׳א

Terumah - Offering - 1

Shemot / Exodus 25:1 - 16

Shemot/Exodus 25:2 Speak to the Sons of Israel and they shall take to Me a portion

דַּבֵּר אֶל־בְּנֵי יִשְׂרָאֵל וְיִקְחוּ־לִי תְּרוּמָה
t'rumah liy v'yik'khu Yisrael B'ney el dabeyr

Here at the start of the instructions concerning the building of the *Mishkan, Adonai* tells Moshe to speak to the people about the materials that will be needed for the construction of the Tent of Meeting. The Lord goes on to stress that the gifts are to come only from those whose hearts motivate them to give. Nevertheless, the words used to describe this process are not necessarily those we would expect: וְיִקְחוּ, they shall take, and תְּרוּמָה, portion. In other contexts, תְּרוּמָה means 'raising' or 'that which is raised' and is used to describe the wave offerings that are waved before the Lord but become the portion for the *cohanim*, eaten by them and their families. Here, as the *parasha* is going to go on to detail, the gifts are to be precious metals, different coloured wools, linen and animal skins. Similarly, if the materials are to be a free-will offering, the use of the word וְיִקְחוּ, they shall take, seems unusual. Rashi explains it to mean 'setting aside', separating the portion to be given from the rest of each person's other possessions.

Rav Sha'ul uses the same words when he writes to the congregation in Corinth, "On the first day of every week let each one of you put aside and save, as he may prosper, that no collections be made when I come", (1 Corinthians 16:2, NASB), in order to prepare a gift of support to be sent to the believers in Jerusalem. See, here too, that the offering is to be a free-will offering as there is to be no public collection or exhortation when Rav Sha'ul gets there, simply a gathering up of that which people have already decided in their hearts to give and set on one side for that purpose.

In these days there is considerable debate about the requirements to tithe, whether the tithe is to be seen as a minimum or maximum, whether collections should be formally taken or boxes discretely provide for people to use, let alone where the offerings are to be given: to a local congregation or to other organisations who compete for our financial support. Some people seem to resent the principle of tithing as a discipline, of being required (or expected) to give away a portion of their money.

Understanding three scriptural principles will help us in our attitude to our finances. The first is that, "God loves a cheerful giver" (2 Corinthians 9:7, NASB) - God is more interested in the state of our hearts and the way we give than how much or how often we give. Secondly, "all things come from You, and from Your hand have we given You" (1 Chronicles 29:14, NASB) - rather than resenting the smaller proportion of our money that we give, focus on the larger proportion that we use for ourselves and the fact that it all comes from and belongs to God anyway. Thirdly, "it is more blessed to give than to receive" (Acts 20:35, NASB) - God's blessing follows those who give and make the kingdom economy flow.

Further Study: Read in full 2 Corinthians 9:7, 1 Chronicles 29:14 and Acts 20:35

Application: How is our attitude to money challenged by the words of Scripture? Do we regularly set aside the Lord's portion and freely lift it before Him as a pleasing and fragrant offering of our lives and love for Him?

תְּרוּמָה ב׳

Terumah - Offering - 2

Shemot / Exodus 25:17 - 37

Shemot/Exodus 25:17 And you shall make a covering of pure gold

וְעָשִׂיתָ כַפֹּרֶת זָהָב טָהוֹר

tahor   zahav   chaporet   v'asiyta

Unlike the ark in most synagogues, which are usually rather like cupboards, with doors or curtains that open at the front, the *Aron Kodesh* - whose plans for construction are described in the previous verses - was in the manner of a box with a lid on top. Rashi makes precisely that comment: "a lid; a covering over the *Aron*, for it was open at the top, and he would lay the lid on it like a board." The word used for 'cover' is derived from the root verb כָּפַר, which in its *Qal* stem means simply "to cover, to overlay". In other stems, the verb is used to mean "to cover over sin, to forgive or pardon, to expiate or make atonements, to purify" and leads to *Yom HaKippurim*, the Day of Atonements.

Whereas the Ark itself was made of wood and then overlaid, inside and out, with gold, the lid was to be made of pure gold with the figures of the *k'ruvim* (cherubim), also of pure gold, mounted on each end. This would have had a significant weight, so that the word כָּבֵד, which is translated as an adjective meaning 'heavy' and a noun 'glory', can be used as a word-play to describe the Ark: it was both heavy and glorious. Its glory was tangible because of its weight.

The purpose of the lid was to cover and seal in the tablets of testimony, Aharon's staff and the jar of manna. Both copies of the contract to be kept together, as well as the two visible signs of God's faithfulness so that every generation would know that God has proved Himself faithful to the covenant, in spite of the people's equivocation. The prophet Jeremiah wrote, "'For this is the covenant I will make with the house of Israel after those days,' says Adonai: 'I will put My Torah within them and write it on their hearts'" (Jeremiah 31:32, CJB). He was looking to the day when the *Torah* would be within our hearts rather than on the tablets of stone and "you people are God's temple and God's Spirit lives in you" (1 Corinthians 3:16, CJB). We

135

have "put our trust in the Messiah and were sealed by Him with the promised Ruach HaKodesh" (Ephesians 1:13, CJB).

Yeshua Himself is now our covering, our atonement. His blood cleanses and purifies us from our sins as we trust in Him. His glory, His heaviness, lies over us like a covering so that when people look at us they see Him. And we too, like the Ark, are open at the top, open to God, but covered by Yeshua our Great High Priest; and inside us is found God's word and promise and the signs of His faithfulness to us: His provision and His authority. His glory rests upon us.

Further Study: Vayikra 17:11; Hebrews 4:14-16

Application: Do you know the weight of God's glory resting upon you in Messiah Yeshua? His promises and His power are available for all those who trust in Him, so that He may cover them with His glory.

תְּרוּמָה ג׳

Terumah - Offering - 3

Shemot / Exodus 26:1 - 14

Shemot/Exodus 26:1 And the Mishkan you will make ... cherubim, the work of a craftsman, you shall make them

וְאֶת־הַמִּשְׁכָּן תַּעֲשֶׂה ... כְּרֻבִים מַעֲשֵׂה חֹשֵׁב

khosheyv ma'aseyh k'ruviym ... ta'aseh ha'mish'kan v'et

תַּעֲשֶׂה אֹתָם:

otam ta'aseh

Commenting on this verse, Rashi says that the images were that of a lion on one side and an eagle on the other. Sifsei Chachamim says that the Cherubim depicted on the curtain were the four images on the *Merkavah*, the chariot, seen by Ezekiel (1:10): a man, a lion, an ox and an eagle. Sforno comments that the curtains were made to reflect the visions seen of God in prophecy: "I saw the Lord sitting on a throne ... seraphim stood above Him" (Isaiah 6:1-2, NASB) and "I saw the Lord sitting on His throne, and all the host of heaven standing by Him on His right and on His left" (1 Kings 22:19, NASB). As the *Mishkan*, the sanctuary, contained the ark - with the mercy seat - the table and *menorah*, the curtains were part of the imagery that the Israelites were instructed to make: "See and make, according to their form that you are shown on the mountain" (Shemot 25:40).

The Bible records people seeing visions of God in many and varied ways, both physical visions of people that looked 'right' and extraordinary visions that stretched their vocabulary to describe. Yet for all the visions that the prophets of old saw, Yeshua told the disciples: "I tell you that many a prophet and many a tzaddik longed to see the things you are seeing but did not see them, and hear the things you are hearing but did not hear them" (Matthew 13:17, CJB). He said this in the middle of telling the Parable of the Sower; after He had told the parable to the crowds, while the *talmidim* were asking Him to explain it to them, and before the explanation itself. What was it that they were seeing that others before them had not seen? Obviously Yeshua Himself, in one sense, but the *Malach Adonai*, the angel/messenger of God, while not frequently seen had been manifest in Israel on a number of occasions, so simply His physical presence was not what Yeshua was getting at. No, rather it was that the people were being taught openly about the Kingdom of God and that the kingdom was being shown to them and made available to them in a greater way than ever before in Yeshua's ministry.

Both John the Immerser and Yeshua started their teaching ministries with the same simple message: "Repent, for the Kingdom of Heaven is at hand" (Matthew 3:2, NASB), "Repent, for the Kingdom of Heaven is at hand" (Matthew 4:17, NASB). John preached "an immersion involving turning to God from sin in order to be forgiven" (Luke 3:3, CJB) as a prelude to entering the kingdom, while "after sunset, all those who had people sick with various diseases brought them to Yeshua, and He put His hands on each one of them and healed them; also demons came out of many, crying, 'You are the Son of God'" (Luke 4:40-41, CJB). The people saw with their own eyes the Kingdom of God in their midst; they could reach out and touch the kingdom with their own hands; they could enter the kingdom right then and there and follow Yeshua, making God's kingdom by acknowledging His rule and authority.

Further Study: Hebrews 11:13-16; 1 Peter 1:10-12

Application: How do you see God? Do you see Him only as high and exalted, surrounded by the heavenly host? Certainly, He is that, but He is also to be seen living and working in and among His people as the Kingdom of God is made manifest - shown to the world - in us.

תְּרוּמָה 'ד

Terumah - Offering - 4

Shemot / Exodus 26:15 - 30

Shemot/Exodus 26:15 And you will make the boards for the Mishkan of acacia wood, standing upright

וְעָשִׂיתָ אֶת־הַקְּרָשִׁים לַמִּשְׁכָּן עֲצֵי שִׁטִּים

shitiym atzey la'Mishkan hak'rashiym et v'asiyta

עֹמְדִים:

om'diym

    While most translations take the word הַקְּרָשִׁים as 'boards' or 'beams', Friedman chooses 'frames'. Davidson reports that the word is a standard masculine plural noun from the root קֶרֶשׁ, which is not used in the text of the Hebrew Scriptures; its use in Arabic is "to cut", so Davidson allows three meanings: 'board', 'plank' or 'bench', the latter of a ship. Brown, Driver and Briggs states that the root means "to be or become firm or solid" and extends the meaning of the noun to include the decking of a ship. The word is used 51 times in the Hebrew Scriptures: mostly here in Shemot 26, where the instructions for the Tabernacle's construction are given, and in Shemot 36 where the construction narrative is related; there is a single occurrence each in B'Midbar 3:36 and 4:31 where the duties of the Levites are described - in all these occurrences, the context is that of the Tabernacle. There is one isolated use of the word in Ezekiel 27:6 where it is taken as the decking of a ship in a lament over Tyre. Its use in the Mishnah (tractate Shabbat) and Shemot Rabbah is also consistent with the components of the Tabernacle.

    So why does Friedman prefer 'frames' to 'boards'? He says: "frames: Trellises - not solid boards or planks. If they were solid, then the linen curtains would be sandwiched between the boards on the inside and the goats' hair and leather coverings on the outside and could never be seen." Friedman seems to be concerned that the curtains - which were made, after all, of "fine twisted linen and blue and purple and scarlet ... with cherubim, the work of a skillful workman" (Shemot 26:1, NASB) - will never be seen or appreciated except during the times when the Tabernacle is dismantled and re-erected during travel; even then, only the priests and the Levites would see them as the people were not allowed to watch the process. All that craftsmanship, the beauty of the rich materials and the embroidery would be lost; simply another layer of covering for the Tabernacle, obscured on one side by solid wood and on the other by the much less attractive layers of goat hair and leather coverings.

Many stories have come down to us, from both the *shtetls* of Eastern Europe and earlier times, of individuals who may themselves have been either rich or poor, who begged alms - charity, *tz'daka* - from the wealthier members of their communities in order to distribute it to the poor, sick and needy. In this way, the donors were isolated from the recipients, often not knowing who had given or to whom. Jewish tradition sets the highest value on charitable giving where neither the recipient or the donor know who each other are, so that it is impossible for the donor to receive any thanks - thus receiving all his reward in the *Olam Haba*, the World to Come - and the recipient should not be embarrassed or feel unable to take an equal place in the life of the community, simply blessing God for His provision.

Yeshua clearly speaks into this idea when He says, "When you give alms, do not let your left hand know what the right hand is doing that your alms may be in secret; and your Father who sees in secret will repay you" (Matthew 6:3-4, NASB). But Yeshua extends the concept beyond the physical giving of charity or doing good deeds: "When you pray, you are not to be as the hypocrites; for they love to stand and pray in the synagogues and on the street corners in order to be seen by men. Truly I say to you, they have their reward in full. But you, when you pray, go into your inner room, and when you have shut your door, pray to your Father who is in secret, and your Father who sees in secret will repay you" (vv. 5-6, NASB).

Here then, perhaps, is an answer to the boards or frames issue. God knows that the decorated linen curtains are there, that they were made for Him; the priests and the Levites, who carry them and put them up and take them down, know that they are there; those who gave the material and did the work know that the curtains are in use. The curtains enlarge the glory of God's presence without being seen on a routine basis, but they are still there, an essential and commanded part of the Tabernacle, the house of God. So should our prayers and giving be also.

Further Study: Ephesians 2:19-22; Hebrews 6:10

Application: Whilst it is sometimes necessary to do things in public, to work together with others, try finding space to spend time alone with God this week; He knows that you are there and He sees you even if you think that you are invisible.

תְּרוּמָה ה׳

Terumah - Offering - 5

Shemot / Exodus 26:31 - 37

Shemot/Exodus 26:31 And you shall make a curtain of blue, purple and scarlet yarn and fine twisted linen

וְעָשִׂיתָ פָרֹכֶת תְּכֵלֶת וְאַרְגָּמָן וְתוֹלַעַת שָׁנִי

shaniy   v'tola'at   v'argaman   t'cheylet farochet   v'asiyta

וְשֵׁשׁ מָשְׁזָר

mash'zar v'sheysh

The word פָרֹכֶת would logically come from a root פָּרַךְ, but such a root is not known in biblical Hebrew. Instead, scholars connect the word to the root פָּרַק, which means "to break off of tear away" - from whence also comes the noun מַפְרֶקֶת, the vertebrae of the neck, literally the place of breaking. Other similar roots share overlapping meanings: פָּרַץ, to break or tear down, demolish; פָּרַר, to break in pieces, annul, abolish; פָּרַשׂ, to break (i.e. bread) or spread; פָּרַשׁ, to divide, disperse, scatter. Sarna gives a probable root meaning of "to bar the way, to mark off an area" and lists other verses that confirm the *parochet's* purpose as a dividing line and screen: פָּרֹכֶת הַמָּסָךְ, the curtain of screening or partition (B'Midbar 4:5); פָּרֹכֶת הָעֵדֻת, the curtain of the testimony (Vayikra 24:3); פָּרֹכֶת הַקֹּדֶשׁ, the curtain of the holy (Vayikra 4:6).

Richard Elliott Friedman considers that the פָּרֹכֶת is a "pavilion", an inner tent. He points out that it is hung on four poles (Shemot 26:32) and provides a cover for the Ark (40:4), that it is over the testimony (27:21); it is even spoken of in Psalm 27:5 and Lamentations 2:6 using the word "sukkah". This confused the sages of the Talmud, who assumed that it had always been a curtain, so were puzzled that the *Torah* describes it as a "sukkah" and being 'over' the Ark (*b*. Sukkah 7*b*). Rashi has commented earlier (to verse 1) about the thickness of this material that is also used for the walls of the holy place: "this was weaving with two sides, so that the designs on either side did not resemble each other", and adds here: "פָּרֹכֶת is an expression of partition - that which separates between the King and the people." Gersonides goes even further: "The curtain was of the same make as the cloths of the Tabernacle except that, since it marked a boundary, it was much thicker - our Sages say, a full hand-breadth thick."

The curtain remained in place, first in the Tabernacle, then in both the first and second temples, as a barrier between the holy place - where the priests would enter each day to perform the divine service: lighting the *menorah*, changing the shewbread and burning the incense - and the most holy place, into which "only the high priest enters, once a year, not without taking blood, which he offers for himself and for the sins of the people committed in ignorance" (Hebrews 9:7 NASB). There was, however, a significant disturbance to the routine at the time that Yeshua was crucified; all three synoptic gospels, in varying degrees, tell us that "the veil of the temple was torn in two from top to bottom" (Mark 15:38, NASB). Some years ago, as a novelty act, it was quite popular to see strong men tearing telephone directories in half, providing they were not too thick! This took significant strength and the knack of knowing exactly how to hold the directory and twist the spine and pages so that a start could be made. Yet the curtain in the Temple simply hung in its place, untouched by human hands, made of heavy embroidered and woven fabric, up to a hand-breadth in thickness. This was more than somebody creeping in and ripping a flimsy piece of net-curtain or muslin; this was a sign from God Himself - for human hands could not have done it - to show that the way between the Holy of Holies, the physical seat of God's presence in the very heart of the Temple, had been made open.

Writing to the Ephesians, Rav Sha'ul addresses the Gentiles and reminds them that they were "at that time separate from Messiah, excluded from the commonwealth of Israel, and strangers to the covenants of promise, having no hope and without God in the world" (Ephesians 2:12, NASB). The court of the Gentiles was the very outermost court in the Temple and Gentiles - whether worshippers of the God of Israel or simply curious tourists - were strictly prohibited from coming anywhere near the altars or the holy places. Sha'ul goes on, "But now in Messiah Yeshua you who formerly were far off have been brought near by the blood of Messiah" (v. 13, NASB). The Gentiles were enabled to come near to God, to approach His presence, because of Yeshua's blood on the execution stake that has opened a way. But there is more: "For He Himself is our peace, who made both groups into one and broke down the barrier of the dividing wall" (v. 14, NASB). Jews and Gentiles - the former forbidden entry to the Holy of Holies just as much as the latter - are now able to enter God's presence. Both walls have been removed: between God and man, and between Jew and Gentile!

Many people today struggle with approaching God. Though desperate to find spirituality and a meaning for their lives, to connect with the eternal that their souls know is out there somewhere, they seem to keep hitting an invisible wall, a glass ceiling. Isaiah tells us, "Your iniquities have made a separation between you and your God, and your sins have hidden His face from you, so that He does not hear" (Isaiah 59:2, NASB). All mankind, Jew and Gentile alike, have to deal with this problem of sin; a wall that we have built with our own hands - so to speak - that has become an insuperable barrier between us and God. How is that densely woven fabric to be parted? "The word of God is living and active and sharper than any two-edged sword, and piercing as far as the division of soul and spirit, of both joints and marrow, and able to judge the thoughts and intentions of the heart" (Hebrews 4:12, NASB). God's word can cut through the barrier of sin and show us God's truth, the forgiveness that is available to us in Messiah Yeshua and make it possible for us to be reconciled to God. Yeshua Himself is the Living Word, the Living *Torah*, who "entered the Holy Place once for all, having obtained eternal redemption" (Hebrews 9:12, NASB).

Further Study: Amos 8:11-12; Hebrews 6:19-20

Application: Do you feel that there is a barrier between you and God, possibly even one that you made, decorated and finely embroidered? Hear the word of God today and allow it to cut through that barrier so that you can be reconciled to God and be able to enter His presence. Yeshua is the key to the door, the blood on the lintel and the gentle calling of the dove; He wants you today!

תְּרוּמָה י'

Terumah - Offering - 6

Shemot / Exodus 27:1 - 8

Shemot/Exodus 27:1 And you shall make the altar [out of] shittim wood

וְעָשִׂיתָ אֶת־הַמִּזְבֵּחַ עֲצֵי שִׁטִּים
shittiym atzey hamizbeyakh et v'asiyta

This phrase throws us immediately into a serious question: how can man make an altar, which is later itself to be consecrated and declared holy, on which to bring holy offerings for atonement, sin and guilt offerings, out of wood? How can anything that man could make be holy and acceptable to God?

Sarna opens the conversation by explaining which altar is in view. Because of its size - the incense altar is only one cubit square - this must be the altar of the burnt offerings, where the twice daily offerings were made. "This altar is also known as 'the altar of bronze' on account of its metal overlay and to distinguish it from the altar of gold, which was used for incense. A third name, found in rabbinic literature, is 'the outer altar'. This name derives from its location and is to be contrasted with the 'inner altar', the golden incense altar that stood in the Holy Place." Sarna also makes the point that the cult[13] could not function without the ritual of sacrifice, so "its presence in the Tabernacle is taken for granted", which is why it referred to here with a definite article - הַמִּזְבֵּחַ - the altar. From archaeology comes the observation that the altar for burnt offerings uncovered in the Judean temple at Arad in the Negev corresponds exactly to the dimensions here. Don Abravanel takes the argument a little further; also starting from the use of the definite article, he comments that "the Israelites knew there had to be one - this was how all the ancients served their gods, by offering sacrifice on an altar". This was how all the primitive religions worked - offering gifts, burnt offerings and libations upon an altar - that marked a total consecration of the offering to the god.

---

13. The performance of the worship ritual, with its sacrifices, offerings, liturgy and procedures

Hirsch connects with the debate conducted by the Sages of the Talmud concerning the dimensions and placement of the altar (*b.* Zevachim 59*b*-62*a*). He summaries that, "for the altar to be used, it had to be square, but its dimensions, length, breadth and height could vary. Nevertheless the height never did and never will change. The altars erected by Moshe, by Solomon and in the second Temple, were all of equal height although the length and breadth rose from the five cubits of Moshe's altar to thirty two cubits in the second Temple." He then quotes Maimonides: "The altar in the Temple of the future, as envisioned and described by Ezekiel will have the same height" (הל' בית הבחירה, II, 5; Ezekiel 43:15). This obsession with detail is typical of the rabbinic debate, but points to two essential truths. Friedman highlights the first: "The quantity and detail in these chapters is an indication that these are authentic descriptions of the Tabernacle and its accoutrements. What motive would there be to make all of this up?" The amount of description of the various components of the tabernacle, its furniture, the clothing of the priests and the ritual of the cult, makes it very unlikely that this would all have been fabricated. If this were not how it was done and what it looked like, there were plenty of witnesses around who would corroborate or deny this account. The text and the following debate confirm the veracity and existence of a real altar. The second truth, however, takes us closer to an answer to our original question. This is one of the reasons that the rabbis debated at such length and with such tenacity: to preserve the divine essence and origin of the specification.

The sanctity of the altar is guaranteed not by the builders - who, even though selected and nominated by *HaShem*, were men - nor by either the building or consecration process, but because *HaShem* has commanded it to be so. Betzalel's gifted obedience to the building instructions is important; Moshe's inspired obedience to the process of consecrating the whole of the Tabernacle assemblage and installing Aharon as High Priest is important. Ultimately, though, the whole process works because God Himself has declared the altar to be holy or "set apart" for Him. He is the one who makes it holy; He declares it to be an acceptable platform for the offering of sacrifice to Him; He stipulates the rules of engagement so that it retains it holiness and is not profaned. Holiness comes from God; it is declared and commanded by Him: "Speak to all the congregation of the sons of Israel and say to them, 'You shall be holy, for I the Lord your God am holy'" (Vayikra 19:2, NASB).

So in our post-Calvary world, where although sacrifice remains the only means of obtaining forgiveness for sin - "All things are cleansed with blood, and without shedding of blood there is no forgiveness" (Hebrews 9:22, NASB) - that obligation is met by receiving and appropriating the sacrifice that Yeshua made on the cross for us, how do we make an altar and what is to go on it? That our worship of God is still to be based around the principle of sacrifice is not open to debate; Rav Sha'ul wrote: "I exhort you, therefore, brothers, in view of God's mercies, to offer yourselves as a sacrifice, living and set apart for God. This will please him; it is the logical 'Temple worship' for you" (Romans 12:1, CJB). But how are we to interpret that? What does that mean in our every day lives?

Even before Yeshua's day, the prophets spoke to articulate what was on God's heart: "I desire mercy, not sacrifice, and acknowledgment of God rather than burnt offerings" (Hosea 6:6, NIV); our sacrifice is to be of ourselves, not in death, but of our lives. Remaining alive, both physically and to God, we offer Him our lives, our lifestyles, our emotions and desires, our finances, our very being, to be a continual and living sacrifice. Dead to the world, yet raised already to new life in Messiah Yeshua, this is how we live out the ancient command of the *Sh'ma*: "Hear O Israel, the Lord our God is One. And you shall love the Lord your God with all your heart, with all your life and with all your essence" (D'varim 6:4-5). We are holy because God has declared us to be so and we are called to prove or demonstrate this each moment of every day by living holy lives that embody His standards of holiness. That is why Rav Sha'ul writes, "I have been crucified with Christ; and it is no longer I who live, but Christ lives in me; and the life which I now live in the flesh I live by faith in the Son of God, who loved me, and delivered Himself up for me" (Galatians 2:20, NASB). Because He lives, we live; because He is holy, we are holy. Our sacrifices are accepted before the Throne because Yeshua Himself - "our great High Priest" (Hebrew 4:14) - accepts them and takes them into the presence of our Father God, they are "golden bowls full of incense, which are the prayers of the saints" (Revelation 5:8, NASB).

Further Study: Shemot 20:24-26; Hebrews 13:10-13

Application: Holiness is not something that we have to achieve; Yeshua has achieved it for us and gives to us. We only have to live out what He has done, so build an altar of your life to offer yourself to God, knowing that no matter where you are, you can be be acceptable to Him when you ask and come in Messiah Yeshua.

תְּרוּמָה ז׳

Terumah - Offering - 7

Shemot / Exodus 27:9 - 19

Shemot/Exodus 27:9 ... at the south side, curtains for the courtyard, fine linen, twisted ...

לִפְאַת נֶגֶב־תֵּימָנָה קְלָעִים לֶחָצֵר שֵׁשׁ מָשְׁזָר

mash'zar sheysh lekhatzeyr k'la'iym teymanah negev lif'at

The curtains provided for the outside perimeter area of the tabernacle generate some interest in the commentators. The word קְלָעִים is a masculine plural noun, from the root קָלַע, which has the slightly surprising meaning "to sling or throw with a sling; to cut out or reject; to cut out or carve" (Davidson); the noun קֶלַע is used as a sling - just twice: "The Lord of hosts will defend them. And they will devour, and trample on the sling stones" (Zechariah 9:15, NASB), "Uzziah prepared for all the army shields, spears, helmets, body armor, bows and sling stones" (2 Chronicles 26:14, NASB) - or a curtain or hanging, eight times in the book of Shemot. Citing the verse, "The cedar of the interior of the House had carvings of gourds and calyxes" (1 Kings 6:18, JPS), Rashbam prefers the 'carve' meaning even at this point, leading us into the suggestion that the curtains were not of solid weave. Ibn Ezra comments that "Unlike the clothes of the Tabernacle, the hangings were made of linen only." Rashi adds that they were "made by braiding, not weaving" and points out that *Targum Onkelos* translates the word by סְרָדִין, netting or grating, the same word used by *Onkelos* for the grating around the altar in verse 4. Nahum Sarna explains, "literally 'plaited, basket work', probably referring to the type of textile manufactured by basketry technique. Linen of this type has been found in Egypt dating to around 2500 BCE." It would seem, then, that the curtains were not opaque, so as to form a complete visual barrier, but were more of a transparent marker, forming a physical boundary while allowing relatively uninterrupted viewing of what transpired inside.

Why would the outer curtains of the tabernacle be made in this way? What is the point of such permeable curtains? Why have them at all if anyone can wander up and look through to see what is happening inside? Wouldn't a row of those ubiquitous sockets laid out on the sand accomplish the same function if delineation of space is the only purpose? Rabbi Samson Raphael Hirsch steps back from the curtains to consider the space that they enclose. He points out that the word translated "for the courtyard", לֶחָצֵר, has a double meaning, being both "beneficial and limiting". The fence provides a "spacious enclosure ... so that the objects of the building are given the space to be developed." Remarking that the equivalent rooms surrounding the sanctuary in the Temple were named "helping rooms/space", Hirsch suggests that the space enclosed by the curtains was not just in front - as in a forecourt - but all around and that the area itself provided space as an essential part of the function of the tabernacle and a place to develop relationship with the Almighty.

In Jewish tradition, one of the names for God is הַמָּקוֹם, which literally means "the place" and is often translated as "The Omnipresent"[14]. This expresses the idea that God is everywhere, that He is not at a place, but is the place; anywhere where His people are and cry out to Him becomes His place. Any place nevertheless has boundaries, so that you know when you are in that place and when you are not in that place. Judaism sees the *Torah* as the boundaries of God's place; when we obey the *Torah* we are in the place and when we disobey the *Torah* we have stepped outside the place. This draws on the above ideas about the nature of the boundary; to allow crossing, the boundary must be porous, but to inhibit crossing inadvertently, it must be substantial. To cross the boundary must be a deliberate action. Similarly, to allow free-will, the boundary must be only partially opaque; it must allow a measure of transparency so that a choice between two alternatives is possible. Notice, however, that the vision through the boundary is partially obscured: those looking in from the outside like the open space, but fear what they think are the restrictions of *Torah*; those looking out from the inside see the temptations of an unrestricted life but fail to see the cost and separation that accompany it.

Rav Sha'ul is very aware of the believer's location. The phrase "in Christ" occurs over 85 times in some 80 verses in his letters. Whether by salutation, "Greet every saint in Christ Jesus" (Philippians 4:21, NASB), to the order of resurrection, "the dead in Christ will rise first" (1 Thessalonians 4:16, NASB), the place of our blessing "the grace that is in Christ Jesus" (1 Timothy 2:1, NASB), or our status and position as believers, "[God] raised us up with Him, and seated us with Him in the heavenly places, in Christ Jesus" (Ephesians 2:6, NASB). Yeshua likened this to being in His hand: "I give

---

14. see, for example, Pirkei Avot 2:14: "one who borrows from man is like one who borrows - מִן הַמָּקוֹם - from The Omnipresent" and the prayer of consolation: "הַמָּקוֹם יְנַחֵם אֶתְכֶם - May the Omnipresent comfort you among the other mourners of Zion and Jerusalem".

eternal life to them, and they shall never perish; and no one shall snatch them out of My hand" (John 10:28, NASB); the boundary prevents any force from outside being able to snatch us away from Him, as Sha'ul memorably proclaims: "For I am convinced that neither death, nor life, nor angels, nor principalities, nor things present, nor things to come, nor powers, nor height, nor depth, nor any other created thing, shall be able to separate us from the love of God, which is in Christ Jesus our Lord" (Romans 8:38-39, NASB). At the same time, because that boundary is porous, we can see outside, be tempted and can choose to step outside as the writer to the Hebrews solemnly warns: "For in the case of those who have once been enlightened and have tasted of the heavenly gift and have been made partakers of the Holy Spirit, and have tasted the good word of God and the powers of the age to come, and then have fallen away, it is impossible to renew them again to repentance, since they again crucify to themselves the Son of God, and put Him to open shame" (Hebrews 6:4-6, NASB). Do not be deceived by the suggestion that those who fall away were never true believers; the text says clearly that they had been made partakers of the Holy Spirit, who is only given to those who repent and believe (Acts 2:38-39). These are believers just like you and I, who have chosen - or been persuaded to choose - to step outside the boundary of the kingdom and have fallen away from Yeshua.

So the question is: where are you? Are you in Messiah, or are you not in Messiah? Sha'ul writes of the need to be "found in Him, not having a righteousness of my own derived from the Law, but that which is through faith in Christ, the righteousness which comes from God on the basis of faith" (Philippians 3:9, NASB). Where will God look for you and will He be able to find you when you call on Him? Peter urges the disciples to "be diligent to be found by Him in peace, spotless and blameless" (2 Peter 3:14, NASB). This takes effort and determination: to avoid the temptations in the world; to keep our whole selves, not just our feet, in Messiah; to be consistent and faithful. But it is our life and our life depends on it!

Further Study: Proverbs 8:29; Joshua 23:16; 1 Timothy 1:16

Application: Turn on your spiritual GPS receiver today and ask the question, "Where am I?" Do you see the signs of life and joy that show that you are "in Christ", in the Kingdom of God and walking according to His commands? Or do you see stress, worry and death as you walk away from the only One who is life? Make no mistake - it is vital that each of us knows exactly where we stand!

Tetzaveh - You shall command

Shemot / Exodus 27:20 - 30:10

רִאשׁוֹן	Aliyah One	Shemot/Exodus 27:20 - 28:12
שֵׁנִי	Aliyah Two	Shemot/Exodus 28:13 - 30
שְׁלִישִׁי	Aliyah Three	Shemot/Exodus 28:31 - 43
רְבִיעִי	Aliyah Four	Shemot/Exodus 29:1 - 18
חֲמִשִׁי	Aliyah Five	Shemot/Exodus 29:19 - 37
שִׁשִּׁי	Aliyah Six	Shemot/Exodus 29:38 - 46
שְׁבִיעִי	Aliyah Seven	Shemot/Exodus 30:1 - 10

תְּצַוֶּה א'

Tetzaveh - You shall command - 1

Shemot / Exodus 27:20 - 28:12

Shemot/Exodus 28:4 They are to make holy garments for your brother Aharon

וְעָשׂוּ בִגְדֵי-קֹדֶשׁ לְאַהֲרֹן אָחִיךָ

akhicha l'Aharon kodesh vigdey v'asu

Aharon the brother of Moshe was to have magnificent garments made for him to wear when he was serving God in the office of *Cohen HaGadol*. These were no ordinary garments; they were to be made from the same materials used for the hangings in the *Mishkan*: "gold; blue, purple and scarlet yarn; and fine linen" (Shemot 28:5, CJB). In a sense, Aharon himself was to be a living part of the fabric of the *Mishkan*, uniquely representing God to man and man to God.

Clothing is an important indicator of the person and what is going on inside him. When Jonah the Prophet was sent to the wicked city of Nineveh, he had only been at work proclaiming God's impending judgment on the city for one day before the king dressed in sackcloth and sat in ashes. More, the king commanded that all the people were to do the same, as well as fasting and crying out to God. The Scriptures tell us that, "when God saw by their deeds that they had turned from the evil ways, He relented and did not bring on them the punishment He had threatened" (Jonah 3:10, CJB).

Clothing is used as an important metaphor in the *B'rit Hadashah* to transition from the physical to the spiritual. Rav Sha'ul wrote to Timothy that instead of being dressed in costly garments and jewelry, "women should adorn themselves with what is appropriate for women who claim to be worshipping God, namely, good deeds" (1 Timothy 2:10, CJB). Similarly, Peter urges both men and leaders to "clothe yourselves in humility towards one another, because God opposes the arrogant, but to the humble He gives grace" (1 Peter 5:5, CJB). Just like the splendid robes of the *Cohen HaGadol* and the sackcloth and ashes, how we appear physically and spiritually before God is an important indication of the attitude of our heart toward Him and those around us.

So much so that Rav Sha'ul wrote to the Colossians: "*clothe yourselves with feelings of compassion, and with kindness, humility, gentleness and patience ... above all these, clothe yourselves with love, which binds everything together perfectly*" (Colossians 3:12,14, CJB). As believers, we might all be wary of wearing the latest Gucci fashions or jewelry from Tiffany's - but how are we doing on the attitude front?

Further Study: Colossians 3:10-15, Ephesians 6:11-17

Application: As you go about your affairs today - what character traits will you be showing to the world? Are they consistent with being a servant of the Most High God, a bond-servant of Yeshua the Messiah?

תְּצַוֶּה ב׳

Tetzaveh - You shall command - 2

Shemot / Exodus 28:13 - 30

Shemot/Exodus 28:13-14 And you shall make settings of gold and two chains of pure gold

וְעָשִׂיתָ מִשְׁבְּצֹת זָהָב: וּשְׁתֵּי שַׁרְשְׁרֹת זָהָב
zahav   shar'sh'rot ooshtey   zahav   mish'b'tzot   v'asiyta

As we shall see in the following verses, this instruction is to start making the breastplate which was to carry the twelve precious stones representing the tribes of Israel. The settings which are spoken of here are to hold the inscribed jewels on to the front of the breastplate. The settings are necessary for two purposes: the first is purely mechanical - it is impossible to mount precious stones directly on to material or fabric securely without either making a hole in them through which to pass the thread, or by enclosing them in so much thread that the stones become obscured. The second is that the setting enhances the jewel by presenting it, holding it forward and at the same time surrounding it by something of value in itself. This is why the settings are to be made of gold; not silver, which although pretty and of value, tarnishes.

In a great chapter of encouragement to Israel, written in the dark days before the exile to Babylon, the prophet Isaiah says: "You will be a crown of beauty in the hand of the Lord, and a royal diadem in the hand of your God" (Isaiah 62:3, NASB). The picture is extended from physical jewels and precious stones in a setting of gold on the breastplate of the *Cohen Gadol* to the whole people of Israel as a crown of beauty in God's hand. Instead of a physical representation, where God sees the jewels to remember the twelve tribes, now Isaiah sees the spiritual reality of Israel held as a crown in *Adonai's* hand. The second image, amplifying the first, is of a royal diadem; not just a crown, a band of gold with a few stones set in it, but an intricate weaving of lattices and designs with stones clustered and grouped to sparkle and shine in the light; a symbol of status and authority; and, as before, held in God's own hand. The setting provides the perfect contrast.

Rav Sha'ul tells us that God also wants to display His glory in us, "For it is the God who once said, 'Let light shine out of darkness,' who has made His light shine in our hearts, the light of the knowledge of God's glory shining in the face of the Messiah Yeshua" (2 Corinthians 4:6, CJB). What a setting! As we "fix our eyes upon Yeshua" (Hebrews 12:2), we see "the radiance of God's glory and the exact representation of His nature" (Hebrews 1:3, NASB). But even that is not enough, for God wants to use us as a setting for His glory as Rav Sha'ul goes on to say: "But we have this treasure in clay jars, so that it will be evident that such overwhelming power comes from God and not from us" (2 Corinthians 4:7, CJB). We are the setting in which God has chosen to display His glory in the world today, that men may see and marvel, not at what we do, but at what God can do through us.

Further Study: Zechariah 9:16; 1 Corinthians 4:9-13; 2 Timothy 2:20-21

Application: Just as God told Moshe to take care to make the right settings for the jewels on the breastplate, so God has taken care in making and selecting each of us to be the setting for His glory in the world. Though we are only flesh and blood now, we have been hand-picked to offset and display Messiah Yeshua to best effect.

תְּצַוֶּה ג׳

Tetzaveh - You shall command - 3

Shemot / Exodus 28:31 - 43

Shemot/Exodus 28:31-32 You shall make the robe of the ephod as blue wool ... it shall not be torn

לֹא ... תְּכֵלֶת כְּלִיל הָאֵפוֹד מְעִיל־אֶת וְעָשִׂיתָ
lo ... t'cheylet k'liyl ha'eyphod m'iyl et v'asiyta

יִקָּרֵעַ
yikareya

The robe, that is to have the row of pomegranates and bells along its bottom edge, is to be made of wool. The colour is also translated 'turquoise' by some versions, in an attempt to convey the word תְּכֵלֶת, which is the name of the mollusc that was used to produce the dye. The robe is worn under the ephod, runs from collar to calf and is to be made all in one piece without any seams or joins. However, it is also to have a hole for the wearer's head to pass through, which must be woven in the fabric, not later cut and edged. The verb יִקָּרֵעַ is in prefix form and *Niphal* stem; the prefix form usually indicates either an action that is incomplete or in the future; the *Niphal* stem indicating a passive voice: the action being carried out upon the subject rather than by the subject. In this case, it should be translated as a command rather than just an observation: "he shall not be torn" in preference to "he will not be torn". This command is number 101 in the list the 613 *mitzvot* compiled by the Rambam. Sforno deduces, by comparing the verb to Jeremiah 22:14 where it is used for cutting out windows - which are long and narrow - that the opening is to be round, rather than simply a split in the weave.

John the Evangelist alludes to this *mitzvah* in his account of the crucifixion, when he records the words of the execution squad: "Now [Yeshua's] tunic was seamless, woven in one piece. They therefore said to one another, 'Let us not tear it, but cast lots for it, to decide whose it shall be '" (John 19:23-24, NASB). Even the soldiers who were crucifying Yeshua unknowingly spoke words that confirmed Yeshua's role as the High Priest of Israel as He offered Himself as a sin offering for all our sin. John goes on to point out that their act of sharing out Yeshua's garments and casting lots for the tunic fulfill the words of Psalm 22: "They divide My garments among themselves; for my clothing they throw dice" (Psalm 22:19, CJB). This is but one of the many remarkable prophecies of the crucifixion to be found in that psalm.

In regular years, this portion is always read around the time of Purim - the feast that celebrates the story of the book of Esther - whose name means 'lots' and serves to remind us that, "One can cast lots into one's lap, but the decision comes from Adonai" (Proverbs 16:33, CJB). It was no accident that Yeshua became our sin offering, just as it was no accident which particular centurion and soldiers were chosen for the execution detail on the day that Yeshua was crucified, so that the centurion could declare his innocence, the jar of sour wine would be there to satisfy a thirst, and that all the other details could be fulfilled. God had prepared not only the large picture but all the smallest detail in advance so that everything worked - even down to not tearing the cloth of the High Priest's robe. "Therefore I told you long long beforehand, announced things to you ere they happened" (Isaiah 48:5, JPS).

Further Study: Psalm 22:1-22; Acts 2:22-25

Application: Today is a day to be certain that just as God arranged all the events we read about in the Scriptures, from the biggest plans to the smallest detail, so He looks after our lives today. Are you uncertain or hesitant? Have you been shaken by a recent event or accident? Know that God knew all about it beforehand and has you in the palm of His hand.

תְּצַוֶּה 'ד

Tetzaveh - You shall command - 4

Shemot / Exodus 29:1 - 18

Shemot/Exodus 29:1 This is the thing that you shall do to them to consecrate them to be priests to Me

וְזֶה הַדָּבָר אֲשֶׁר תַּעֲשֶׂה לָהֶם לְקַדֵּשׁ אֹתָם
otam l'kadeysh lahem ta'aseh asher hadavar v'zeh

לְכַהֵן לִי
liy l'chaheyn

Now that the details for the priestly uniforms have been described, *HaShem* proceeds to tell Moshe how he is to install Aharon as the anointed *Cohen Gadol*, High Priest, and his sons as priests, to be holy and set apart for God. This ritual actually takes place in Vayikra chapters 8-9. Nahum Sarna points out that "Moshe is to preside over the ceremonies, during which he will act as the sole priest." Moshe was neither the first-born in his family (the old order) - Aharon was Moshe's older brother - nor of the sons of Aharon (the new order) - being his brother - yet by divine command he is to act as a priest on this occasion, in order to induct Aharon as the *Cohen Gadol*. Once Aharon is installed, Moshe backs away and does not serve as a priest again, yet this occasion is enough for the Psalmist to record that "Moshe and Aharon were among His priests" (Psalm 99:6, NASB).

From this we can learn the importance of ordination, so that people whom God has called to serve Him in various ways can be recognised and set apart - their calling by God acknowledged - by the people amongst whom they serve. In some parts of the Body, this is done by formal ordination of priests or rabbis, a professional clergy; in other parts it is "setting in" of elders and/or deacons. Some groups recognise new house-group leaders by calling them out to the front of a meeting, introducing them and praying for them, while others are less formal and simply make an announcement in the weekly bulletin. Whatever the level of formality or the names and titles involved, the same process is taking place: peoples' calling by God is being recognised and they are being set apart to serve Him in some particular capacity. At Mt. Sinai, when our people heard God Himself speak to them, Israel was ordained as "a kingdom of priests and a holy nation" (Shemot 19:6), God's "special possession among all the peoples" (v. 5) and some of that function was fulfilled each year at Sukkot (the feast of Tabernacles) when part of the sacrifices offered each day during the festival was on behalf of the nations of the world.

Within the people Israel, the Levites were set apart for the service of the Tabernacle, to serve God on behalf of all the other tribes; within the Levites, the priests were set apart for the offering of the sacrifices and the daily service in the presence of God; while just one man - the High Priest - was chosen by God to represent the whole nation in the annual act of atonement, entering the presence of God in the Holy of Holies. So also within the Body of Messiah, there are levels of formal heirarchy, be it bishop, priest and deacon; superintendent, minister and deacon; overseer, elder, house-group leader; or ministries that have a board or a council of reference - all are set apart by God and equipped by Him to carry out the ministry that he has called them to, whether full-time, part-time or spare time!

More importantly, however, to each and every one of us, is the truth that we have all been set apart by Yeshua as believers, for the gospel. Each of us has been called out of the world - "out of the darkness into His glorious light" (1 Peter 2:9) - so that we may serve Him both at an individual level, sharing the gospel and good news of the Kingdom with those that God brings into our path, but also as members of His Body, building each other up, "in order to spur each other on to love and good deeds" (Hebrews 10:24, CJB). So that we can carry out this calling, God has equipped, empowered and commissioned each of us with His *Ruach* - Spirit - in specific and deliberate measure to fulfil the "life of good actions already prepared by God for us to do" (Ephesians 2:10, CJB).

Further Study: Isaiah 61:1-3; 1 Corinthians 3:16-17

Application: Consider today how you have been called and appointed by God. His calling is not without purpose and effect, so wherever you are, and whatever you are doing, know that He has chosen you and set you apart to serve Him in the way and place that He has given you. Just as Aharon was unique - the only High Priest - so you are unique: the only person to serve God exactly where you are and as you can do.

תְּצַוֶּה ה'

Tetzaveh - You shall command - 5

Shemot / Exodus 29:19 - 37

Shemot/Exodus 29:19 And you shall take the second ram

וְלָקַחְתָּ אֶת הָאַיִל הַשֵּׁנִי
ha'sheyni ha'ayil eyt v'lakakhta

This phrase starts a section of text that deals with the ram of ordination, that runs through until verse 34. Unlike the first ram, verses 15-18, which is a whole burnt offering, only part of this animal is burned upon the altar, the rest belongs to the priests. The daubing of the blood on the right ears, right thumbs and right foot big toes (v. 20) is paralleled only in the instructions for the cleansing of one who has *tzara'at*: "The priest shall then take some of the blood of the guilt offering and the priest shall put it on the lobe of the right ear of the one to be cleansed, and on the thumb of his right hand, and on the big toe of his right foot" (Vayikra 14:14, NASB). According to Sarna this suggests that the purification function for *tzara'at* may well be at work here, purifying the priest for his service to God. He goes on, "The singling out of the ear, hand and foot may well symbolise the idea that the priest is to attune himself to the divine word and be responsive to it in deed and direction in life."

Hirsch draws attention to the way the ritual symbolises and confirms the *cohen* in his role of sanctification and holiness before God. In the same way as the first ram was completely given up for God, symbolising the total dedication of the priest's life - his very being - in surrender to God, His *Torah* and His will, so the blood of the second ram symbolises the surrender of the priest's living faculties to God's service. Hirsch explains that the blood is touched to "the ear through which they hear and understand, the hand by which they achieve, the foot by which they go where they will" and is then thrown upon the altar in a graphic illustration of the priest himself - remembering that the priests and Levites serve God as the redemption offering for all the firstborn of Israel - thrown upon the altar. As the blood is given up as profane and by being splashed against the altar becomes holy, so the priests although profane must give up their lives at the altar and find

163

them anew in the service of God. Hirsch then makes the following remarkable statement: "The ram offering must not remain merely an external ritual, the identification must become concrete and real in the actual rebirth of the actual ear, the actual hand and the actual foot. The soul (represented by the blood), the personality, of the priest-to-be must actually begin its devotion and surrender by this giving-itself-up to the altar ... it is only in the giving-up of his own self that the priest, and also the garments of the priest, receives its holiness."

The crucifixion stake is the central focus point of Yeshua's earthly ministry. Although it came almost at the end of His time on earth, it is clearly pointed to during the approach; for example, we find John telling us that, "the Spirit was not yet given, because Yeshua was not yet glorified" (John 7:39, NASB). As Yeshua and the disciples are coming down the mountain from the Transfiguration, He tells them, "Tell the vision to no-one until the Son of Man has risen from the dead" (Matthew 17:9, NASB); when "some Greek-speaking Jews" (John 12:20, CJB) wanted to see Yeshua after He had formally entered Jerusalem, He answered them, "The time has come for the Son of Man to be glorified" (John 12:23, CJB). At the cross, as Yeshua gave Himself as a ransom for all of us that have, do and will believe in Him, He fulfilled the image of the first ram at the ordination of the High Priest in total surrender to God: "I am the Good Shepherd. The good shepherd lays down his life for the sheep ... and I lay down My life on behalf of the sheep" (John 10:11,15, CJB). In this way, Yeshua became our High Priest, the *Cohen Gadol*; He received His office and ordination: "When Messiah appeared as a high priest of the good things to come, He entered through the greater and more perfect tabernacle ... through His own blood He entered the holy place once for all, having obtained eternal redemption" (Hebrews 9:11-12, NASB).

But what about the second ram? Rav Sha'ul writes, "Even if my life blood is poured out as a drink offering over the sacrifice and service of your faith, I will still be glad and rejoice with you" (Philippians 2:17, CJB). He appears to have the idea in view that we too - as believers in Messiah - are to be a part of this ordination process. He compares our lives to that of Yeshua when he says, "Live a life of love, just as also the Messiah loved us, indeed, on our behalf gave Himself up as an offering, as a slaughtered sacrifice to God with a pleasing fragrance" (Ephesians 5:2, CJB). Sha'ul seems to be suggesting that our lives also ought to be some kind of sacrifice, following the model of Yeshua. Finally he explains when he writes, "I exhort you, therefore, brothers, in view of God's mercies, to offer yourselves as a sacrifice, living and set apart for God" (Romans 12:1, CJB).

Yeshua, who adopted the role of the first ram, wholly and completely surrendered to God on the crucifixion stake - yet resurrected and exalted to the right hand of God (cf. Philippians 2:8-11) - invites each of us to be the priests identified with the second ram, whose blood was poured on the altar yet reborn to holiness in Him; we are to exchange our lives at the altar for a calling and ordination as priests and ministers of the Most High God, dedicated to serving Him. As Yeshua said: "If anyone wishes to come after Me, let him deny himself, and take up his cross, and follow Me. For whoever wishes to save his life shall lose it; but whoever loses his life for My sake shall find it" (Matthew 16:24-25, NASB).

Further Study: Luke 9:23-27; Romans 8:12-17

Application: Have you heard God's call to "take the second ram", to draw near to the altar and surrender your all to Him? Whether you are already a believer or whether you are still wondering whether to take that step, now is the time to draw closer to God in Messiah Yeshua and surrender more of yourself to Him.

תְּצַוֶּה 'ו

Tetzaveh - You shall command - 6

Shemot / Exodus 29:38 - 46

Shemot/Exodus 29:38 And this is what you shall do upon the altar:
sheep, a year old, two for a day, continually.

וְזֶה אֲשֶׁר תַּעֲשֶׂה עַל־הַמִּזְבֵּחַ כְּבָשִׂים בְּנֵי־שָׁנָה
shana b'ney k'vasiym hamizbeyakh al ta'aseh asher v'zeh

שְׁנַיִם לַיּוֹם תָּמִיד:
tamiyd layom sh'niym

Later to be known as עוֹלַת הַתָּמִיד - the regular burnt offering - or
even just הַתָּמִיד - the regular - this text lays the foundation of the sacrificial
system: the morning and evening sacrifice that is to be made each and every
day, *Shabbat* included, as a point and time of meeting between *HaShem* and
the people. Abravanel asks, "Why are only the 'regular' offerings
mentioned here and none of the other offerings that the Israelites were
eventually be instructed to make?" He then answers his own question: "The
altar and the priestly service in general are not for sin offerings - better that a
man should never sin and have no need to bring one - but for this regular
offering in thanks to God for what He did for His people". The Ba'al
HaTurim points out that the initial letters of the phrase שְׁנַיִם לַיּוֹם תָּמִיד -
two each day, continually - make the number 730, which is the number of
lambs that will be offered (2 x 365) in each solar year!

Sarna comments that the importance of the daily offering grew
through time. It heads the list of public offerings in B'Midbar 28-29, and its
re-instatement after the return from Babylon preceeded even the
construction of the Second Temple. Its suspension by the Selucid king
Antiochus Epiphanes in 167 BCE was regarded as a disaster. Prophesied by
Daniel (8:11-12, 11:31, 12:11) and recorded by the Maccabees (1
Maccabees 1:41-45), the Mishnah includes this as one of the five disasters
that occurred on and are still remembered on the fast of 17th Tammuz (*m.*
Ta'anit 4:6). The memory was still so current in Yeshua's time that He was
able to re-prophecy about the "abomination of desolation" (Matthew 24:15).

Ibn Ezra emphasises that one lamb was to be offered in the morning and one in the evening, while Don Isaac Abravanel considers the specific gifts for which Israel was to thank God each day. He connects the morning offering with the spiritual gift of the *Torah*, which was given "as morning dawned" (Shemot 19:16), and the evening offering with the physical gift of the Exodus from Egypt, which was marked by the slaughter of the *Pesach* lamb "at twilight" (Shemot 12:6). The prayer services that take place in the synagogue each day still commemorate these two offerings, with the central prayer - the *Amidah*, or Standing Prayer - being considered a replacement , in lieu of the Temple, for the offering of the lamb. Although it contains some stanzas of petition, which are not said on *Shabbat*, this prayer is framed by thanksgiving and praise of *HaShem*, declaring His holiness and power, remembering some of the specific acts that He performed for our people and blessing His name. There are passages in the Jewish writings that suggest that early oral forms of some of these prayers may pre-date the destruction of the Second Temple or even come from the time of the Babylonian Exile.

Rav Sha'ul encouraged the early believers to continue in the same way. "In everything give thanks, for this is what God wants from you who are united with the Messiah Yeshua" (1 Thessalonians 5:18, CJB); thanksgiving was to be a major part of worship: "Always give thanks for everything to God the Father in the name of our Lord Yeshua the Messiah" (Ephesians 5:20, CJB), "as you sing psalms, hymns and spiritual songs with gratitude to God in your hearts" (Colossians 3:16, CJB). Just as in the *Amidah* - stanzas of petition surrounded by praise and thanksgiving - our prayer is to be a blend of thanks for what God has already done and requests for His continued involvement in our lives: "First of all, then, I counsel that petitions, prayers, intercessions and thanksgivings be made ... this is what God, our deliverer, regards as good; this is what meets His approval" (1 Timothy 2:1-3, CJB). Indeed, Sha'ul continues: "That is, everything you do or say, do in the name of the Lord Yeshua, giving thanks through Him to God the Father" (Colossians 3:17, CJB).

In our busy lives, constantly under pressure and on the run from one thing to another, we need to maintain a healthy balance between thanksgiving and requests. We need to avoid the somewhat prevalent "I/We" focus that is to be found in much modern worship music; sometimes these songs talk more about us than about God and concentrate on our feelings rather than on praise of God. Instead of asking God to give us a nice feeling when we think about Him, we should devote ourselves to truly worshipping Him and let our feelings catch up later. God is to be worshipped at all times and places, even when our feelings would forbid it: "Don't worry about anything; on the contrary, make your requests known to God by prayer and petition, with thanksgiving" (Philippians 4:6, CJB).

Further Study: Colossians 4:2; Psalm 55:16-18; Isaiah 63:7

Application: Have you become too focused on yourself during prayer? Are your conversations with God more about you than about Him? What not start a change by coming before God just to thank Him twice a day - morning and evening - to revolutionise your prayer life.

תְּצַוֶּה ז׳

Tetzaveh - You shall command - 7

Shemot / Exodus 30:1 - 10

Shemot/Exodus 30:1 You shall make an altar, [for] the burning of incense

וְעָשִׂיתָ מִזְבֵּחַ מִקְטַר קְטֹרֶת
k'toret   mik'tar miz'beyakh v'asita

As usual, there are a number of unusual things here that draw the commentators' attention. The word מִזְבֵּחַ - altar - is formed from the verb root זָבַח, to slaughter, with a מ prefix to make a noun signifying the place where an an action of slaughter takes place, hence 'altar'. Nahum Sarna points out that it is strange to use a word that essentially means place-of-slaughtering for the incense altar, which is quite specifically used only for incense and not for any animal sacrifices[15]. The same word-formation technique is used for מִקְטַר, literally "the place of raising an odour by burning": מ + קְטַר; and קְטֹרֶת is another noun from the same root, formed by appending a ת to make a feminine singular noun: incense. These two nouns are in a construct, giving the literal clumsy English wording, "the place of raising an odour by the burning of incense", which we smooth out to "for the burning of incense". *Targum Onkelos* actually changes the first of these nouns into a verb - לְאַקְטָרָא - an Aramaic *Af'el* infinitive, "to burn".

Rashi comments that the purpose of the altar is "to offer up on it the raising of the smoke of burning spices". Later in the same chapter, Moses is given more details about the spices: "And the Lord said to Moshe: Take the herbs stacte, onycha, and galbanum - these herbs together with pure frankincense; let there be an equal part of each. Make them into incense, a compound expertly blended, refined, pure, sacred" (Shemot 30:34-35, JPS). The herbs or spices are combined according to a deliberate and pre-arranged recipe, not a haphazard arrangement of whatever was to hand on any given

---

15. Although once a year, the high priest makes atonement for the incense altar by touching the horns of the altar with the blood from the atonement sacrifice on *Yom Kippur*.

day. The Israelites are forbidden to use the same recipe for themselves: "And the incense which you shall make, you shall not make in the same proportions for yourselves; it shall be holy to you for the Lord. Whoever shall make any like it, to use as perfume, shall be cut off from his people" (vv. 37-38, NASB). The first mix was carried out by no less a person than Betzalel, the master-craftsman who made the tabernacle and all its furniture and accoutrements: "[Betzalel] prepared the sacred anointing oil and the pure aromatic incense, expertly blended" (Shemot 37:29, JPS).

Why did such careful and particular care need to be taken over something that was, at a basic level, simply burned to make smoke and a smell? It is suggested that the smell would not even be very pleasant to the human nose. The Ramban makes two suggestions. The first is that the incense was to act as an atonement, to stop the spread of plague. In Moshe's blessing for the tribe of Levi, he says that "they shall offer incense for your nose" (D'varim 33:10); elsewhere the word for 'nose' is also translated as 'anger'. In the story of Korah's rebellion, "Then Moshe said to Aharon, 'Take the fire pan, and put on it fire from the altar. Add incense and take it quickly to the community and make expiation for them. For wrath has gone forth from the Lord: the plague has begun!' Aharon took it, as Moshe had ordered, and ran to the midst of the congregation, where the plague had begun among the people. He put on the incense and made expiation for the people; he stood between the dead and the living until the plague was checked" (B'Midbar 17:11-13, JPS), it is Aharon's burning of incense that causes the plague to stop.

Ramban's second suggestion is that "They must know that My Glory [often translated 'presence'] will not pardon your offences and be careful of My Glory". As the incense is burned "near the ark of the testimony, in front of the mercy seat that is over the ark of the testimony, where I will meet with you" (Shemot 30:6, NASB), this teaches "that the burning of the incense involves an encounter with the *kavod*, the Glory or Presence, of God." The idea of meeting with God is confirmed by the next verses which instruct: "Aharon shall burn fragrant incense on it; he shall burn it every morning when he trims the lamps. And when Aharon trims the lamps at twilight, he shall burn incense" (vv. 7-8, NASB) juxtaposed with "It shall be a continual burnt offering throughout your generations at the doorway of the tent of meeting before the Lord, where I will meet with you, to speak to you there. And I will meet there with the sons of Israel, and it shall be consecrated by My glory" (29:42-43, NASB). The offering of the incense is to be a part of the ritual conducted by the priests every morning and evening, when God has promised that He will meet with Israel, to speak with them and His Glory will be manifested.

The Psalmist takes the next step in the development of the idea: "May my prayer be counted as incense before You; the lifting up of my hands as the evening offering" (Psalm 141:2, NASB). David here connects his prayers and the lifting of his hands to the incense made at the morning and evening sacrifices. Rabbinic Judaism uses this thought to claim that the central prayer[16] at each of the three daily prayer services[17] - and the additional services on the holy days[18] - is acceptable to God in place of the sacrifices that would have been made at the Temple. Since the physical temple is no longer available and its destruction must have been permitted by God, the rabbis say, yet Israel is still under an obligation to bring the morning and evening offering, God must be prepared to accept it in an alternative form. This must be prayer.

Finally, to complete the chain, the writer of Revelation tells us about the twenty four elders in heaven, each of whom "held a harp and gold bowls filled with pieces of incense, which are the prayers of God's people" (Revelation 5:8, CJB). Here is the explicit connection: the prayers of God's people - and notice that it does not say that these people are Jews or believers in Messiah, simply that they are God's people - are pieces of incense to be offered to God. A few chapters later, we see what happens to the incense/prayers: "Another angel came and stood at the altar with a gold incense-bowl, and he was given a large quantity of incense to add to the prayers of all God's people on the gold altar in front of the throne. The smoke of the incense went up with the prayers of God's people from the hand of the angel before God" (8:3-4, CJB). The prayers intermingle with the incense and go up as a pleasing aroma before God.

If then, the incense is made with such care and precision, not available for ordinary use, shouldn't we take similar care over our prayers? This is not to say that prayers should always be liturgical, although good liturgy can be a powerful way for God's people to come together in praise and thanksgiving, or that prayers need always be in formal or Elizabethan language. On the contrary, informal and spontaneous prayer is an essential part of every believer's prayer life and relationship with God, both individually and in groups or congregations. What is does say, on the other hand, is that prayer should be deliberate and intentional. As Rabbi Eliezer said: "Know before whom you stand" (*b. Berachot* 28*b*); we should always be aware that we are talking to God: a blend of the Father who loves us, the Master of the Universe and the friend who is "closer than a brother" (Proverbs 18:24, NASB). In all events, He wants to hear from us, but most importantly, we should remember that our prayers involve an encounter with the Glory or Presence of God. We should expect and relish His presence as He engages with us!

Further Study: Shemot 29:45-46; Psalm 63:1-8; Luke 24:50-53

---

16. Known as the *Shemone Esrei* - The Eighteen Benedictios - or the *Amidah* - The Standing Prayer. It is often abbreviated simply to The Prayer.
17. Shacharit, Mincha and Ma'ariv - Dawn, Gift (made at 3pm) and Evening.
18. i.e. Musaf - Additional or Added

Application: Are you a shopping-list prayer or a marathon-walker prayer? How can you deepen your relationship with God in prayer - perhaps you could explore different forms or types of prayer and see if they work for you. Press on and keep working at it; it is God's desire that all of us should know Him in that intimate way.

כִּי תִשָּׂא

Ki Tissa - When you take

Shemot / Exodus 30:11 - 34:35

רִאשׁוֹן	Aliyah One	Shemot/Exodus 30:11 - 31:17
שֵׁנִי	Aliyah Two	Shemot/Exodus 31:18 - 33:11
שְׁלִישִׁי	Aliyah Three	Shemot/Exodus 33:12 - 16
רְבִיעִי	Aliyah Four	Shemot/Exodus 33:17 - 23
חֲמִשִׁי	Aliyah Five	Shemot/Exodus 34:1 - 9
שִׁשִּׁי	Aliyah Six	Shemot/Exodus 34:10 - 26
שְׁבִיעִי	Aliyah Seven	Shemot/Exodus 34:27 - 35

כִּי תִשָּׂא א׳

Ki Tissa - When you take - 1

Shemot / Exodus 30:11 - 31:17

Shemot/Exodus 30:12 When you take a census of the sons of Israel to number them

כִּי תִשָּׂא אֶת־רֹאשׁ בְּנֵי־יִשְׂרָאֵל לִפְקֻדֵיהֶם

lif'koodeyhem Yisra'el b'ney rosh et tisa kiy

What an interesting way to take a census! Although *Targum Onkelos* translates the word תִשָּׂא as 'taking' or 'you take' (Aramaic תְקַבֵּל, as also in Vayikra 19:17 and B'Midbar 1:49), the root נָשָׂא means to raise or carry. It has many specialised or derived meanings, but a plain or literal meaning of this text could say that *Adonai* told Moshe that the way to number the sons of Israel is to lift their heads. Although the Lord's instructions go on to describe the mechanism of the half-shekel, collected in Yeshua's day as the Temple Tax (Matthew 17:24-27) and still remembered in the synagogue cycle every year on *Shabbat Shekalim*, the passage seems to carry the idea that this is not to be an anonymous or faceless count, but that each individual matters. In the following verses, *Adonai* stresses that the rich do not pay more, nor the poor less - each human being, each soul, has the same value before God - and Moshe is not simply to collect the money as a ransom for the people; he is to look each person in the face so that they can know that they each have value, have each paid their own half-shekel and have been each atoned for.

There are several lists of names in the Bible: some are genealogies, some are lists of people who came or went on a journey or migration, others are lists of people who did certain functions. Without trying to read too much into them, it is important we see that the Scriptures are teaching us that every individual is important. Whether a high priest or a king, down to the door-keepers and ash-collectors in the Temple, even people of whom we know nothing except that they were somebody's son and somebody's father - they all played their part in fulfilling God's purposes and being His people, our people.

Little wonder, then, that Rav Sha'ul writes, "For now we see obscurely in a mirror, but then it will be face to face. Now I know partly; then I will know fully, just as God has fully known me" (1 Corinthians 13:12, CJB). Whilst our view of God is partly obscured or hidden - for "no man can see My face and live" (Shemot 33:20), He sees and knows each one of us personally and individually. When Yeshua was talking with the disciples, Philip asked Him, "'Show us the Father and it will be enough for us.' Yeshua replies to him, 'Have I been with you so long without you knowing Me, Philip?'" (John 14:8-9, CJB). It is in Yeshua, in knowing Him face-to-face that we find our true worth and know true atonement with God, when He raises our heads and we see in His eyes that we are important to Him.

Further Study: Luke 12:4-7; Job 22:21-28

Application: With the passage of time, it is easy to lose sight of just how much we matter to God and how He desires eye-to-eye soul contact with us. Today, lift up your face to God and ask Him to renew that freshness in your relationship with Him.

כִּי תִשָּׂא 'ב

Ki Tissa - When you take - 2

Shemot / Exodus 31:18 - 33:11

Shemot/Exodus 31:18 And He gave to Moshe, as He finished with him ... the two tablets of stone

וַיִּתֵּן אֶל־מֹשֶׁה כְּכַלֹּתוֹ ... שְׁנֵי לֻחֹת הָעֵדֻת

ha'eydoot lookhot sh'ney ... k'chaloto Moshe el vayiteyn

The word translated "as He finished with him", כְּכַלֹּתוֹ, is in *defectiva* spelling, without a ו to carry the *holem* vowel between the ל and the ת. Rashi points out that with a change of only one vowel the word would have been כְּכַלָּתוֹ, which means "like His bride". This could suggest that *HaShem* gave Moshe, as the representative of the people, the two tablets as a *ketubah* - or marriage contract - following a marriage: between Israel and God as bride and groom. *Chazal* say that Moshe achieved the closest possible relationship between man and the *Torah*, like that of man and wife (Tanchuma 18).

Working with the picture of Israel as *Adonai's* bride, the Rabbis saw great significance in the last phrase of the verse "As a bridegroom decks himself with a garland, and as a bride adorns herself with her jewels" (Isaiah 61:10, NASB). The jewels, they explain, are the twenty four books of the *Tanakh* - and a *Torah* scholar is to be familiar with all the parts of the *Tanakh*, as Israel is to adorn herself with the jewels of God's word; the *Torah* itself being the crown (Tanchuma 16). The prophet goes on to say, "And as the bridegroom rejoices over the bride, so your God will rejoice over you" (Isaiah 62:5, NASB). As God's people study His word and put it into practice, as we demonstrate our commitment to Him, spending time with Him, working on our relationship with Him, so He delights in us and rewards us with His presence.

As the pages of the Bible turn, into the gospels that tell us of Yeshua, we find John the Immerser talking about Yeshua: "The bridegroom is the one who has the bride; but the bridegroom's friend, who stands and listens to him, is overjoyed at the sound of the bridegroom's voice. So this joy of mine is now complete" (John 3:29, CJB). John is clearly identifying Yeshua as the bridegroom. But who is the bride now? Who is to be the bride of Messiah?

Rav Sha'ul answers this question in his letter to the Ephesians when he talks about the relationships between husbands and wives, drawing his analogy from Messiah and His bride, the Body: "Husbands, love your wives, just as the Messiah loved the Messianic Community, indeed, gave Himself up on its behalf, in order to set it apart for God, making it clean through immersion in the mikveh, so to speak, in order to present the Messianic Community to Himself as a bride to be proud of, without a spot, wrinkle or any such thing, but holy and without defect" (Ephesians 5:25-27, CJB). We are the bride of Messiah, being prepared in this time of betrothal, having been given the *Ruach HaKodesh* as our *ketubah* (Ephesians 1:13-14) until the great marriage feast when Yeshua returns for us (Revelation 19:7-9).

Further Study: Matthew 25:1-12; Ephesians 5:21-32

Application: During the time of betrothal, a bride-to-be prepares for marriage. She gets ready all that she will need to start being a wife to her husband when they are married. How are we preparing for the time of Yeshua's return when He comes back to claim His bride?

כִּי תִשָּׂא 'ג

Ki Tissa - When you take - 3

Shemot / Exodus 33:12 - 16

Shemot/Exodus 33:12 And Moshe said to Adonai, "Look! You say to me ..."

וַיֹּאמֶר מֹשֶׁה אֶל־יהוה רְאֵה אַתָּה אֹמֵר אֵלַי
eylay omeyr atah r'eyh Adonai el Moshe vayomer

This verse comes at the start of a powerful block of text describing the revelation of some of *HaShem's* attributes to Moshe. Hirsch says, "At no part of the *Torah* does translation and explanation have to tread with greater care and diffidence than at the context of verses 12-23, for here we are led to the extreme limits of man's knowledge of God." The previous verses have narrated the incident of the Golden Calf, God's intention to wipe out the Israelites and start again with Moshe, and Moshe's self-sacrificing intercession for the people, before God says that the people are to go ahead, to enter the Land, but that He is not going with them lest He should destroy them on the journey, so He will send an angel with them instead. It is at this point that Moshe starts talking to God.

The first word that Moshe says, רְאֵה, is in imperative form: Look! or See! as if Moshe is taking the Lord to task: "Now see here!" Sforno interprets this as a plea: "'See!' means 'watch over us and do not conceal Your face from us over this!'" Moshe realises that without God's personal attention and presence, the project will fail; not only does God need to be personally involved, but the people need to be aware that He is still in control of them, their situation and their future. If God withdraws His face from direct contact, the life and spirit of the people will drop - they will cease either to be a witness for God or to be capable of carrying out His commands.

Rashi, on the other hand, has Moshe take a more diplomatic tack: "'Look!' means 'focus Your eyes and heart upon Your words!'" Rashi projects Moshe drawing God's attention to the inconsistency of what He has just said. God appears to be taking His hand off the tiller and leaving Moshe in charge, supported by an angel to administer the miracles where necessary.

"Look!" Moshe says, "this doesn't add up; we're not going to be able to do it without You and our failure will rebound on You - it's Your name and Your reputation that are going to take the hit." Appearing to yield to Moshe's logic, *HaShem* agrees that He will go with the people after all and then allows Moshe to ask for and receive an outstanding revelation of His glory. Moshe's boldness and *chutzpah* win through.

In Luke's gospel, Yeshua tells His *talmidim* the parable of the widow and the dishonest or corrupt judge. Although the judge ignored the widow for a long time, eventually he gave in: "because this widow bothers me, I will give her legal protection, lest by continually coming she wears me out" (Luke 18:5, CJB). Now, of course, Yeshua is not saying that God is like the unrighteous judge - *chas v'shalom* - but He is encouraging His disciples to engage with God. Whichever way you read Moshe, he refused to disengage and accept an angel instead of God; he persisted, reminding God of what He had already promised, and God rewarded his perseverance not only with a direct answer to the immediate question, but with a generous further revelation and relationship. Yeshua calls us to the same pattern of persistence and reward.

Further Study: Isaiah 62:6-9; Luke 11:5-13

Application: Have you been finding it difficult hearing from God lately? Do you struggle to engage with Him in a meaningful way? Push on today and insist; even be bold or daring - God values our determination to maintain communication with Him and will come through for you.

כִּי תִשָּׂא 'ד

Ki Tissa - When you take - 4

Shemot / Exodus 33:17 - 23

Shemot/Exodus 33:17 for you have found favour in My eyes and I have known you by name.

כִּי מָצָאתָ חֵן בְּעֵינַי וָאֵדָעֲךָ בְּשֵׁם:
b'sheym va'eyda'acha b'eynay kheyn matzata kiy

    The text presents an interesting idea that seems to run counter to many of the more evangelical views about salvation and the relative positions of God and man. The Calvinist position of mankind's total depravity, intended to describe man's unregenerate state before salvation, but often extended in contemporary teaching to say that man can never earn any favour before God by his words or actions because everything must be of grace - from God to man - would declare it impossible for Moshe to have earned any credit or standing with God by his actions and behaviour. Yet, nonetheless, this text is the reason God gives for granting Moshe's request that His presence should continue to accompany the Children of Israel as they travel to the Promised Land in spite of the episode of the Golden Calf. Moreover, it appears to be the foundation of Moshe's extraordinary request to see God's glory, and of God's at least partial granting of that request.

    Rabbi Hirsch addresses the issue, commenting, "since I chose you, you have shown yourself worthy of being chosen, and have been endowed with ever-growing talents." This places the emphasis back on what God has done: choosing Moshe and then giving him more abilities as he learns to use those he has already been given. At the same time, it allows room for the original meaning of the text: that Moshe himself has worked and been active, rather than simply passively letting things happen around him - and this is surely in character with the overall narrative of the text over the 40 years that Moshe led Israel, from the start at the Burning Bush, until his death after seeing the Land from Mt. Nebo.

    Taking a more relaxed translation, Friedman points out that God is echoing back the words of Moshe's request, thus confirming His acceptance of Moshe's point. The text seems to be agreeing that Moshe has been sufficiently active in his relationship with God that he has actually been able to bring something to the table that God has found acceptable; more - that God considered this a basis for trusting Moshe's opinion and granting his request as a reward for his *chutzpah* in being so strong on the people's behalf.

So what does it mean to find favour in God's eyes and how is this done? Is this something that we can or should do? Does this come from us or is it something that comes from God? Without any explanation of what had been before, an angel appeared to a young girl - therefore, relatively uneducated and without formal *Torah* study - in Nazareth: "Shalom, favoured lady! Adonai is with you! Don't be afraid, Miryam, for you have found favour with God" (Luke 1:28,30, CJB). We get more of a clue some verses earlier, when Luke describes Zechariah and his wife Elizabeth who were to be the parents of John the Baptist: "Both of them were righteous before God, observing all the mitzvot and ordinances of Adonai blamelessly" (Luke 1:6, CJB). When the angel of the Lord appears to the mother-to-be of Samson she is told, "You will conceive and bear a son. Now, therefore, be careful not to drink any wine or other intoxicating liquor, and don't touch anything unclean" (Judges 13:3-4, CJB). Setting aside the specifics, these examples all seem to support that there is a significant component of human action, obedience, deliberate choice involved in finding favour in God's eyes.

So much so that Rav Sha'ul writes, "For we are God's fellow workers" (1 Corinthians 3:9, ESV); he sees Apollos and himself working alongside God Himself: preparing the ground, sowing the seed, watering the crop and God giving the growth - no doubt an echo of Yeshua's words, "The harvest is plentiful but the labourers are few; therefore pray earnestly to the Lord of the Harvest to send labourers into His harvest" (Matthew 9:37-38, ESV). But Yeshua went further saying, "No longer do I call you servants, for the servant does not know what his master is doing; but I have called you friends, for all that I have heard from My Father I have made known to you"(John 15:15, ESV). Not only do we pray for workers, but we should expect to be workers and to find favour with God by so doing.

Further Study: Mark 16:20; 2 Corinthians 6:1

Application: How, then, are you working with God today? What has He called you to partner with Him to accomplish? If you are uncertain or unsure, ask the Lord to help you see or confirm the ways in which you are to labour with Him, so that we may all take our part in the work of the kingdom and find favour in God's eyes.

כִּי תִשָּׂא 'ה

Ki Tissa - When you take - 5

Shemot / Exodus 34:1 - 9

Shemot/Exodus 34:1 Hew for yourself two tablets of stone, like the first ones

פְּסָל־לְךָ שְׁנֵי־לֻחֹת אֲבָנִים כָּרִאשֹׁנִים

kari'shoniym avaniym lukhot sh'ney l'cha   p'sal

HaShem's instructions here to Moshe start the re-instatement of the covenant. The following verses contains parallels to the original giving of the covenant when the people first arrived at Sinai: the tablets are replaced; Moshe is told to be ready, as the people were told to be ready; access to the mountain is restricted; the Lord again comes down in Sinai and through fear the people back away. On this occasion, however, Moshe rather than God is to prepare the tablets of stone; the verb פְּסָל is a *Qal* imperative from the root פָּסַל, which means to cut or hew stone, to carve wood. God is going to do the writing, as He did before, but Moshe has to prepare the stone.

Rashi comments rather tartly, "You broke the first ones, you carve yourself other ones," as if *HaShem* is petulantly stamping His foot and berating Moshe for breaking the first set of tablets, but then goes on to relate a parable from Midrash Tanchuma to show that Moshe's actions had been correct. However, this points to an important aspect of this re-instatement: Moshe - representing the people - has to contribute to the process, rather than just being given a second set of tablets; he, or whoever is delegated to actually work the stone, has quite a bit of skilled physical labour to do in order to have the covenant restored.

"Carve ... like the first: like them in kind and size," adds Ibn Ezra, who then goes on to list the seven ways in which Sa'adia Gaon claims that the second set of tablets outshone the first. Ibn Ezra is not impressed, however, and points out that "the writing was God's writing" (Shemot 32:16, JPS) making them equivalent in that respect. He then asks, since God created the first set, whereas Moshe crafted the second set, how can Moshe's work be of a higher standard or holiness than God's! There is also debate among the commentators as to whether the first set contained the commandments as found in Shemot 20 with the second set containing the form in D'varim 5, or whether the writing was identical.

The physical considerations, however interesting, should not hide what is happening at a relationship level. In the previous chapters, God has given Moshe a set of tablets containing His covenant with our people but, barely before the ink is dry, the people have made an idol - a golden calf - and are worshipping it at the foot of the mountain while Moshe is still on his way down. God decides to obliterate the people and start again with Moshe, but Moshe pleads for the people and God relents; three thousand people are killed by the Levites who answer Moshe's call to stand for the Lord and God sends the people on their way to the Land with only an angel as guide rather than His presence, after sending a plague among the people because of their sin. Once more, Moshe intercedes, pointing out that it is only the presence of God among them that distinguishes the people of Israel from the other peoples; God not only agrees that He will come with them personally, but rewards Moshe's request to see His glory by a private theophany while he stands in a cleft of the rock. It is in that context that Moshe is told to bring two tablets so that God may write the covenant again for the people. This is a moment of re-making the covenant that was only so recently made and almost immediately broken.

Hirsch, in a fine piece of writing, comes so close and yet just fails to grasp the key to the matter that one might suggest that he chose his words deliberately to avoid open expression while seeing it in his own mind's eye: "The condition for the return to the original direct and intimate relationship between God and Israel is that Israel should again take up God's Law in their midst as the one mediator for this relationship. As Israel had broken this Law, it is up to them to hand God the blank tablets, and by that the Law may be written afresh on the new tablets by the Finger of God." As we have seen from the text, though, it is God who is taking the initiative here by instructing Moshe to bring two new tablets, it is God who is going to take the initiative again when He says, "I will make a new covenant with the house of Israel and with the house of Judah" (Jeremiah 31:30, CJB), and it is God who took the initiative of sending Yeshua to resolve the issue of sin once and for all: "there is but one Mediator between God and humanity. Yeshua the Messiah, Himself human, who gave Himself as a ransom on behalf of all, thus providing testimony to God's purpose at just the right time" (1 Timothy 2:5-6, CJB).

Hirsch's next sentences, however, are exactly on target: "Our transgressions in no wise alter the contents of the Divine Law. God does not modify or reform the *Torah* to accommodate our weaknesses. Unaltered, the *Torah* awaits our conversion and return." Grace is neither easy or cheap; it cost Messiah His death on the crucifixion stake and it costs us everything that we have in surrender to God as we follow Yeshua. Yeshua made this clear when He taught: "The kingdom of Heaven is like a merchant on the lookout for fine pearls. On finding one very valuable pearl he went away, sold everything he owned and bought it" (**Matthew** 13:45-46, CJB).

Further Study: John 15:9-10; Ezekiel 37:24-28

Application: God is calling people today to bring Him their hearts, so that He may forgive their sin and write His law inside them. Have you brought your heart to God, for this is something that only you can do, and are you committed to keeping the commandments of Yeshua so that you remain in covenant with God?

כִּי תִשָּׂא ו׳

Ki Tissa - When you take - 6

Shemot / Exodus 34:10 - 26

Shemot/Exodus 34:10 Behold, I am making a covenant: before all your people I shall do wonders

הִנֵּה אָנֹכִי כֹּרֵת בְּרִית נֶגֶד כָּל־עַמְּךָ אֶעֱשֶׂה
e'e'seh   amcha kol   neged   b'riyt   koreyt anochi hineh

נִפְלָאֹת
nifla'ot

The word נִפְלָאֹת - a *Niphal* participle form, feminine plural - comes from the root verb פָּלָא, which has a consistent set of meanings such as "to be extraordinary", "to be wonderful, marvellous" (Davidson). The participle, therefore, working from the literal "things being wonderful" is usually translated "wonders" or "wonderful, great things" (e.g. Daniel 11:36). The text, then, records *HaShem* speaking to Moshe and telling him that He is making a covenant, and that the covenant explicitly includes doing wonders before the people. Yet the immediately following chapters and verses record no such wonders until, perhaps, "the cloud covered the Tent of Meeting and the glory of HaShem filled the Tabernacle" (Shemot 40:34) right at the end of *parasha* Pekudei. This caused the commentators to try to explain away *HaShem's* words in the light of the following text.

Rashi goes perhaps the furthest, claiming that the word נִפְלָאֹת is derived from the different root - פָּלָה - which means to separate or distinguish. This enables him to translate the phrase as: "before all your people I shall make distinctions", and point to Israel being set apart from all the other nations. Rashbam extends that to suggest that *HaShem* was going to distinguish Moshe from all the rest of the people, because of the way Moshe's face would shine when he had been talking with *HaShem*. Ibn Ezra is prepared to accept the meaning "wonders" but suggests that this refers only to the miracles already performed in Egypt. The Sforno is uncomfortable with taking the argument that far and instead comments that only the generation of Moshe saw the wonders because they were only done in Moshe's merit. This idea is amplified by Hirsch who declaims that Moshe's ministry was a unique creation in the history of the world, so was not subject to the normal physical rules of the universe, thus allowing miracles and wonders as long as Moshe lived.

1 Kings 18 records the confrontation between Elijah and the prophets of Ba'al and Asherah on Mt. Carmel. Throughout the episode, the people show resistance to Elijah's challenge. Elijah starts by asking the crowd of witnesses who have gathered to see what happens, "How long will you hesitate between two opinions? If the Lord is God, follow Him; but if Ba'al, follow him.' But the people did not answer him a word" (1 Kings 18:21, NASB). The people might have seen lots of ritual before, but were not interested in taking a position. Elijah's logic seemed reasonable, but the people refused to commit themselves. The story is well known, but let's pick it up again immediately after the fire fell from heaven at Elijah's request: וַיַּרְא כָּל־הָעָם

וַיִּפְּלוּ עַל־פְּנֵיהֶם - "and all the people saw and they fell on the faces" (v. 39). The Hebrew text tells us something important about the way the people reacted: the first verb - וַיַּרְא - is singular, while the second verb וַיִּפְּלוּ is plural. All the people saw, as one, the fire fall; there was no getting away from that - everyone present had seen it. But a typical crowd reaction followed: some of the people hit the deck instantly, others took a little longer and some - either curious or skeptical - didn't want to do it at all; they only lowered themselves reluctantly to the ground when they saw that everyone else already had and realised that they would be extremely obvious to everyone else if they remained upright. Even in the face of an open miracle, there were those who didn't want the consequences that would follow - having to acknowledge and worship *HaShem* rather than Ba'al - and so tried to deny the miraculous wonder that had been performed. Elijah's subsequent flight the next day from Jezebel's threats shows that he too recognised that even miracles were not enough to change the dominant nature of the culture of Israel.

Man has always had a tendency to downgrade God to fit his own expectations. From the very beginning, Eve's sin in the Garden of Eden came about because the enemy caused her to downplay God's words because of logic. Throughout history we can see the same scenario being played out again and again. The gifts of the Holy Spirit have been suppressed for centuries - apart from odd bubbles of life - because their operation wasn't in line with the expectations of the church, be that clergy or laity. They remain suppressed by a significant block of churches, the cessationalists, who are forced to downgrade the words of Yeshua and Rav Sha'ul in order to support their claim that the gifts were only intended for the apostolic age and have now been withdrawn because the "perfect" has come (1 Corinthians 13:10) in the form of the New Covenant scriptures. Many believers live stunted spiritual lives because their expectations of the way God works have been shaped and constrained by the traditions of the church since the time of the Enlightenment, when reason triumphed over faith and the supernatural was declared impossible because God was bound just as much by the physical laws of nature as man is. It is no coincidence that such disbelief in the supernatural is also often found hand-in-glove with replacement theology, which denies that God's covenant with Israel continues or that Israel is to play any other part in the eschatalogical outworking of the ages.

Charles Haddon Spurgeon, the mighty preacher of Victorian England, was involved - in the closing years of his life and ministry - in what became known as the Downgrade Controversy. In 1887-88 Spurgeon was increasingly concerned about the advance of Higher Criticism and other liberal attacks upon the veracity and authenticity of the Bible, in particular upon its inspiration. He saw that many educated people were moving over to accept the prevailing scholarship which saw the Scriptures as nothing more than the writings of man and not inspired by God - if indeed there was a God at all - and that this position was being taught to the next generation of ministers in training. After a series of articles in his magazine "Sword and Trowel" and bruising but private correspondence with the council of his denomination, Spurgeon felt that he had no alternative but to resign from the Baptist Union. He could no longer, in spite of many years of close personal friendship in some cases, fellowship with those who denied the inspiration and truth of the gospel or, by remaining quiet within the Union, condone their teaching. The leaders of the Union and lecturers in the Union colleges had downgraded their vision of God to match the circumstances and experience of their lives, rather than focusing on the truth of God's word and lifting their lives to conform with that truth.

In our lives today we too face the same challenges. Rival attractions vie for our attention and favour, be that Amazon, Facebook or simply radio and television. There is a constant torrent of material in every public arena that seeks to deny God, to encourage us to be more materialistic and buy more stuff, and to downgrade what faith we have to what society considers reasonable. But the same God who provided for our people in the wilderness, sent the fire on Mt. Carmel and - most importantly - raised Yeshua from the dead, is still active and working in His world to call men into relationship with Himself and enlist them as workers in His vineyard. Whom will you believe - the god of this age (the Devil) or the God who made the whole universe and has cut His covenant with us?

Further Study: Joshua 24:14-15; 2 Corinthians 4:16-18

Application: Have you allowed the world to shrink your ideas about God? Has He become tame to you because the world says that you shouldn't expect any more? Why not turn to God today and ask Him about a small miracle to set you back on track again?

כִּי תִשָּׂא ז׳

Ki Tissa - When you take - 7

Shemot / Exodus 34:27 - 35

Shemot/Exodus 34:27 ... for according to these words I make covenant with you and with Israel.

כִּי עַל־פִּי | הַדְּבָרִים הָאֵלֶּה כָּרַתִּי אִתְּךָ בְּרִית
b'riyt   itcha karatiy ha'eyleh hadvariym   piy   al kiy

וְאֶת־יִשְׂרָאֵל:
Yisra'el   v'et

Our exploration begins with an affirmation by Don Isaac Abravanel: "You thought that I would give you a new set of commandments to purge them of the sin of the Calf? No, the commandments are the same as in the covenant of chapter 24 [when Moshe first wrote down the words of *HaShem* and goes up the mountain to receive the first set of tablets that *HaShem* has written]." Although phrased as a question that he puts in *HaShem's* mouth, Abravanel's point is straightforward; *HaShem* has not changed, so His covenant has not changed, the *Torah* has not changed. The undeniable fact that the Israelites sinned over the Calf does not alter *HaShem* or His position. Our belief in God is founded upon exactly that characteristic: God is, by His own words, constant and does not change. "For I, the Lord, do not change; therefore you, O sons of Jacob, are not consumed" (Malachi 3:6, NASB).

Targum Onkelos takes the argument a step further. In his translation of the verse, he changes the text to read: "with the words of these statements I made a covenant with you and with Israel". *Onkelos* is saying that the very words are what makes the covenant; they themselves, the words of the *Torah* - in their precise form - are the covenant between God and Israel. It is precisely this understanding that has led to centuries of detailed analysis of the Hebrew text, the word ordering and spelling, the added punctuation and vocalisation provided by the *Masoretic* pointing that preserved the traditional pronunciation and emphasis.

Rabbi Hirsch, on the other hand, insists that the covenant is more than just the words; that the words are just the written baseline upon which the covenant is built. "It is not merely the fixed written words as they stand before our eyes, on which our covenant with God is to be established, but the full and living meaning of the spirit as had been explained to Moshe before the 'letter' had been fixed." He even goes as far as saying that "although it is a welcome bearer of thoughts and ideas it is nevertheless, by itself, a danger to the completeness, the life and truth of the thoughts." Hirsch senses - without knowing Yeshua, the Living Word - that mere words on a page do not make a covenant or a relationship; more is required.

Nahum Sarna takes us on again, by commenting on the last few words of the verse: "with you and with Israel: this unexpected order signals the transition to the final episode, which concentrates on the exaltation of Moshe. It reflects his role as the dominant figure in dealing with the apostasy and in successfully interceding with God on Israel's behalf." Sarna is suggesting that Moshe has become the mediator of the covenant; the one who explains how it works, applies it to everyday situations and acts as the enforcer as well as the advocate when things go wrong. By this thought, Moshe has become the lynch pin of the covenant; he is the interface between God and our people. Without Moshe, the covenant would not work.

Rav Sha'ul is clearly aware of the debate in his time. While he confirms the role of Moshe as the mediator of the Sinai covenant: the *Torah* was "ordained through angels by the agency of a mediator, until the seed should come to whom the promise had been made" (Galatians 3:19, NASB), at the same time he points forward to the time when another would come. Explicit use of the word 'mediator' of course comes in the well-known verse, "For there is one God, and one mediator also between God and men, the man Messiah Yeshua ... the testimony borne at the proper time" (1 Timothy 2:5-6, NASB); Yeshua is the mediator who, born at the proper time, takes over the mediator role that Moshe had been holding until He came. Without Yeshua - the high priest and king of Israel, the inheritor of the promise, the fulfillment of prophecy - the covenant does not work.

Have both the Jewish and Christian communities nevertheless cast the written word in concrete so that it has become an inflexible and often sterile source of inspiration when read through the lens of dogma and tradition? Sha'ul warns that "the letter kills, but the Spirit gives life" (2 Corinthians 3:6, NASB); a warning that surely applies today as much as it did when he wrote it. He goes on, "to this day whenever Moses is read, a veil lies over their heart; but whenever a man turns to the Lord, the veil is taken away" (vv. 15-16, NASB). This is conveniently taken by many Christians to apply only to what they think of as dead Rabbinic Judaism, entirely missing the point that when Sha'ul wrote, Moshe was the Scriptures and as Yeshua commented, "it is these that bear witness of Me" (John 5:39, NASB). Unregenerate man - and, frankly, often even regenerate man - has exactly the same reaction to the words of the gospel; when anyone reads from or quotes the words of Scripture, eyes glaze and people turn away, because they do not know what they are hearing. A veil remains over their heart.

The Scriptures are a source of life, because they point us to the source of all life. The writer to the Hebrew tells us that "the word of God is living and active and sharper than any two-edged sword, and piercing as far as the division of soul and spirit, of both joints and marrow, and able to judge the thoughts and intentions of the heart" (Hebrews 4:12, NASB), but we have to be prepared to hear them speak to us. When we read and listen to the written word, we need to hear through the lens of the *Ruach*, the Holy Breath of God, who brings the words to life within us and applies them afresh to our hearts as Yeshua promised He would: "the Helper, the Holy Spirit, whom the Father will send in My name, He will teach you all things, and bring to your remembrance all that I said to you" (John 14:26, NASB).

It is the words of Yeshua that make covenant with us. His words are the living water that well up inside us (John 4:14) and bring us His life in abundance (John 10:10). We ignore His words at our peril; we distance ourselves from His blessing when we treat the Scriptures casually; we kill the covenant when we study the Scriptures only as an academic exercise without letting the Spirit wash us with their meaning. God is constant and does not change; His word is not dated or old-fashioned. On the contrary, it touches our souls and makes covenant with us in every way and every age. We must not dilute it or dumb it down, we must not pull its punches as if it is too strong for the people we meet - some of them need that knock-out blow! - and we must allow the Spirit room and liberty to work. For it is according to these words God makes covenant with mankind.

Further Study: Jeremiah 11:2-5; Mark 4:3-9

Application: How do you hear the Bible as you read it each day? Do you filter the words through a lens - cultural, archeological, denominational? If so, then you may only have half the story and so, half the covenant. Ask God today to let you hear His words "in the raw", straight from His mouth, so that He may make His full covenant with you.

וַיַּקְהֵל/פְּקוּדֵי

Vayakhel - And he assembled / P'kudei - Accounts

Shemot / Exodus 35:1 - 40:37

- in leap years, the two *parashiyot* are read separately; in regular years, they are read together -

רִאשׁוֹן	Aliyah One	Shemot/Exodus 35:1 - 29
שְׁלִישִׁי	Aliyah Three	Shemot/Exodus 37:17 - 29
רְבִיעִי	Aliyah Four	Shemot/Exodus 38:1 - 39:1
שִׁשִּׁי	Aliyah Six	Shemot/Exodus 39:22 - 43
שְׁבִיעִי	Aliyah Seven	Shemot/Exodus 40:1 - 38

וַיַּקְהֵל - Shemot/Exodus 35:1 - 38:20

שֵׁנִי	Aliyah Two	Shemot/Exodus 35:21 - 29
חֲמִשִׁי	Aliyah Five	Shemot/Exodus 36:20 - 37:16

פְקוּדֵי - Shemot/Exodus 38:21 - 38:20

שֵׁנִי	Aliyah Two	Shemot/Exodus 39:2 - 21
חֲמִשִׁי	Aliyah Five	Shemot/Exodus 40:1 - 16

וַיַּקְהֵל/פְּקוּדֵי א׳

Vayakhel - And he assembled / P'kudei - Accounts - 1

(In a leap year this could be read as Vayakhel 1)

Shemot / Exodus 35:1 - 29

Shemot/Exodus 35:1 And Moshe assembled the people of Isra'el

וַיַּקְהֵל מֹשֶׁה אֶת־כָּל־עֲדַת בְּנֵי יִשְׂרָאֵל

Yisra'el   b'ney   adat   kol   et   Moshe vayak'heyl

The *parasha* starts with an interesting word: וַיַּקְהֵל, *vayak'heyl*, translated as 'he assembled'. It is interesting because the spelling is *defectiva*: the consonants are correct for the *Qal* stem, but the basic *Qal* stem is never used in the *Torah* because it is impossible directly to gather people together, by hand, as it were, particularly not a group as large as the whole community of Israel. Rather, the verb is in the *hif'il* stem, whose normal spelling can be seen in Job 11:10 or B'Midbar 20:10. The *hif'il* stem is used to indicate cause - Moshe caused the people to gather together by speaking to them, in order to teach them. Moshe gave out instructions that the people were to assemble so that he could address them and the people gathered themselves together.

So it is that we find God Himself gathering together, or choosing, the people of Israel for a purpose: "But the Lord has taken you and brought you out of the iron furnace, from Egypt, to be a people for His own possession, as today" (D'varim 4:20, NASB). God has chosen and called out a people so that they might be His people, His own people, and so that He can have relationship with them. "And the Lord has today declared you to be His people, a treasured possession, as He promised you ... and that He shall set you high above all the nations which He has made, for praise, fame and honour, and that you shall be a consecrated people to the Lord your God" (D'varim 26:18-19, NASB). God has caused us, as a people, to exist and to be gathered together for and before Him, so that He would have a people of His very own, a chosen and special people set apart for Him.

When the time came for Him to be revealed, Yeshua the Messiah initially confirmed the call on our people, "Go to the lost sheep of Israel" (Matthew 10:6, NASB), but then extended the call to choose a remnant from the nations who would also be separate and set apart for Him: "Go therefore and make disciples of all nations" (Matthew 28:19, ESV). Rav Sha'ul confirms Yeshua's purpose when he writes, "[Yeshua] gave Himself for us, that He might redeem us from every lawless deed and purify for Himself a people for His own possession, zealous for good deeds" (Titus 2:14, NASB). Peter echoes this in his letter to those in the *Diaspora*: "you are a chosen race, a royal priesthood, a holy nation, a people for God' own possession, that you may proclaim the excellence of Him who has called you out of darkness into His marvellous light; for you once were not a people, but now you are the people of God" (1 Peter 2:9-10, NASB). God has done something that is impossible for man to do - He has called together and assembled a people from all nations, tribes and tongues to be His holy people, a part of His body, in these days.

Further Study: Shemot 34:8-9; Ephesians 1:13-14

Application: Thank God today that He has gathered you, made you a part of His remnant in Messiah Yeshua and is gathering His people from all over the world as One New Man in Yeshua.

וַיַּקְהֵל ב׳

Vayakhel - And he assembled - 2

(In an ordinary year this could be read as Vayekhel/Pekudei 1)

Shemot / Exodus 35:21 - 29

Shemot/Exodus 35:21 Every man came whose heart lifted him

וַיָּבֹאוּ כָּל־אִישׁ אֲשֶׁר־נְשָׂאוֹ לִבּוֹ

libo n'sao'o asher iysh kol vayavo'u

This phrase starts the recounting of the building of the *Mishkan*, with the various contributions coming from those who wanted to give - a voluntary offering. In *parasha Terumah* God told Moshe to take up a collection from the people, but that he was only to "accept a contribution form anyone who wholeheartedly wants to give" (Shemot 25:2, CJB). Now at the start of the giving, we hear of those who came to give: those whose hearts lifted them - those who were inspired, motivated from the heart. The Sages saw the heart as the seat of the emotions, the persona, the real person as opposed to the brain, where the intellect or reasoning was seen to dwell. God spoke into and gave conviction to the heart. Consequently, the heart was the centre of the being, the motivator; if you wanted to do something then you would find a way. All appeals were made to the heart, for if the heart was swayed, then the rest of the body would follow.

In the scroll of Jeremiah, we find the Lord speaking about the human heart: "The heart is more deceitful than all else and is desperately sick; who can understand it? I, the Lord, search the heart, I test the mind, even to give each man according to his ways" (Jeremiah 17:9-10, NASB). This gloomy assessment seems to be echoed in the words of Yeshua: "For from within, out of the heart of men, proceed the evil thoughts, fornications, thefts, murders, adulteries, acts of coveting and wickedness, as well as deceit, sensuality, envy, strife, pride and foolishness" (Mark 7:21-22, NASB). What a contrast with the generous hearts among our people who gave so much for the building of the *Mishkan* that they had to be told to stop.

Yeshua told the well-known story of the sower who went out to sow and then explained to his *talmidim* how the story worked. Luke's record tells us, "those beside the road are those who have heard; then the devil comes and takes away the word from their heart, so that they do not believe and be saved" (Luke 8:12, NASB). Then, after the rocky soil and those crowded by thorns, the good soil represents those "who have heard the word in an honest and good heart and hold fast and bear fruit with perseverance" (v. 15, NASB). It would seem that our heart attitude is the key to understanding this. It isn't a matter of what we know, what we understand, what we can prove or reason out, but how we respond in the very depths of our being - from our hearts - to God that makes the difference. The Puritan divines waxed lyrical about the dangers of an unrepentant or unregenerate heart. As Rav Sha'ul straightforwardly said, "If you confess with your mouth that Yeshua is Lord and believe in your heart that God raised Him from the dead, you shall be saved" (Romans 10:9, NASB). Where the heart leads, the mouth follows.

Further Study: Matthew 15:15-20; Matthew 12:33-37

Application: Where is your heart today? Do you rejoice in God and bring Him an acceptable sacrifice from a heart that is open and generous towards Him, or are you not yet at that place?

וַיַּקְהֵל ה׳

Vayakhel - And he assembled - 5

(In an ordinary year this could be read as Vayekhel/Pekudei 2)

Shemot / Exodus 36:20 - 37:16

Shemot/Exodus 36:22 So he did for all the beams of the tabernacle

כֵּן עָשָׂה לְכֹל קַרְשֵׁי הַמִּשְׁכָּן:

ha'Mishkan kar'shey l'chol asah keyn

We are now in the portion of the *Torah* that describes the building of the tabernacle by Betzalel and Oholiav, leading a team of artisans and craftsmen. It is an almost verbatim repetition of God's instructions given in previous chapters, substituting "he did" for "you shall do". It is also one of the sparser areas for the commentators, most of whom let the text go by with just the occasional comment about a wording or order difference between the instruction and its fulfillment. Nachmanides comments to the whole section that, "All this repetition is an affectionate and distinctive way to say that God took pleasure in the work, and mentioned it in His *Torah* many times to multiply the reward for those engaged in it." Certainly for several complete chapters, pride of place is given to Betzalel, so that apart from the occasional comment that everything was done "as Adonai had commanded Moshe" (Shemot 39:7, 21, 26, etc.), all the action is focused on the craft team.

This particular text comes at the conclusion of the making of the first plank or board for the tabernacle, "fifteen feet long and two-and-a-quarter feet wide" (36:21, CJB). In the following verses, up to verse 30, Betzalel is to make 48 planks in all: 20 for the south side, 20 for the north side, 6 for the west side and two extra to reinforce the corners. Forty eight planks, all exactly the same, but of very plain and simple design, is quite a lengthy and not very exciting job for a master craftsman; there is very little scope for imaginative design skills or innovative decoration and finishing in 48 identical wooden planks which are, in any case, about to be overlaid with gold. Perhaps that is why the text emphasises the detail of Betzalel's work - even though repetitive and relatively mundane - he finishes the job without comment or complaint, to the exacting standards of both Moshe - his line-manager - and the Lord Himself.

Shortly before the destruction of Solomon's temple, when Jerusalem was - as it were - living on borrowed time after Nebuchadnezzar had reduced the kingdom of Judah to a client state and left Zedekiah as a vassal king, Jeremiah wrote to the first wave of exiles who had been taken to Babylon, the artisans and craftsmen, the merchants, the wealthy aristocracy, priests and civil servants. In the letter, Jeremiah urges the exiles to "Build houses and plan to stay. Plant gardens and eat the food you produce. Marry and have children. Then find spouses for them and have many grandchildren" (Jeremiah 29:5-6, NLT). God is giving the people a long-term charge to stay where they (now) are, to build new lives as a people in exile, to be a witness for Him there. Babylon is to be their home - there has been a Jewish community in Babylon and its successor, Baghdad until modern times - and they are to get on with the work there. God warns them, "'Do not let the prophets and mediums who are there in Babylon trick you. Do not listen to their dreams because they prophecy lies in My name. I have not sent them,' says the Lord. 'The truth is that you will be in Babylon for seventy years. But then I will come...'" (29:8-10, NLT). "Rabbi Tarfon said, 'You are not required to complete the task, yet you are not free to withdraw from it'" (*m.* Pirkei Avot 2:21); the job goes on and we each have our part to play in advancing the work of the Kingdom of God, even though we do not necessarily see the fruit of our labours.

We find Yeshua saying similar things to His *talmidim* as He sends them out to preach and teach in the towns and villages of the Galil: "Truly I say to you, you shall not finish going through the cities of Israel until the Son of Man comes" (Matthew 10:23, NASB). Although He was sending them out in a local sense, as His representatives while He Himself was still teaching in the same cities (cf. Matthew 11:1), He was alerting them to the size and magnitude of the task of the kingdom: they would not finish it in their lifetimes, but they were to do their part in that work while they could. Interestingly, it is in recent years that we have seen the kingdom advancing again among God's ancient people; one of the "signs of the times" that warns us of the approach of Yeshua again. How amazed Peter, John and James would have been to think that it would be two millenia before Yeshua returned. How puzzled Rav Sha'ul, who wrote "For you yourselves know full well that the day of the Lord will come just like a thief in the night" (1 Thessalonians 5:2, NASB) to one of the early churches, would be to find we are still waiting for that "day of the Lord" to come, hundreds of generations after he wrote.

Although making boards for the tabernacle might not be the most exciting job, it had to be finished off properly, or the tabernacle would not stand correctly. Betzalel had to start, continue and finish the task. Yeshua asked, "Who is the faithful and sensible servant whose master puts him in charge of the household staff, to give them their food at the proper time? It will go well with that servant if he is found doing his job when his master comes" (Matthew 24:45-46, CJB). In the parallel passage in Luke's gospel, Yeshua goes a little further: "Happy the slave whom the master finds alert when he comes! Yes! I tell you that he will put on his work clothes, seat them at the table and come serve them himself! Whether it is late at night or early in the morning, if this is how he finds them, those slaves are happy" (Luke 12:37-38, CJB).

Further Study: Matthew 16:27-28; Mark 13:9-13

Application: Are you making planks for the tabernacle? Do you have a job that the Lord has given you and, although not high profile or glamorous, you know it needs to be done; that - so to speak - the Lord depends on you? Now is the time to persist, to be sure that you move steadily on with the work, even if the end is not in sight, so that you may be ready when He comes and be found faithfully engaged in His business.

וַיַּקְהֵל/פְּקוּדֵי ׳ג

Vayakhel - And he assembled / P'kudei - Accounts - 3

(In a leap year this could be read as Vayakhel 6)

Shemot / Exodus 37:17 - 29

Shemot/Exodus 37:17,22 And he made the menorah ... all of her beaten of one pure gold

וַיַּעַשׂ אֶת־הַמְּנֹרָה ... כֻּלָּהּ מִקְשָׁה אַחַת זָהָב

zahav   akhat   mik'shah   koolah ...   ham'norah   et   vaya'as

טָהוֹר
tahor

    As said previously, the commentators are almost universally silent for several chapters during this *parasha*, which relates the building of the *Mishkan* and the construction of all its furniture, decorations and utensils. Many people have suggested that this report section is really very similar to the instruction section several chapters earlier, so that it is not necessary to re-comment on material that has already been covered. In doing so, however, it is all too easy to miss the singular event that is inserted between the command and its fulfillment: the incident of the Golden Calf.

    The Hebrew word used for the construction of the *menorah*, מִקְשָׁה, comes from the root קָשָׁה, which means "to be hard, harsh, severe or difficult". The various nouns and adjectives that are derived from that root imply something that is hard or unyielding, difficult, stubborn or even obstinate. The masculine noun מִקְשֶׁה means a wreathing or plaiting of the hair and is seen in Isaiah 3:24 - "instead of well-set hair, a plucked out scalp" (NASB). The noun used here is feminine and is deemed to mean a piece of turned work. Gesenius relates it to the Arabic קָשָׁא, which means to take off bark, especially by turning. But what does all that add to the picture? Isn't it obvious from the description of the *menorah*, with all its cups, flowers, petals and stems, that it would be extremely difficult to make from one piece of gold, however pure?

The Golden Calf incident, a clear example of *avodah zorah* (strange, forbidden worship) before the ink on the covenant document was even dry, caused a major rupture in the relationship between God and our people. It was repaired at the cost of 3,000 lives, Moshe offering to be blotted out of the covenant and God at first refusing to accompany the people into the Land. Yet only in the next *parasha* (i.e. this *parasha*), we find the construction of the *Mishkan* proceeding exactly as God originally prescribed. God's purposes were greater than and outlived the breakdown; His instructions survived and persisted over the hiatus. God forgave the people their sin - although there were clearly consequences that needed to be faced - and re-commissioned them with a fresh set of tablets, witnessing to the covenant. So the *menorah* was hard work to craft; as the unity among the people was hard to produce; the material of the *menorah* was stubborn and unyielding as the heart of the people could be.

God wanted to heal the wound; He wanted to re-commission the people and He is still in the 'restart' business today. After the stunning victory over the priests of Ba'al at Mt. Carmel, Elijah ran away when threatened by Jezebel, Ahab's queen; he was met at Mt. Horeb by *HaShem* and re-commissioned to finish the job, because there was still work to do. Peter, after he had denied Yeshua three times was met on the sea-shore and re-commissioned by Yeshua in his role of apostle and leader, because he still had work to do.

Further Study: 1 Kings 19:9-18; John 21:15-22

Application: Have you slipped up, or deliberately sinned, causing a relationship breakdown between you and God? If so, then know that God wants to repair that relationship; He can forgive your sin - no matter how great - in Yeshua, and wants to re-commission you in the service of the kingdom. For there is work to be done and you are the one to do it.

וַיַּקְהֵל/פְּקוּדֵי 'ד

Vayakhel - And he assembled / P'kudei - Accounts - 4

(In a leap year this could be read as Vayakhel 7)

Shemot / Exodus 38:1 - 39:1

Shemot/Exodus 38:1 And he made the altar of the burnt offering of acacia wood

וַיַּעַשׂ אֶת־מִזְבַּח הָעֹלָה עֲצֵי שִׁטִּים
shittiym atzey ha'olah miz'bakh et vaya'as

In describing this detail from the narrative of the construction of the tabernacle and all its furniture, the text uses two cultic technical terms: altar and burnt offering. מִזְבֵּחַ, altar, here with its vowels shortened in construct form, is derived from the root זָבַח, to slaughter - most often for sacrifice, sometimes for eating (see 2 Chronicles 18:2), also in divine judgement (Ezekiel 3:17-19, 2 Kings 23:20) - so that the altar is defined as the place for sacrificial slaughter. Altars were built by many biblical characters and in many places: Noah; Avraham at Shechem, Bethel and Hevron; Yitz'khak at Beer Sheva; Ya'akov at Shechem and Bethel; Moshe at Rephidim and Horev; and many others. This matches the command given to Moshe: "You shall make an altar of earth for me ... in every place where I cause My name to be remembered ... you shall not build it of cut stones ... and you shall not go up by steps to My altar" (Shemot 20:24-26, NASB) - multiple altars, made of earth or uncut stone, without steps. By the time Israel is about to enter the land, that freedom has narrowed, "But you shall seek the Lord at the place which the Lord your God shall choose from all your tribes, to establish His name there for His dwelling, and there you shall come, and there you shall bring your burnt offerings, your sacrifices, your tithes ..." (D'varim 12:5-6, NASB), to be just one place, and sacrifice is forbidden away from that one place.

עֹלָה, burnt offering, here preceded by the definite article הָ, comes from the root עָלָה, to go up, ascend or climb, which is also the origin of the word 'aliyah' to go up - immigrate - to the Land, or to go up to the *bimah* (or platform) in synagogue. The burnt offering then, is the offering that goes up, because it is entirely consumed in flames on the altar and it arises as a fragrant aroma before the Lord (B'Midbar 28:2) as the priest makes it go up as smoke upon the altar (Vayikra 1:9,13,17).

Given the precision and quantity of the instructions given in the *Torah* concerning the various sacrifices, the places and occasions where and when they should be offered, and the way in which this is to be done, how should we relate to this manifestly important part of God's relationship with our people? How, as believers in Messiah Yeshua, who the Scriptures tell us changes not (Hebrews 13:8), and "the Father of lights with whom there is no variation or shadow due to change" (James 1:17, ESV), do we respond to this clear call for sacrifice? The rabbis of the *Talmud* struggled with the obvious fact that God had allowed the Temple - the place of sacrifice - to be destroyed and concluded, since the commands to bring sacrifice were given as a permanent ordinance throughout our generations, that there must be another way to do this. They put these words in God's mouth: "When Israel recites the Scriptural order of the offerings, I will consider it as if they had brought the sacrifices and I will forgive their sins" (*b*. Megillah 31*a*). Also, "Rav Yitz'chak said: The *Torah* writes 'this is the Torah of the sin offering' (Vayikra 6:18) to imply that whoever involves himself in the study of the sin offering is regarded as if he had actually brought a sin offering" (*b*. Menachot 110*a*). So the morning prayer service includes reading passages from the *Torah* that deal with the washing in the laver, the removal of the ashes, the daily burnt offering and the incense to substitute for the physical daily offerings prescribed, but no longer possible, in Shemot 29:38-46.

As New Covenant believers we recognise Yeshua as our sin offering: "we have been separated for God and made holy, once and for all, through the offering of Yeshua the Messiah's body" (Hebrews 10:10, CJB), but the requirement for sacrifice remains. Rav Sha'ul writes, "I exhort you, therefore, brothers, in view of God's mercies, to offer yourselves as a sacrifice, living and set apart for God. This will please Him; it is the logical 'Temple worship' for you" (Romans 12:1, CJB). How do we do this? Rav Sha'ul tells the Philippians, "I have received from Epaphroditus the gifts you sent - they are a fragrant aroma, an acceptable sacrifice, one that pleases God well" (Philippians 4:18, CJB). In John's vision we read, "Another angel ... was given a large quantity of incense to add to the prayers of all God's people on the gold altar in front of the throne. The smoke of the incense went up with the prayers of God's people from the hand of the angel before God" (Revelation 8:3-4, CJB).

Further Study: Ephesians 5:1-4; Mark 12:32-33

Application: How will you respond to God's call for sacrifice in your life? That call is different and yet the same for all of us, whether in material things, money, time or prayer, service and worship. What matters is finding out what is pleasing to God in your life and giving it wholeheartedly to Him.

פְקוּדֵי 'ב

P'kudei - Accounts - 2

(In an ordinary year this could be read as Vayekhel/Pekudei 5)

Shemot / Exodus 39:2 - 21

Shemot/Exodus 39:2 ... gold, silver, and purple and scarlet yarn and twisted linen

זָהָב תְּכֵלֶת וְאַרְגָּמָן וְתוֹלַעַת שָׁנִי וְשֵׁשׁ

v'sheysh shaniy   v'tola'at   v'ar'gaman t'cheylet   zahav

מָשְׁזָר:

mash'zar

    The Bavli Talmud explains how the various threads and yarns in this colour mixture were combined in groups of six, eighteen and twenty four, and how the gold was beaten thinly into a sheet then then cut up into threads and woven into the strands of yarn (*b.* Yoma 72*a*). The blending was perfect, according to a precise formula which prescribed the exact numbers of each coloured thread and the amount of gold to be included as the groups of threads were woven and re-combined. Great care was taken with the handling and presentation of the materials that the people had given to the Lord for the building of the *Mishkan*, its furniture and the official clothing of the High Priest.

    Neither were these materials cheap or common place. The *techelet* blue is the same colour that was used as a single thread in the *tzitzit*, or fringes, worn on the corners of every four-cornered garment (B'Midbar 15:38); made from a mollusc, this colour has been lost for over a thousand years and has only recently been rediscovered. Purple was a colour only worn by the very rich throughout the ancient world because of the cost of the dyes and dying process. Scarlet, sometimes translated crimson, was a very strong and permanent dye extracted from the 'tola' worm, which is why it is used by the prophet Isaiah as picture of sin: "though your sins are as scarlet, they will be white as snow" (Isaiah 1:18, NASB). Finely twisted white linen took a long time to prepare and weave, combing out all the woody stems and seeds of the flax plant to get the clean white fibres to spin the thread. Gold has always had value and was the most costly of the precious metals known in biblical times.

The people in the desert brought of their very best for the "freewill offering from the heart" for the *Mishkan* and all its accoutrements. Then they gave again of their skills in building, carving, weaving and assembling these materials into a structure and garments that were to reflect the glory of God in their midst. We see the same dedication, design and craftsmanship in the synagogues and cathedrals of the Middle Ages - buildings which still defy the skills of modern architects in their intricate design and sheer lofty grandeur - dedicated to the glory of God.

How much more then should we today offer of our best to God, presenting it the best and most effective way to reflect His glory and bring Him pleasure. Rav Sha'ul wrote: "I exhort you, therefore, brothers, in view of God's mercies to offer yourselves as a sacrifice, living and set apart for God. This will please Him; it is the logical 'Temple worship' for you" (Romans 12:1, CJB).

Further Study: Malachi 1:6-14; 1 Corinthians 11:20-22

Application: How do you view what we are and bring to God, be it ever so much or ever so little? What care do we take as stewards over what is His while it is in our charge? Resolve today to give Him the very best you have - yourself - and keep it in spotless condition for Him always.

וַיַּקְהֵל/פְּקוּדֵי ו׳

Vayakhel - And he assembled / P'kudei - Accounts - 6

(In a leap year this could be read as Pekudei 4)

Shemot / Exodus 39:22 - 43

Shemot/Exodus 39:33 And they brought the Mishkan to Moshe

וַיָּבִיאוּ אֶת־הַמִּשְׁכָּן אֶל־מֹשֶׁה

Moshe   el   hamishkan   et   vayaviyu

On the surface, this seems a perfectly normal concluding step to the preparation and construction of the Tabernacle. The previous verse says that, "all the work of the Tabernacle of the Tent of Meeting was completed; and the sons of Israel did according to all that the Lord had commanded Moshe; so they did" (Shemot 39:32, NASB). What could be more natural than to bring everything that they had made to Moshe for his approval before moving on with the next step? The following verses summarise all the different classes of components and furniture that had been made and prepared, almost repeating verse 32 as verse 42: "So the sons of Israel did all the work according to all that the Lord had commanded Moshe" (NASB). Finally, the section ends with a record of Moshe examining all the work and agreeing that they had done it all correctly, before blessing the people and the craftsmen.

Nevertheless, that narrative does not satisfy a number of the commentators who want to know why the workmen did not assemble the Tabernacle before calling in Moshe to do the final assessment. Would it not have been more fitting, they imply, for Moshe to have inspected the fully erected Tabernacle and be sure that it did assemble correctly and see with his own eyes that all the pieces did fit together and were accurately balanced? Presumably the craftsmen had in fact assembled parts of the Tabernacle before, as they were making it, to check the fit and precision of their work! Rashi comments, "And they brought the *Mishkan*: because they were unable to erect it ... for no man was able to erect it because of the weight of its beams." He then cites a *midrash* that has Moshe miming the erection of the Tabernacle while the beams and pillars miraculously lift themselves into place (Tanchuma 11). Rashi concludes, "this is the meaning of הוּקַם הַמִּשְׁכָּן - "the Mishkan was set up" (Shemot 40:17, later); it was set up on its own". The later use of a passive verb, *Hof'al* affix, allows the commentators to consider that no human hands were involved.

Nechama Leibowitz takes the argument another stage. Quoting the Alshikh, who said: "In the construction of the Tabernacle the Israelites were not even expert in the work, which was executed miraculously of its own accord through Divine Providence", she comments, "This principle may, however, be said to apply equally to every performance mentioned in the *Torah* since we know that man can accomplish nothing by himself but only by the grace of God, as it is stated: 'But you shall remember the Lord your God, for it is He who is giving you power to make wealth!' (Devarim 8:18, NASB)". Although Leibowitz considers the latter reference to be given in the context of "the every day tasks of field and vineyard", she nevertheless extends the argument to cover every activity in which mankind is involved, from the smallest personal action to big, formal, corporate plans and events. This position is, of course, strongly echoed by the more conservative church commentators who also see - based upon different premises and verses - a complete dependence on God's grace for man to do or accomplish anything.

We can see the same principle at work in the story of the feeding of the five thousand in Matthew's gospel. As the story starts, the people have been with Yeshua most of the day and He has been healing whoever was sick among the crowd. As evening starts to draw in, the *talmidim* come to Yeshua and, pointing out that it is both late and a remote place, ask Him to dismiss the crowd so that they can go and get food in the local villages. Unexpectedly, Yeshua responds by telling the *talmidim* to feed the people themselves, right there. This confuses the disciples: "'All we have with us,' they said, 'is five loaves of barley and two fish'" (Matthew 14:17, CJB). As if that would feed more than a few of the huge crowd (see v. 14)! But Yeshua is not disconcerted: "He said, 'Bring them here to Me'" (v.18, CJB), and after telling the people to sit down on the grass, He makes the normal blessing "... *hamotzi lechem min ha'aretz* - who brings forth bread from the earth", breaks the bread and calmly tells the *talmidim* to hand it round to everyone. In something of an understatement, Matthew dryly comments that "They all ate as much as they wanted, and they took up twelve baskets full of the pieces left over. Those eating numbered five thousand men, plus women and children" (vv. 20-21, CJB). Setting aside the interesting question of where the twelve baskets came from to collect the left-overs, or the sound ecological principle of picking up the left-overs rather than just leaving them lying about on the ground, we have the astounding fact that a crowd approaching ten thousand in number had all been fed to surfeit from five loaves and two fishes. Either the disciples had hurriedly run a human supply chain into the local villages and bought up every loaf to be found for a thirty mile radius, or a very open and public miracle had been performed. The miracle actually sounds the more credible of the options!

The process here started with two phrases: "All we have is five loaves and two fishes" and "Bring them here to Me". God used the same principle 600-700 years earlier when the widow of Zaraphat had to give her last small loaf of bread and a cup of water to Elijah before the pot of meal and the cruise of oil became never-ending (1 Kings 17:8-15). So it is with the Israelites in our text from the *Torah*: they had to bring what they had to Moshe, God's appointed agent of the moment, for approval and acceptance, before the miracle of assembly took place. Exactly the same principle applies in our lives: if we want to see miracles wrought in our midst, if we want to see dramatic growth in the Kingdom of God, if we truly long to see God glorified in our everyday lives, then we have to bring everything to Him; we have to hand it over and wait to see what He will do, trusting that He wastes nothing and that His word never returns to Him void without accomplishing what He has determined (Isaiah 55:11).

Further Study: B'Midbar 11:21-23; Proverbs 10:22

Application: Do you long to see God moving in your life and affecting those around you? Then the time has come to bring everything that you have to Him and lay it down before Him so that He can work the miracle today.

פְּקוּדֵי 'ה

P'kudei - Accounts - 5

(In an ordinary year this could be read as Vayekhel/Pekudei 7)

Shemot / Exodus 40:1 - 16

Shemot/Exodus 40:2 In the day of the first month, in the first of the month, you shall raise up the Tabernacle

בְּיוֹם־הַחֹדֶשׁ הָרִאשׁוֹן בְּאֶחָד לַחֹדֶשׁ תָּקִים

takiym la'khodesh b'ekhad   ha'rishon ha'khodesh b'yom

אֶת־מִשְׁכַּן

mish'kan   et

Moshe is told to erect the tabernacle himself, since he is the only person who has seen the vision of the heavenly tabernacle shown to him on Mt. Sinai - he alone knows the exact position and sequence of all the elements. Moreover, he is told to erect the tabernacle on the first day of the year, two weeks short of the first anniversary of the Exodus from Egypt and nine months since arriving at Sinai. The phrase "in the first month" ties up with the instructions given to Moshe before the Exodus itself: "This month shall be the beginning of months for you; it is to be the first month of the year to you" (Shemot 12:2, NASB); Gersonides confirms: "Nisan makes more sense as the beginning of the year than does Tishrei, for at that time the sun moves closer to inhabited areas, plants and fruit are renewed and all life rejoices."

A recurring theme within Judaism is that of the lunar cycle being a reminder that repentance and renewal are always available. As the new moon faithfully re-appears each cycle, so man can always turn to God and experience a "new moon" in his spiritual life. Similarly, the waxing and waning of the moon is seen as a demonstration that just as God restores or revives the moon, so He will give revival and restoration for the low points in our lives if we will turn to Him. Hirsch looks back to the Exodus, commenting that it was the new moon that hung in the sky to announce the birth of our people as a nation and our freedom from slavery in Egypt, starting the calendar, the year and the month. How appropriate, he continues, that the formal erection and inauguration of the tabernacle should be on the same new moon in the calendar, exactly one year later. "The new moon of the arising of the nation is to be also the new moon of the entry of the Shechinah, the fulfillment of 'I will dwell among them' in which the natural redemption first finds its completion."

While Moshe was given the responsibility of raising the tabernacle for the first time, and the priests and Levites would pack, transport and re-assemble the tabernacle on a sometimes daily basis as our people travelled, this process was itself a sign of what God Himself was going to do with the people over the centuries that followed. As we moved into the Land, went through periods of rebellion and revival, through exile and return, so God Himself would pack up, move and then restore the people. So it continues to today, through two millennia of exile, expulsion, pogrom, interspersed with times of study, peace and prosperity until it is time to move on again. From the golden days of the Spanish era before the expulsion in 1492, to the *yeshivot* of Old Europe before the *Sho'ar*, the people of Israel have always been a sign to the nations of God's presence in the world. Neither is that process yet complete for God says, "'In that day I will raise up the fallen tabernacle of David, and wall up its breaches; I will also raise up its ruins, and rebuild it as in the days of old; that they may possess the remnant of Edom and all the nations who are called by My name', declares the Lord who does this" (Amos 9:11-12, NASB). This is to be both a physical action, with the partial and as yet imperfect restoration of Israel as a nation in its own land with Jerusalem as its capital, living in peace and harmony; it is also to be a spiritual action, then the nation turning to God on a previously unimagined scale, restoring the spiritual fortunes of Israel declaring not a narrow exclusiveness but the glory of God to the world.

How do we know this is going to happen? How can we be sure that God is still interested? Because of the critical step in the process that we just skipped over. During His earthly ministry, Yeshua made it clear to the disciples what was going to happen to Him: "He began teaching them that the Son of Man had to endure much suffering and be rejected by the elders, the head cohanim and the Torah-teachers; and that He had to be put to death; but that after three days, He had to rise again. He spoke very plainly about it" (Mark 8:31-32, CJB). So widely known was this teaching that immediately after the crucifixion and Yeshua's burial, "the head cohanim and the P'rushim went together to Pilate and said, 'Sir, we remember that that deceiver said while He was still alive, "After three days I will be raised." Therefore, order that the grave be made secure until the third day; otherwise the talmidim may come, steal Him away and say to the people, "He was raised from the dead"; and the last deception will be worse than the first'" (Matthew 27:62-64, CJB). In spite of their precautions, of course, Yeshua did rise from the dead for Rav Sha'ul tells us: "He was raised on the third day, in accordance with what the Tanakh says; and He was seen by Peter, then by the Twelve; and afterwards He was seen by more than five hundred brothers at one time, the majority of whom are still alive. Later He was seen by James, then by all the emissaries; and last of all He was seen by me" (1 Corinthians 15:4-7, CJB). It is because He Himself rose from the dead that we can have faith in His promise to us: "Yes, this is the will of the Father: that all who see the Son and trust in Him should have eternal life, and that I should raise them up on the Last Day" (John 6:40, CJB). This promise is for us, for Israel and for all who believe in Him.

Further Study: Isaiah 60:1-3; Malachi 4:2

Application: Where have you put your trust? Are you trusting in the work of your hand, the building that you have erected by your own labour, or are you trusting in the promises of God, knowing that the building He erects will last forever?

וַיַּקְהֵל/פְּקוּדֵי ז׳

Vayakhel - And he assembled / P'kudei -
Accounts - 7

(In a leap year, this could be read as Pekudei 5)

Shemot / Exodus 40:1 - 38

Shemot/Exodus 40:2 In the day of the first month, on the first of the month, you shall establish the Tabernacle, the Tent of Meeting.

בְּיוֹם־הַחֹדֶשׁ הָרִאשׁוֹן בְּאֶחָד לַחֹדֶשׁ תָּקִים
takiym lakhodesh b'ekhad ha'rishon hakhodesh b'yom

אֶת־מִשְׁכַּן אֹהֶל מוֹעֵד:
mo'eyd ohel Mishkan et

The phrase בְּיוֹם־הַחֹדֶשׁ הָרִאשׁוֹן - literally: in the day of the month, the first - seems an awkward way to start this series of instructions from *HaShem* to Moshe. Which month is being described here? Is it the biblical month of Aviv, designated as the first month of the year in Shemot chapter 12, now called Nisan in the Jewish calendar, or is it the month of Tishrei to line up with the rabbinic idea of the creation of the world? The Sages seem to reach consensus here that it is Aviv, just a twelvemonth after the Exodus from Egypt and nine months after the theophany at Mt. Sinai, while our people are still encamped at the mountain. The next phrase, the two words בְּאֶחָד לַחֹדֶשׁ - literally: in the first to the month - is taken to mean the day of *Rosh Chodesh*, the New Moon; a fortnight short of one year after the night of the Exodus itself.

There is also some debate over the context of the word תָּקִים - *Hif'il*, prefix, 2ms, in *Qal* "to rise, rise up, flourish, prosper", in *Hif'il* "to set up, establish, make to stand". The meaning seems clear enough: *HaShem* is telling Moshe to put up the Tabernacle. The debate is over how often Moshe did this during the inauguration week of Aharon and his sons. Was it just the once and, once up, it stayed up for the week; or was it seven times, each morning, taking it down again at night; and, if the latter, was it just once a day or several times each day for the three times of sacrifice, so as to demonstrate exactly how it was done and where the pieces went? There is general agreement that the day being spoken of here is at the end of that week, so that either way this would have been the last time that Moshe erected the Tabernacle before it was handed over into the care of the *cohanim* - the priests - and the Levites.

The last question that is commonly asked about this text is why it is necessary at all. It is followed by a detailed list of the components of the Tabernacle and its furniture - hadn't Moshe commissioned and overseen their building and, in just the previous verses, officially received and checked them before blessing the craftsmen? Why should *HaShem* now need to tell Moshe to put them up? Nahum Sarna suggests that "He personally is charged with this task because the entire enterprise is based on a celestial image or prototype that had been shown to Moshe on Mt. Sinai. Hence, he alone possesses a mental image of the completed whole." Again, here we have a hint at the idea of Moshe teaching the priests and Levites where everything goes so that they will get it right when they become responsible for the building up and taking down of the Tabernacle on a regular basis, but we are still left unclear why *HaShem* found it necessary to walk Moshe himself through the instructions all over again.

Step forward to an event in the gospels. Yeshua and three of the *talmidim* have been up a mountain, experiencing Yeshua's transfiguration; they come down to rejoin the others and "as they came up to the crowd, a man approached Yeshua, kneeled down in front of him, and said, 'Sir, have mercy on my son, because he is an epileptic and has such terrible fits that he often falls into the fire or into the water. I brought him to your talmidim, but they couldn't heal him'" (Matthew 17:14-16, CJB). What is this all about? Why is there an issue? Hadn't Yeshua given the disciples authority to handle this sort of thing? The text certainly seems to say so: "Calling together the Twelve, Yeshua gave them power and authority to expel all the demons and to cure diseases; and he sent them out to proclaim the Kingdom of God and to heal" (Luke 9:1-2, CJB; cf. Matthew 10:1). Yeshua calmly deals with the situation, casting a demon out of the man's son so that he is healed. Then we get the anxious debrief: "The talmidim went to him privately and said, 'Why couldn't we drive it out?'" (Matthew 17:19, CJB). There were still nine of them there, only three had gone up the mountain with Yeshua; wasn't that enough? Besides, they had been out and done this sort of thing before on their own, both as twelve and even seventy. Luke tells us that, "The seventy came back jubilant. 'Lord,' they said, 'with your power, even the demons submit to us!'" (Luke 10:17, CJB), so much so that Yeshua replies, "I saw Satan fall like lightning from heaven" (v. 18, CJB), rejoicing that the powers of the enemy have been impacted by the disciples' faith and actions. Yet in the next breath He reminds them: "Remember, I have given you authority; so you can trample down snakes and scorpions, indeed, all the Enemy's forces; and you will remain completely unharmed" (v. 19, CJB). But isn't that just what they had been doing? Yeshua even starts with the word "remember"; He has already said this, but He is saying it again.

We miss something if we fail to see that the disciples - yes, the Apostles - were human and needed frequent reminders of their instructions and the gifts and authorities they had been given. Even after successful ministry trips all over the Galil, they still hadn't reached the full measure of faith. Here is Yeshua's answer to their question: "Because of your little faith. For truly, I say to you, if you have faith like a grain of mustard seed, you will say to this mountain, 'Move from here to there,' and it will move, and nothing will be impossible for you" (Matthew 17:20, ESV). Do we hear that? After between two and three years of ministry with the Master Teacher Himself, up hill and down dale, dragging all through the dust of the Galil, seeing Yeshua healing everyone who came to Him and casting out every demon, then being sent out to do the same themselves and bringing back a report that made Yeshua rejoice, still He rebukes them for their lack of faith. Just before He ascends into heaven, Yeshua reminds the disciples, "And these signs will accompany those who do trust: in My name they will drive out demons, speak with new tongues, not be injured if they handle snakes or drink poison, and heal the sick by laying hands on them" (Mark 16:17-18, CJB). This itself is a repeat of the words He used just a few weeks before in the run-up to the Last Supper: "I tell you that whoever trusts in me will also do the works I do! Indeed, he will do greater ones, because I am going to the Father" (John 14:12, CJB). Just like Moshe, the disciples needed to hear it time and again in order for it to become a confident part of their faith walk.

And what about us? Are we any different from the Apostles? We haven't had the advantage of three years personal full-time ministry training from Yeshua in the flesh; most of us haven't seen as many miracles in a lifetime as they saw in a week. Perhaps that is why Rav Sha'ul writes that, "And He gave the apostles, the prophets, the evangelists, the shepherds and teachers, to equip the saints for the work of ministry, for building up the body of Christ, until we all attain to the unity of the faith and of the knowledge of the Son of God, to mature manhood, to the measure of the stature of the fullness of Christ" (Ephesians 4:11-13, ESV); God gave the instructors, encouragers and leaders that He knew we would need if we were to measure up to the standard of Yeshua. That is why we need to keep on hearing words of encouragement and - where necessary - rebuke, to keep us steady in our walk. It is also why we need to keep putting our faith into practice, getting out there, getting our hands dirty, touching and healing people just as Yeshua did, and - yes - failing occasionally so that we learn to do it right. We depend on the Holy Spirit to empower us and show us who and how to touch, but we are the Tabernacle builders in this generation. Just as Moshe was told, "Now build the Tabernacle", we are told, "Now build My kingdom". The instructions are to hand, the people are watching to see how to do it, we have been given the parts and the authority; what are we waiting for?

Further Study: Acts 19:13-16; Romans 15:18-19

Application: From the very largest to the very smallest, everyone has a part to play. From the smallest bronze socket to the *menorah* or the *parochet* (curtain), every piece of the Tabernacle was essential to make it assemble correctly. Where are you in that process? What is your role? As you hear the call to build, seek God's directions for your life and get plugged in!

Biographies

Abravanel - Don Isaac Abravanel, 1437-1508, Statesman and biblical commentator; born in Lisbon, died in Venice; claimed descent from King David; wrote commentaries on the whole of the Hebrew Scriptures

Alshikh - Rabbi Moshe Alshikh, 1508-1600, spent most of his life in Safed, Israel; famous for his commentary on the *Torah*, which was a record of his popular *Shabbat* sermons

Ba'al HaTurim - Rabbi Yaakov ben Asher, 1269-1343, born in Cologne, Germany; lived for 40 years in and around Toledo, Spain; died *en route* to Israel; his commentary to the Chumash is based upon an abridgement of the Ramban, including Rashi and Ibn Ezra; it includes many references to *gematria* and textual novelties

Gersonides - Rabbi Levi ben Gershom, Gersonides or Ralbag, 1288-1344; famous rabbi, philosopher, mathematician and astronomer/astrologer; born at Bagnols in Languedock, France; wrote a commentary on the *Torah* and a parallel to Maimonides' *Guide For The Perplexed*

HaGriz - Rabbi Yitzchak Zev Soloveitchik, died 1959; also known as the Brisker Rav

Hirsch - Rabbi Samson Raphael Hirsch, 1808-1888, German rabbi of Frankfurt am Main, author and educator; staunch opponent of the Reform movement in Germany and one of the fathers of Orthodox Judaism

Ibn Ezra - Abraham Ibn Ezra, 1089-1167, born in Tudela, Spain; died in the South of France after wandering all around the shores of the Mediterranean and England; a philosopher, astronomer, doctor, poet and linguist; wrote a Hebrew grammar and a commentary on the Bible

Ibn Janah - Jonah Ibn Janah (c. 990 - c. 1050);a Spanish scholar famed as a Hebrew grammarian and lexicographer; his principal work was the two-volume *Book of Exact Investigation*, a Hebrew grammar and lexicon, written in Arabic

Nechama Leibowitz - 1905-1997, born in Riga, graduate of the University of Berlin, made *aliyah* in 1931; professor at Tel Aviv University; taught *Torah* for over 50 years

Rabbi Akiva - Akiva ben Joseph, c.50-c.135; one of the third generation of the Mishnaic Sages, who were active between 70 and 135; although starting life as an ignorant shepherd, he became perhaps the most central authority quoted in the Mishnah; known by some as the "father of the Rabbinic Judaism"

Rabbi Eliezer - Rabbi Eliezer ben Hyrcanus was one of the most prominent tannaim of the 1st and 2nd centuries, a disciple of Rabbi Johanan ben Zakkai and a colleague of Gamaliel II, whose sister he married

Rabbi Tarfon - one of the third generation of the Mishnaic Sages; actually served in the 2nd Temple and pronouned the Aaronic Benediction there; an adherent of the school of Shammai yet with a reputation for leniency

Rambam - Rabbi Moshe ben Maimon or Maimonedes, 1135-1204, Talmudist, philosopher, astronomer and physician; author of *Mishneh Torah*, Guide for the Perplexed and other works; a convinced rationalist

Ramban - Rabbi Moshe ben Nachman of Gerona or Nachmanides, 1194-1270, Spanish rabbi, author and physician; defended Judaism in the Christian debates in Barcelona before making *aliyah* to *Eretz Yisrael*

Rashbam - Rabbi Shmuel ben Meir, 1085-1158, born in Troyes, France; grandson of Rashi; his commentaries focus on the *p'shat* (plain) meaning of the text

Rashi - Rabbi Shlomo Yitzchaki, 1040-1105, French rabbi who wrote commentaries on the *Torah*, the Prophets and the *Talmud*, lived in Troyes where he founded a *yeshiva* in 1067; perhaps the best-known of all Jewish commentators; focuses on the plain meaning (*p'shat*) of the text, although sometimes quite cryptic in his brevity

Sa'adia Gaon - Sa'adis ben Yosef of Faym, 882/892 Egypt - 942 Bagdad; a prominent rabbi, Jewish philosopher, and exegete of the Geonic period

Sforno - Rabbi Ovadiah Sforno, 1470-1550, Italian rabbi, philosopher and physician; born in Cesena, he went to Rome to study medicine; left in 1525 and after some years of travel, settled in Bologna where he founded a *yeshiva* which he conducted until his death

Bibliography

Books by Author

Abraham Even-Shoshan, *A New Concordance of the Bible*, Kiryat Sefer Publishing House, Jerusalem 1988 (Hebrew only)

Benjamin Davidson, *The Analytical Hebrew and Chaldee Lexicon*, Samuel Bagster & Sons Ltd, London 1850

Brown, Driver and Briggs, *Hebrew and English Lexicon*, HoughtonMiflin and Company, Boston 1906

Israel Drazin & Stanley M Wagner, *Onkelos on the Torah - Exodus*, Gefen Publishing House, Jerusalem 2006

Michael W. Holmes, *The Apostlic Fathers - Greek Texts and English Translations*, 3rd edition, Baker Academic, Grand Rapids MI, 2007

Paul Jouon, T. Muraoka, *A Grammar of Biblical Hebrew*, Subsidia Biblica, Rome 2005

Nahum Sarna, *The JPS Torah Commentary - Exodus*, Jewish Publication Society, Philadephia 1989

Richard Elliott Friedman, *Commentary on the Torah*, Harper Collins, San Francisco 2003

Books by Title

Authorised Daily Prayer Book, New translation and Commentary by Chief Rabbi Dr. Lord Jonathan Sacks, Harper Collins, London 2006

Be'er Yitzkhak - a book of commentary and response by Rabbi Yitzchak Elchanan Spector, 1817-1896, the Rabbi of Kovno

Gesenius's Hebrew Grammar - Edited E.Kautzsch, Translated by A E Cowley, Oxford University Press, 1910

Gur Aryeh - A commentary by the Maharal on Rashi's *Torah* commentary

Mekhilta - The earliest known halakhic midrash or commentary on (parts of) the book of Exodus; formally named for Rabbi Ishmael and therefore set around 100-135CE, it was redacted some years after his time; quoted many times in the Bavli *Talmud* as "Rabbi Ishmael taught ..."

Midrash Rabbah - a collection of *aggadic* commentaries upon the *Torah* and some other books of the Bible most used in worship; different volumes have been collated in written form between the 4th and 13th centuries CE; they contain both very early oral material from the sages of the 1st and 2nd centuries and glosses and inserts down to the 1200s

Midrash Tanchuma - a collection of *midrashim* on the *Torah* collected and published in the ninth century

Mishnah - the collection of Jewish law and customs codified (collected and written down) under the auspices of Rabbi Judah the Prince around the year 200 CE

Pirkei Avot - literally "Chapters of the Fathers", although usually "Ethics of the Fathers"; one of the tractates of the *Mishnah* that includes many pithy proverb-like sayings attributed to the sages who contributed to the *Mishnah*

Septuagint - Also known simply as LXX, the Septuagint is a translation of the whole of the Hebrew Scriptures into Greek that was probably done during the 1st century BCE by members of the Jewish community in Alexandria to have the Scriptures in their "first" tongue; the quality is mixed - some parts, such as the *Torah*, were in frequent use and are quite well rendered, other parts were less used and the translation is rather patchy and shows signs of haste; it was widely deprecated by the early rabbis who generated the story of its being translated under threat of death by 70 Jewish scholars on the orders of Ptolemy

Shem Tov Matthean text - George Howard, *Hebrew Gospel of Matthew*, Mercer University Press, Macon GA, 1995. This is a set of Hebrew manuscripts for the Gospel of Matthew, traceable to a 14th century Spanish Jew, Shem Tov Ibn Shaprut. Its earlier provenance is unknown, but it clearly contains some very early portions of Hebrew text intermingled with mediaeval rabbinic accretions. Eusebius wrote in the 3rd century that the Jewish believers of his time had a version of Matthew's gospel in Hebrew; this is confirmed by Jerome, who writes of such a manuscript in the Alexandrian library, that he had consulted on a number of occasions. The Shem Tov manuscripts may contain original readings from this Hebrew Matthew or may simply be a slightly later translation of Matthew into Hebrew.

Shemot Rabbah - one of the components of the *Midrash Rabbah* collection (the Great Midrash), probably compiled around 1000-1100 CE from the oral teachings of any of the early sages - some named, some anonymous - with later glosses and references to other collections such as the Pesikta de Rab Kahana

Sifsei Chachamim - a super-commentary to Rashi's commentary on the Pentateuch; written by Shabbetai ben Joseph Bass, 1641-1718, an educated man and printer of Jewish books in Breslau

Talmud - literally, instruction or learning; the distilled writings of the early sages, a composite of the *Mishnah* and the *Gemarah* an extensive commentary to the *Mishnah*; two talmuds exist: the Jerusalem Talmud, from around 400-450, compiled in the Land of Israel; and the Babylonian Talmud, from around 550-600, compiled in the jewish communities in Babylon

Tanakh - the Hebrew Scriptures: *Torah* (Instructions/Law), *Nevi'im* (Prophets) and *Ketuvim* (Writings)

Vayikra Rabbah - one of the components of the *Midrash Rabbah* collection (the Great Midrash), probably compiled in Israel the 5th or 7th centuries CE from the oral teachings of any of the early sages - some named, some anonymous; makes reference to *B'resheet Rabbah*, the Pesikta de Rab Kahana and both the Jerusalem and Babylonian *Talmud*

Vulgate - a translation of both the Hebrew and greek Scriptures to Latin that was undertaken - at least in significant part - by Jerome between 382-405 CE; it was unusual in being a fresh translation from the best available Hebrew and Greek texts rather than working from the *Septuagint*; it does include some exegetical material and a rather paraphrased style

Yalqut Shimeoni - a compilation of older *aggadic* on most of the books of the Hebrew Bible; probably produced in the early part of the 13th century CE, possibly by Rabbi Simeon Kara who lived in Southern Germany

Glossary

acharit hayamim - literally, the last days

Adonai - literally, "My Lord" or "My Master"; although appearing in the Hebrew text as a word in its own right, widely used as a elusive synonym to avoid pronouncing the tetragrammaton - יהוה - ineffable or covenant name of God; where this appears in a text, and is being read in a worship context, it will be pronounced as *Adonai*

Af'el - the causitive voice of Aramaic verbs, corresponding to the Hebrew *Hif'il*

Amidah - The Standing Prayer, see *Shemoneh Esrei*

anthropomorphism - ascribing human qualities - emotions, attributes or physical characteristics - to God or an inanimate object

Aramaic - a member of the Northwest family of Semitic languages, heavily cognate with Hebrew. Aramaic script - also known as Assyrian Square Script - replaced the earlier paeo-Hebrew script which was more like Phoenician in appearance. The majority of the *Talmud* is written in Aramaic as are parts of Daniel and Ezra

Aron Kodesh - literally: the holy Ark

B'rit Hadashah - New Covenant

b'rit milah - literally, the covenant of circumcision, used to refer specifically to the circumcision of male children on the eighth day after birth

chas v'shalom - Hebrew phrase understood to mean "God forbid!"

Chazal - an acronym: "Ch" stands for "Chachameinu", Our Sages, and the "z" and "l" correspond to the expression "Zichronam Livrocho", "of blessed memory"; this is catch-all that often refers to the authoritative opinion in the *Talmud*, sometimes just the collected wisdom of the Sages in years past

chutzpah - the original Hebrew word means "insolence, audacity or impertinence"; colloquially, "nerve" or "gall" *cohen* (pl. *cohanim*) - priest, so *cohen gadol* or *Cohen HaGadol*: High Priest

defectiva - a "short" form of spelling Hebrew words without any helper consonants to indicate pronounciation

Diaspora - from a Greek word meaning to scatter or disperse, this is the name given to the Jewish people scattered in exile throughout the world, as opposed to the part of the Jewish people that now live in *Eretz Yisrael*

Eretz Yisrael - the Land of Israel

gematria - a system of assigning a numerical value to a Hebrew word or phrase (using the numerical values of the letter) in order to connect it to other words and phrases having the same numerical value; produces some interesting results but can be abused to generate spurious connections

hapax legomenon - Greek phrase meaning "something said once"; a word that has only one instance of use within a body of literature. In the Bible, a word that either is only used once, in any form, or - less strictly - a particular form that is only used once

HaShem - literally, "The Name"; widely used as a elusive synonym to avoid pronouncing the tetragrammaton - יהוה - ineffable or covenant name of God; where this appears in a text, and is not being read in a worship context, if will be pronounced as *HaShem*

Hitpa'el - the reflexive or iterative voice of a Hebrew verb

Kotel - literally "wall"; the Western Wall - the part of the western retaining wall of the Temple platform in Jerusalem that is exposed and visited by thousands of Jews each week; one of the closest accessible places to the Holy of Holies of the Second Temple

Malach Adonai - literally "The Messenger of the Lord" or "Angel of the Lord"; thought by some scholars to be a pre-incarnation appearance of Yeshua

masorete - The Masoretes were groups of scribes and scholars in Tiberias and Jerusalem - *masorete* meaning guardian or keeper of tradition - in the 8th - 9th centuries; they preserved the traditional pronunciation, chanting and breathing of the Hebrew Bible text, lest it should be lost and future generations unable to read and interpret the consonantal text

Masoretic Text - the standard Jewish text of the Hebrew Bible, as annotated with vowels and trope marks by the *Masoretes* in the 9th century; devised by Aaron ben Moses ben Asher in Tiberias, these pointed texts are preserved in the Aleppo Codex and the Leningrad Codex

menorah - the seven-branched candle-stick or lamp holder that was set in the holy place in the Tabernacle

*Midrash (*pl. *midrashim)* - literally, study or investigation; the technique of *Midrash* is to interpret or study texts based on textual issues, links to other verses and narratives; as a class it includes both *halachic* (law-based) and *aggadic* (story or narrative) material which often fills in many gaps in the biblical material

Mishkan - literally, "place of dwelling/presence"; the Tabernacle

*mitzvah (*pl. *mitzvot)* - literally, command or commandments

Niphal - the passive voice of a Hebrew verb

Olam Haba - the world to come

*parasha (*pl. *parashiyot)* - one of the traditional names for the divisions into weekly portions of the Hebrew Bible; the *Torah* contains 54 portions, each with its own name taken from one of the first few words in the text

Parochet - the thick curtain that hung in the Temple as a division between the Holy Place - which was accessible to all priests throughout the year - and the Holy of Holies, where only the High Priest could go, once a year; described as being a cubit or more in thickness and decorated in rich colours and designs

Pesach Hagaddah - the order of words and actions that take place at a Passover seder; compiled originally between 170 and 280 CE, tradition suggests by Rabbi Judah himself; the oldest complete manuscript dates to the 10th century

Pi'el and *Pu'al* - the emphatic or stressed voices (active and passive, respectively) of a Hebrew verb

plene - the full or extended spelling of spelling Hebrew words; done by inserting extra consonants (typically, *vav*, *yod* or *hay*) into a word to indicate pronunciation

P'rushim - Pharisees

Qal - literally, light; the unmodified or unenhanced version of a Hebrew verb; the simplest meaning of a Hebrew verb root

Qohelet - the Hebrew name for the book of Ecclesiastes

regalim - the pilgrimage festivals: Passover, *Shavuot* and Tabernacles

Rosh Chodesh - literally, "head of the month"; the day of the New Moon feast, to be marked by the blowing of silver trumpets; declared by the *Sanhedrin* in Jerusalem after having received reliable testimony from two witnesses that the new moon has been sighted

Ruach HaKodesh - literally, "Spirit or Breath, the Holy"; most common Hebrew name for the Holy Spirit

Sanhedrin - the most senior court in biblical Israel, with seventy one members; recently re-founded in the modern state of Israel

Shabbat - the 24 hours from sunset Friday to sunset Saturday, the seventh day of the week; literally "the ceasing" because as Jews we cease from any kind for work during those hours

Shabbat Sheckalim - the day each year when the half-shekel tax for the upkeep of the Temple was collected; now set as the shabbat before the first of Adar (Adar II in a leap year); the *Torah* portion Shemot 30:11-16 is read

Shacharit - literally "dawn"; the name of the early morning prayer service

Shaliach (pl. *shlichim*) - literally 'one sent'; depending on the context, from a representative to an amabassador; in a gospel context, 'apostle'; modern usage 'emissary'

Shavuot - literally "weeks"; the name of the bibical Feast of Weeks at the end of the fifty days of the counting the *Omer* (sheaf) from *Pesach* (Passover)

Shemoneh Esrei - literally, "The Eighteen" because it originally contained eighteen stanzas or blessings; the central prayer of the three daily prayer services. Also known as the *Amidah* - "standing" or simply "the prayer", the rabbis determined that this prayer was the act of service that replaced the sacrifices in worship after the destruction of the Second Temple

Sh'ma - the first word of D'varim 6:4 "Hear!", used to refer to the whole verse, the passage from 6:4-11, or the three paragraphs 6:4-11, 11:13-21 and B'Midbar 15:37-41 which are recited at each of the three prayer services in the synagogue each day

Sho'ar - the Holocaust

shofar - ram's horn trumpet

shpiel - Yiddish; a usually high-flown talk or speech, especially for the purpose of luring people to a movie, a sale, etc.

shtetl - a diminutive of the Yiddish word "stot" meaning "town", so "little town"; used to refer to the many small towns with a significant Jewish population that existed in Eastern Europe before the Holocaust

*talmid (*pl. *talmidim)* - student or disciple

Targum - literally, translation or interpretation; two principle *targums* are known: *Targum Onkelos*, a translation with some paraphrase of the *Torah* into Aramaic; *Targum Jonathan*, a translation with rather more paraphrase of the Prophets into Aramaic. They were probably made between 200-400 and were used in the reading and study of the Hebrew scriptures: one line or verse in Hebrew, followed by the same line or verse from the Targum. Important early witnesses to the text and translation into a closely connected cognate language

tetragrammaton - the four letter covenant name of God: יהוה yod-hay-vav-hay; never pronounced as written within the Jewish tradition and never vowelised with a correct set of vowels to prevent pronunciation

Torah - the first in the three parts of the Hebrew Bible (with Prophets and Writings); from the root יָרָה, to throw or teach; often translated 'law' but probably better 'instruction'; used at a minimum to describe the five books of Moshe, often expanded to include the whole of the Hebrew Bible, the *Talmud* and the Jewish writings, so that it can be used as a totally encompassing term

tzaddik - a righteous man

tz'daka - originally "righteousness", but commonly since Second Temple times, "charity"

tzara'at - Hebrew word for skin disease; often translated - incorrectly, since it bears no relationship to the latter disease - as leprosy

tzitzit (pl. *tzitziyot*) - tassles; worn (as per B'Midbar 15:38-40) on the four corners of a garment

yeshiva (pl. *yeshivot*) - Jewish religious school/college where the syllabus is almost exclusively studying the *Torah* and the Jewish writings

Author Biography

Although professionally trained and qualified as a software engineer, Jonathan's calling to the Messianic Jewish ministry started in the mid-90s after a season of serving as a local preacher in the churches of North Devon. He was ordained "Messianic Rabbi" by Dr Daniel Juster and Tikkun Ministries, and has served as a Tikkun network congregational leader in England for some years. Now the founder and director of Messianic Education Trust - an educational charity and ministry that works to share the riches of the Jewish background of our faith in Messiah with the church, while teaching Yeshua as the Jewish messiah - he lives in the south-west of England with his wife, Belinda, and three of his four daughters. There he contributes to the local body of believers by being involved in the Exeter Street Pastors project.

You can follow the work of Messianic Education Trust and read the weekly commentaries as they are produced each week, on the MET website at:

http://www.messianictrust.org

When You Lie Down & When You Rise Up

Daily Readings Following The Weekly Torah Portions

Rabbi Jonathan Allen

www.elishevapublishing.co.uk

Lightning Source UK Ltd.
Milton Keynes UK

175417UK00001B/1/P